On Heaven's Lake

A Year in New China

Justin Hempson-Jones

First published 2011 in the United States, United Kingdom, Germany,
France, Italy

This edition first published 2012

ISBN 9781469996486

Printed and bound in Charleston, South Carolina, USA

To Rachael and Andrew,

with love

1. *Running*

The airport was new, the trains were new. So were the motorway flyovers, the cars that flew on them, and the Doric columned towers, golf courses, and service stations that flanked them. The van from Educated People University, wasn't. It was battered and dirty and broke down twice on the slow lane of the Shanghai to Hangzhou expressway. Educated People University's foreign liaison officer owned teeth better polished than his shoes - which sparkled. He sat facing us smiling somewhere between charming and helpless, like a child who had just tied his own shoelaces for the first time. His name was

'Lou Da' he said, 'meaning Sophisticated Temple'. I later discovered 'Big Building' was more accurate.

Lou Da held up a pamphlet titled *'Law of the People's Republic of China on entry and exit of Aliens'*. This he handed over with two hands.

'Welcome to invest, work, study and live in Hangzhou!' it began on page one *'...We, division in charge of foreign affairs, introduce to you this pamphlet, hoping that you could work smoothly and live happily!'* It added, as an afterthought, *'Thanks!'*

Outside passed towers and hangars, factories and cranes; then came fields and the concrete bunkers that passed for peasant homes. There were no artisans painting porcelain bowls nor thickets of Bamboo. Just this East coast countryside: Three thousand years of agriculture fast being digested by industry, the farmland plugged with production lines, apartment blocks, shopping malls - everything the citizens of a modern state would require.

Time out from cramped tubes and red eye: a year to go for Kristel and me. A year in China, the workshop of the world; where peasants became consumers and communists became property magnates...Hangzhou was a star around which the Chinese world once orbited, a former centre of the imperial China, generator of Chinese culture - where poets, musicians and writers had once worked under the willow shade. This mellow glory of the Southern Song and their capital had been cut short by barbarian tribes, by foreigners who had not been kept safely beyond the wall. Hangzhou's light had failed: it had been raped and pillaged and ransacked and plundered. During the Great

1

Taiping rebellion two centuries back it had been burned right to the ground by the imperial troops who had liberated it. Its recent economic rise completed it as a metaphor for the entire country, the fall of *Tanxia*, all under heaven and the rebirth of the nation state of China. It was the town in which we would live.

The countryside continued repetitively: allotment, bunker, allotment, bunker. It passed in a bitter stench of burnt tyre, here and there in the odd housing estate - cloned houses built for the stampeding middle classes. They were detached, with smoked glass windows, spires topped by little gold-coloured orbs...We hit a pothole. The landscape had changed. I must have drifted off for the plains now blazed behind, outlines of hills smudged the horizon. Then the motorway frayed and merged into broken city streets crowded with bicycles and taxis three wheeled pedi-cabs - and people. Everywhere people. Despite this the northern outskirts of Hangzhou seemed a wilderness. It was something to do with all the dust and construction work, the chronic lack of foliage.

Against a descending yellow pall vehicles and men cast silhouettes.

'Sunlight reflecting through mist. From the lake' claimed Lou Da. This though was truly myth. For the mist came not from the lake, but rose from the chimneys and flues of the city, from suburban industry, and the satanic mills downtown. Modern Hangzhou had risen from ashes: the squat housing blocks streaked with damp, the construction sites on every corner in various repair - hives of strengthening rod and drill bit, or abandoned shells. Behind all the crowds there were ramshackle shops of concrete and corrugated iron, the occasional glass fronted showroom or restaurant replete with gaudy signboards of characters and odd fragments of English.

Here came towers, malls - and the lake. The West Lake haunted by writers, poets, and statesmen. Three hundred years previously the Great Qing emperor Qianlong had holidayed on its shores, the same ones on which forty years back Red emperor Mao had recuperated from illness. In the summer it was still apparently a place besieged: by hordes of domestic tourists unleashed by the economic boom. For now though it lay shrouded, cloaked in 'mist'. Marco Polo claimed to have seen the lake and its city. He came by horse train and called it 'without doubt the finest and most splendid city in the world'. These days Hangzhou was more easily reached by motorway and damned by the Shanghainese as 'the Garden of Shanghai'.

'We are home!' crowed Lou Da. He pointed triumphantly at the security guard saluting outside a blockhouse. The windows poked out of it like pits in the skin of an orange. Kristel gripped me by the shoulder and said

'Home. It's a urinal!'

'I guess it does look a little functional'

Three hawkers peered in through the gates with frost on their breath. They stood hunched by outdoor carts, their gas canisters and portable stoves, the woks for frying noodles and wicker baskets for steaming dumplings. A Dog and a couple of chickens rooted around in a pile of trash. An itinerant labourer slogged past carrying a sack of cement. Students scurried quickly between buildings.

'Did you read page 2?' asked Lou Da "Aliens shall abide by Chinese law and shall not endanger the national security of China, harm its public interests or disturb its public order' it says' Lou Da said.

'The German teacher did not read this book properly. In class he told students lies about Tibet. China does not mistreat Tibetan people. He said Taiwan should be independent…So we sent him home'. Matthias had been this German's name. The University of Educated People had asked him to clear up and leave China.

'Also he talked about sexual intercourse in his classes' Lou Da waved his finger dismissively. 'The girls were very upset'.

Chang Wen waited there too at the foot of the urinal.

'I told Cheng Hualing I was studying today. That is the only way she would let me out' he said, laughing the laugh of embarrassment. 'She has been talking marriage and children. But first, she says, I need a house and a real job. Teaching is not good enough. My future is in business. Everybody's future is in business she says'. We had met Wen in the UK. He had been studying International Relations with hopes of joining the Chinese diplomatic service. Since returning he taught English at a local college.

'Are you ready for all that?' I asked.

He laughed as we shook hands - another ironic little hiccough.

'It is my time' he began 'My girlfriend says she cannot wait forever. In China we say 'Girls marry to please their parents'. But my mother also has been complaining. My father. My grandparents'

'Yes?'

'...and my Aunts. And my Aunts' husbands. Some of my neighbours. And all of my colleagues'.

The flat was five floors up. Lou Da unlocked the door - three rooms, spacious and clean. The whitewashed walls had been overlaid with selotaped mountain scenes.

'You are not married. But we will let you live together' Lou Da offered graciously, the product of new China. For he was a '79 baby like me, birthed alongside reform and opening.

'The Communist Party Secretary was not happy. But I said to her this is old thinking. How can trade prosper without students learning English? How can students learn English without English teachers?' He lifted his finger 'We don't need men from Africa. We need good English teachers from the West who must live as they wish'

'You don't need men from Africa?'

'We once employed a man from Ghana. I could not understand him. So how could the students understand?' He shook his head 'Also, he was a danger to the girls'.

Lou Da didn't care to expand on this comment. When I tried to probe he instead raised a hand.

'Tomorrow read the booklet' he said.

'I'll come back as soon as I can' promised Chang Wen, a bear next to Lou Da.

Together they turned through the door and headed downstairs. We walked to the kitchen window sitting above the sink and the gas canister and watched them enter the street, the beamer and the beefcake vanishing into the masses - students, itinerants, hawkers.

Chang Wen had wrangled positions for us here at Educated People through his father's contacts. Then he had come round with a camera.

'Lou Da will not hire the ugly' he'd said 'he wants to be certain you foreigners will not frighten the students. And no men who look like women'. The results were posted first class. The answer was rapid: acceptable looks. No men looking like women. There were requests for more paperwork, which flew to China and back, stamped, with the university's red official seal - a ring of delicate characters surrounding the waning star of international communism. There were queues at the embassy to receive the 'Z' class visa for 'foreign experts'.

And here we were, two more joining one thousand three hundred million.

Structure

Dawn was breaking and light began to frame the monstrous administrative block across the street. The telephone blared. I found a receiver hiding under the desk and picked it up.

'I can show you around campus' suggested the voice, which was *grinning*.

'When?' I asked

'Now'.

So I woke Kristel - who had been pretending quite vainly not to notice the phone - and the two of us threw on some clothes. Lou Da waited outside.

Educated People it seemed, was a place of never-ending construction, a sort of permanent revolution in structures. It had been built in two clear stages. The early generation left from the idealism of revolution - functional boxes all around six stories high, faced in toilet tile and lined up together at right angles as though order might somehow mitigate their ugliness. They included the main administration block, teaching blocks, the girls dormitories, the teachers dorms - which included our foreigners' quarters. The new classroom blocks and boys dorms found themselves estranged on the other side of windswept parkland - the tarmac pathways and yellowed grass. They were quality structures of hardwood floor and smoked glass (the pink tiling we would overlook) standing firm whilst the day's tide of students began to surge in and out.

Above all of this rose a tower: thirteen marble plated storeys still swarming with itinerants.

'Big Building…' I began

'Not big building!' he interrupted, wagging a stern finger 'in English, Elegant Pagoda. My name means Elegant Pagoda'.

'You said Lou Da meant Sophisticated Temple' Kristel pointed out.

5

'Please' he said slowly, as though explaining to someone with a grievous head injury 'Lou Da is classical Chinese'. This of course, did not explain anything.

'That is the new library' he stated making artful use of the distraction tactic and gesturing pompously at the tower 'the old library will become two classrooms. The stock of books from our current library will fit into just one floor of the new one'.

Meanwhile the itinerants fitted a few windows. Others scampered in droves around the library's base, clearing away strengthening rods, draining deep puddles. Some fitted grass turf and flowers. Whole trees brought in on the back of flat bed trucks were transplanted. They were building the pyramids, these dishevelled packhorses, males from the surrounding countryside. But by dusk these itinerants had melted off campus and back to cabins to light lamps, cook and drink. Some of them played cards and most of them smoked. Despite the cold they almost looked cosy inside their temporary homes.

Later at the bottom of our stairwell I discovered waiting a tiny girl in pigtails and platform trainers.

'Betty' she said her name was, and she was a Chinese English teacher.

'We will be neighbours' she sang in a fit of high pitched giggle 'We can call each other from the windows, I will cook food, invite you for tea. You will never be lonely'.

But the entrance to Betty's part of the block was on the opposite side to ours. The foreigners entered their side of the block by one door. The Chinese entered theirs by another. Our quarters included air-conditioning, Italian power shower, washing machine, microwave, leather armchairs: it was the kind of place you could invite the neighbours to, for whisky and cigars. It soon turned out that the flats of native Chinese teachers contained a bed, desk, and chair. They showered together and used a communal washing machine. We were separate castes.

Discipline

Early morning, blaring phone, grinning voice. This was becoming a bit of an alarming trend.

'Mr. Yao requests you for dinner' said the voice.

'When?'

'Now'

Lou Da ushered us across the way to the University's plushest restaurant. Here he pushed me past the bow-tied waiters loitering forlornly, and into a private room. Mr. Yao, the Vice President sat in a velvet chair bowed in ribbons of gold. He also faced the door, the privilege of the most important diner. Mr. Gong, the balding head of languages was especially excited to meet Kristel since he had in the 1970s lived in Paris studying French language and culture.

'In China the communists let the students here make life difficult for people like me. So it was a good time to be away' Mr. Gong began fluently 'Then I saw the students rise in France, I thought maybe trouble followed me' he scoffed 'I was a vain man!' Mr. Gong suddenly flicked a glance across the table, and recomposed himself.

'Lou Da is also learning French' he added superfluously. Lou Da beamed across the table. Something about this seemed strangely menacing.

After that, Mr. Yao began to speak and Mr. Gong opened his mouth only to translate.

'China is a great civilisation' began the Vice President, raising his empty glass 'It has been brought low before. But we learned how to stand on our own. Then we learned how to open to the world' he took a theoretical swig. 'The University of Educated People rises just like our nation. And like China itself, we too will rise to greatness.' Everyone on the table began to agree vigorously, a little assembly of nodding dashboard dogs.

'We continue to follow in the footsteps of Elder Wang' continued Mr. Yao. The nodding ceased abruptly. Mr. Wang was a peasant who had risen to become Vice-Governor of Zhejiang and conceived of the University of Educated People in some moment of brilliance. Amidst the flux of reform and opening, Mr. Wang had used all his *guanxi* to set it up. It had been difficult, but Mr. Wang knew about toil and back breaking effort from a former life. His vision was born, and Educated People opened as one of the first institutions in the country to fund itself privately.

Mr. Gong was struggling to look interested, and only the effort at translation seemed to be keeping him going. I assumed they had all heard it before. Mr. Yao talked about his expectations for the coming year:

7

educated People would be granted permission to enrol level 5 students who paid for their own tuition; all seven thousand of Educated People's students would be selected from the towns and villages of Zhejiang province; there would be an expansion of compulsory English; fees were to rise...

Rather unpredictably, Mr. Yao hit the air with his fists.

'There needs to be more discipline for our students!' he shrieked. Perhaps he was attempting to wake everyone up. And with this, Mr. Yao suddenly emerged as a man of ultimate modesty. His self-control sounded modest and so did his imagination. He bore the hallmarks of a modest career technocrat, the industrious type who had faithfully obeyed his superiors: but now was his time, Mr. Yao's turn to be listened to.

Eggplant

It was on the fourth morning that I heard the front door open. I got up to investigate and was only a little surprised to find a middle aged woman standing out there in our kitchen. She wore the kind of hair that suggested styling by a toaster, and the way in which she brandished a mop did not increase my confidence. Only when Lou Da stuck his head round the corner did I relax a little.

'She says hello by the way' he explained casually, pulling himself out into the open and plonking himself on a kitchen chair.

'Her name is Mrs. Ho' he said. Mrs. Ho was already about her business, mopping the place, chatting merrily to herself. I stood there mute in my underwear, just watching Lou Da while he sat at my table taking in the walls and the taped bits of scenery.

'A Swiss man lived here' said Lou Da 'But he went home early. His mother was ill. That's why these pictures are up' Lou Da gestured at the walls 'Mrs. Ho thought it might stop Ernest getting homesick. Didn't do much good'. Mrs. Ho interrupted. Lou Da pretended not to hear her, but translated anyway.

'Mrs. Ho always says she knows all about homesickness because the university took away her home' he said 'That is why they gave her the job she says. So they could replace her family home with a university'.

'She is homeless?'

'No, no' said Lou Da brightening 'she lives out there in the new town now. But she used to be - because they had to knock down her house!' he laughed. Mrs. Ho did not seem to understand she was being mocked. Instead she span off towards the bedroom in which Kristel was pretending to sleep. I did not attempt to stop her.

Mrs. Ho lived just beyond the campus walls, out there in the neighbourhood. It seemed to claw at the campus walls: rubbish, shacks and bobbing locals, the houses of ceramic plates with their windows plastered in metal grilles.

'...a triple murder is being investigated in *Yunnan* province...' stated the English language channel, China Central Television 9. A student had smashed his roommates up with a hammer after losing a game of cards. The suspect was on the run and unconfirmed sightings placed him in just about every town in China.

Perhaps he was down there in the neighbourhood, that disorderly warren. Perhaps he was hiding out amongst the boiler houses from which locals bought hot water for tea, under the stalls of vegetable and doomed chicken, or inside the restaurants savaged by construction workers and students - all armed with disposable chopsticks. Maybe he would make his home in the shipping container sized incinerators and the apartment block sized drainage ditches; he would stalk the sidewalks of mud and mislaid concrete strewn with building materials and trash. Anyone may have holed up amongst the wood stacks and barber shops, the flower stalls, and the colourful newsagents filled with the communist party's diverse mouthpieces. One individual became a particularly tiny needle in this haystack, amongst the cyclists and mopedists, pedicabs, taxis, trucks, buses; an inconspicuous entity amongst the storming pedestrians, bartering, complaining, hollering, whilst the columns of tricycling peasants rode between them hauling trailers of goods straight in from the smallholdings: cabbage, pumpkin, giant marrow, soya bean sprouts, carrots and thin, spindly aubergines about which Lou Da later asked

'Why do Americans call these eggplants? They look more like fingers than eggs'

Washing

The French had thrown up a supermarket on the end of the road, beside the elevated expressway. It boasted trolley parks and sliding doors.   Inside stood a magazine stand, a photo developer, rows of checkouts serving columns of customers: everything seemed to be in its rightful place.

This turned out to be illusory .   There were deep freezes of meat, cling wrapped bar coded portions of beef, pork and dog; strings of intestine and sacks of stomach.   The customers close by were hollering amongst the salted chicken and the soy braised duck hanging from hooks in the beak. It was quieter in the entire aisle dedicated to dried fish where folks were otherwise engaged sniffing at the squid in plastic pic'n mix drawers. They poked too at live fish and wriggling shrimp swimming in open tanks, and harassed the river turtles trapped inside string bags.

I could only watch this circus stupidly while the counter girls stared back. They laughed at this lost foreigner, covering their mouths with their hands - after all, who had not been to a supermarket before? And then...

'That is the polite way. No smiling please girls' intervened Lou Da, who was starting to seem omnipresent. He too had turned up to shop with his girlfriend along with all of these other hooligans. The girlfriend's name was Zhou Mei-xie, and she was a pretty little thing from a tiny village deep in the mountains. Mei-xie had warmed to city life, and enjoyed hauling Lou Da around in a shopping trolley. Graciously he indulged this hobby of hers, yanking items brutally from the shelves like some gangly sort of child.

Lou Da began to turn up in many of the places we visited - firstly at the outdoor market just down the street.

'How convenient' he said leading me off by the arm down the biscuit aisle 'I'll show you how to get home. Mei-xie wants to take the Japanese text books that were left in your room'

And by the boiler house.

'Ah yes. I was just thinking my students would like it if you could write them emails from my office'

'Today is Saturday' I said.

'Yes. The students are all free on Saturday'

And on one watery morning when he ambushed us as we left the foreigners' block.

'Time for an official photo?' he asked, caressing a camera with his intellectual's hands.

'I'll have to go back. I left my shoes' I said.

'Cheese?'

'Shoes'

'Of course say cheese. Smile for the camera. Cheese!'

The very same evening came a knock at the door. Behind it, stood the sparkling teeth.

'I've come to give you a Chinese lesson' claimed Lou Da. But it soon became transparent that what Lou Da was actually after, was a French lesson.

We soon learned that there were only a very few occasions on which Lou Da might go out of his way to avoid us. Usually these would be late at night when we heard patter leading to the empty flat above. At such times I suddenly became quite excited about seeing Lou Da. And when I opened the front door, there he would be, caught on the stairs, framed in the light while Mei-xie winced behind him.

'We have come to do some washing in the spare flat' he claimed. The washing always took all night.

Ghosts

There were others who shared the same communal entrance, who shared the caste. The Chinese knew us as *waiguorren*, foreign country people; *laowai* - old foreigners; or occasionally, when the situation called for a spot of casual racism, as *gui* - ghosts. There was space in our block for 12 households, but presently only three flats contained occupants.

Professor Darling and his wife Emma lived downstairs we discovered on the fifth day. Darling had five degrees and came from Texas. Emma collected matchbox adverts and came from California. Professor Darling seemed keen to impress on us how much he just did not like American Republicans. He especially did not admire the administration of President George W Bush.

'A fascist rabble!' he said they were.

'In fact all of this progress, this advancement, the change in people's lives here in China...it is all down to the vision of the communists' he reckoned.

'Democracy?' he asked rhetorically, dropping an eyebrow 'Black Americans are still oppressed. I grew up in the South. I can tell you it's still racist as hell. But now we yanks demonise *these* people, the Chinese.

We've got rid of the soviets' he said 'and we don't get enough of a kick picking on the niggers anymore'

Professor Darling was a man fired by faith. He hated organised religion and Christian evangelicals, he disliked corporations, stock markets, and businessmen. By the end of my gin martini his whole body trembled with an excitable rage. Emma squeezed his hand.

'Now calm down Frank' she said. 'This kind of talk is no good for your condition'.

Apart from us and the Darlings there was David. He was a heavyset youth with floppy hair and a penchant for dieting. David's mother was Hungarian, his father, Chinese. He had been brought up in the UK.

'I fit in better here though' he said, and I wondered just how lost he was. Over jellyfish salad and fried cow intestine in a local canteen he talked about fitness regimes and colonic irrigation. Finally he leant back with satisfaction, resting his arms behind his head.

'But foreigners who live in China are always running from something' he claimed 'what is it for you two?'

Coincidentally I began my own jogging schedule during which I started to notice some of the neighbourhood fixtures. Mrs. Ping was the local key grinder. She was a buck-toothed woman who lived in a garden chair outside the school gates.

'Mrs. Ping's husband left her' Lou Da told me 'ran off with a noodle seller who worked on the other side of the road'. She had a young son. Sometimes he sat passively beside her, other times he played in the drains. Always the machine grated and the keys cut.

Opposite Mrs. Ping sat Mr. Hong, the ancient bin tender who owned neither teeth or shirt. He did though own a wicker hat and skin as thin as rice paper which sagged from his frame like washing hung out to dry. Mr. Hong lived outside Mr. Zha's fast food buffet and tended the bins, raking out anything of value and holding the rest of the trash in quarantine.

'His family starved in the Great Leap Forward' said Lou Da 'he has no relatives left'. Despite leaving the fields, Mr Hong had refused to learn Mandarin, the language the government had been imposing on the people since the beginning of his lifetime.

Through the fumes my routes took me, past people and

construction sites and supply stores where whines and sparks span out from unprotected electric saws at work on the pavement. Running in the city was the behaviour of a madman. Or perhaps worse in China, an eccentric. There was an easy explanation. I was a *laowai*. And they were both.

I ran on the road when the crowds became too thick, keeping company with the taxi drivers dodging heedless pedestrians, and the rickety carts playing chicken with the buses. I passed young women with babies in their arms and giggling, shielding once more their mouths; there were shy children, smoking workers and aimless beggars. Occasionally the labourers waved, the schoolboys screeched *'Hullo!'* All this at the sight of a foreigner - a running foreigner! I smiled as often as possible so they would realise I was not so dangerous. That at this point in time I was not intending to burgle their homes or rob them in the streets.

I ran through the flea market with its winking tailors and the exercise park around which the winos hung. In the early mornings I ran past the coveted green spaces where the elders practiced *Tai Chi*. After sundown I ran through smoky pool halls, past the pyjama-garbedwomen in slippers shuffling out to gossip at the boiler houses, past the men who stumbled out in their underpants to call them back inside. I ran too past the hawkers peddling street food and the brothels that advertised in pink lamplight.

I ran past Lou Da and Mrs. Ho; past Betty in her platforms and Mr. Gong with his flask of tea. I ran past the lanky flatbread seller who screamed *'Laowai lai le!'* (the old foreigner has arrived!) past the soup ladies that stank of chicken and cabbage, past a greasy dumpling seller with curtain hair and muddy hands. I ran through the hordes of itinerants on the construction sites, and the columns of sewer labourers whose chants floated from open manholes. I ran past cranes and frenetic building sites. Sometimes too Kristel ran with me so we were two runners amongst the dust, noise, and mess. Wherever we ran in Hangzhou the hum of activity was constant and unending. It would turn out to be the same across the new China's highways and byways. No one escaped. It seemed everyone was in this together, in this race to keep up.

2. chalk

The dogs that often hung around the local rubbish bins strangely disappeared around the same time as the lantern festival opened in a flurry of fireworks. Rockets were unleashed from the rooftops, the streets, in the parks and across the waterways, until the heavens took on a permanent lurid stain. All this because once a homesick palace maid had cunningly persuaded the Emperor to appease a vengeful God with fire before escaping unnoticed amongst all the chaos she had caused. The truth of the matter was not verifiable, since the festival's origins lay in the legends emerging from before history - which could be dated back quite some way back: to the first records of the Shang dynasty at least, to characters written on turtle shells about one and a half millennia before the birth of Christ.

Betty called.

'How do you find the festival?' she asked

'Interesting' I said 'How do you find it?'

She giggled.

'It is old thinking' she said 'perhaps just a big waste of money'.

Then Year of the Dog was upon us. And Betty called again.

'Best wishes for Year of the Dog' she said 'Do you like the celebrations?'

'Yes' I lied. Businesses opened in more flurries of fireworks over the lunar New Year since it was an auspicious time for opening.

'How do *you* like them?' I asked.

'Aah' she said 'Old thinking. I do not like them so much'

As everyone was having too much fun, the fireworks did not stop. At night, lantern festival celebrations blazed. In the early hours, year of the dog business openings began. This routine continued for days, and I wondered how many more would pass until we would be allowed to sleep.

In northern Hangzhou it seemed foreigners were still something of a curiosity. From the locals came staring and plenty of giggling. One firecracker cheered day in the midst of the dual celebrations we were walking home from the supermarket when a stooped old couple hobbled from behind a boiler house and forced us to a halt. The two of them lunged forward to nose excitedly around the boxes of groceries we had just bought at the supermarket. What sort of curious items might *waiguorren* procure...? Moon Beans? Unfortunately nothing quite as exciting as that - just cabbage, a fillet of pork and a few other bits and pieces that regular Chinese people might eat. They shambled off disappointedly and let us be about our business.

It was a continual assault, this China. It was a place of drastic interference. It was beginning to seem a bit of a foolish idea, living amongst such a curious racket.

Being Busy

The demolitions began a little while later, starting with the four storey block across the road. Built in the early 1950s, it had been supposed to shine as an example of modern style at the height of communist optimism. Now it was abandoned and grimy, a hollow tooth. The photographic developer had already vacated the premises, and so had Professor Darling's hairdresser.

'He was real old style' said the professor one morning on the staircase, scratching his nose. There was no longer space for this kind of barber in the new China, the kind where one size of haircut fit everyone.

The solution arrived early one morning about the same time as the first explosions of the day signalled the birth of another restaurant or internet café. The itinerants arrived, and by first light each day they had swarmed all over the building. Posturing in absurdly unsafe positions, they started to bludgeon the concrete. They worked with enthusiasm and without pause. The pounding of deconstruction ricocheted off the faces of surrounding buildings and amplified into our bedroom. Often this provoked Kristel to get up and throw cutlery about in a fit of rage.

The first day of term opened with this glorious choir of fireworks and concrete pounding. I heard Kristel shriek from the shower. Electricity was being rationed across Hangzhou Northeast sector. A new coal fired power plant opened once a week across China. It was not enough to provide for the power strains of a biting winter. Some of the most enthusiastic gamers had already been kicked out of the paralysed internet cafes: hopefully they might finally go home to wash. Of course, there were only cold showers waiting.

Armed with a *'Hold Your Dreams!'* notepad from the

supermarket, I downed a green tea, hopped the stairs. Mrs. Ho stood in my way. She brandished a broom.

'Yes?' I asked. She smiled broadly, uttered something indecipherable, and removed herself from the stair. I was then out to the road dodging bicycles and pedestrians, past the security guards and the demolition team, amidst the shoals of students and through the main doors of Block B of the north campus, where a red banner proclaimed in yellow characters

'Cultivating People Intellectually and Morally!'

I heard the students of my first class from the end of the third floor corridor. They were so loud they drowned out the work of the sledgehammers outside, truly a frightening feat. This was my first ever class. Forty two students, all lurking in room 325. I stepped up to the podium and assailed the blackboard with my name. The chatter ceased. My flock huddled tightly together, trying to keep out the cold. A few of them seemed to be suffering from colds too - the *ganmao*. Most of the students coped with *ganmao* all winter. It spread voraciously in cramped dormitories and on crowded streets.

I was from an island called Britain I said. I told them I came from a large family, and liked to snowboard, which was sliding down a mountain on a piece of wood. No-one blinked. There was time for a few introductions and a little role-play. Then the bell sounded and the students filed out. An hour had passed, leaving my jacket covered in dust from the mess of chalk I'd broken and crushed in the execution of duty.

I'd have to stop asking about families. I had gotten around half the room. There was only one answer

'There are three people in my family, mother, father, and me'. Only a wiry imp called Fei Lian differed. 'I've got four brothers!' he shouted to sniggers. The parents of my students had been among the first to face sanctions for giving birth to second children under the one child policy: fines and forced sterilisations. From the countryside came reports of late term abortions. Peasants had had their homes dynamited. They were almost entirely singletons, floundering at the bottom of an inverted 4-2-1 pyramid, the future breadwinner for up to six elders. They were a generation of spoilt 'little emperors' - the *xiao huangdi* mocked in the Chinese press.

Still in this first encounter I had debatably more success than

Kristel. She had spent most of the first lesson trying to pronounce her students' Chinese names until deciding to give up in the face of laughter. They produced for themselves English names - included amongst them Freud, Marx, and one 'Big Hammer'. There was a shy little creature 'Satan'.

> 'Your name is Saturn?'
> 'Satan.'
> 'Satan. Are you sure?'
> 'Yes'
> 'Ok. Thank you Satan'

Later that day, we stopped at Mr. Zhang's cosy internet café where the toilets were never clean and the twenty four hour lock-ins illegal. It was a haven for unkempt men who gamed frantically and smoked double happiness cigarettes. I decided to browse the website of the University of Educated People. Interestingly, I discovered that the teachers of the English department had written biographies about themselves. This one caught my eye:

> *It's my pleasure to meet you here. I come from Britain. Besides, I am a good snowboarder. Concerning my interest - travel, I have been to whole European countries and US New Zealand Mexico Sri Lanka etc. My dream used to be working and travelling in China. And this dream has come true. Thank Educated People University gives me the good opportunity to know about China and make friends with you.*

And so did this one:

> *Hi, I am a French girl born in a small city near the capital, Paris. In early age I was sent to US to be educated and later take the degree from British University. Apart from being bi-lingual, I can also speak Spanish. Sport is my hobby, especially diving and swimming which can make me more healthy and smart.*

I recognised these two...they were us. Incidentally, we had not seen Lou

Da recently either, but I suspected he had been very busy.

Dinner Parties

We both became used to the routines of school life: a demolition wake up, the unknown chat from Mrs. Ho the broom wielder, a five minute walk to class, and a battle with the chalk. Time on the campus of Educated People was expressed in sound. Aside from the morning wake up calls, class bells signalled the ends of periods, midday was marked by the theme tune from Chariots of Fire belting over the University Radio, the end of the school day signalled by its abrupt demise. The evening was less well-defined, with the scattered hollering and the odd honk from the street.

Because of this, Lou Da was a big fan of University Radio.

'At the weekends I find it hard to arrange my day. We just had this new speaker system installed' he said 'We could use it seven days not just five. There is not one place on the whole campus where it cannot reach!' I truly believed this most East Asian boast. Being inescapable was the sound system's proudest feature…this unique competition of noises, constant and all-encompassing, the reminder to the Chinese and their guests that we were all alive as one amongst the teeming anthills of the landscape. Silence seemed to have become the enemy, the reminder of being separated from the hive - of loneliness and perhaps death. Peace became a scarcity inside our apartment at all hours of the clock - not least when it all got a bit much and the kitchenware found itself displaced.

Next class, I asked my students where they wanted to be in two years time. Fei Lian grinned mischievously, and said 'I'll play basketball in the US like *Yao Ming*'. A round faced girl threw up a spindly hand. Her name was Chang Er. Her hair was drawn into pig-tails which were the longest I had ever seen.

'We used to need the eight bigs' she began 'but now we want more'. Television, refrigerator, stereo, camera, motorbike, furniture set, washing machine and electric fan: the 'eight bigs', the important things in life. Once more the answers for the rest of the class were similar. The favoured replies were '*become a manager*', and '*make lots of money!*' China's leadership had been wringing its hands over this generation. The youth of today weren't interested in building the socialist paradise. I didn't imagine their role models were Presidents, Prime Ministers, or Communist theorists. Stars like Yao Ming were a little more exciting. The Communist President, Deng Xiaoping, had set this state of affairs in motion. He said

> *'To become rich is glorious!'*

At the end of class a beanpole called Tian Fei skipped over. She was striking for her deeply tanned skin - which in China marked her out as coming from peasant stock. She was not quite pretty, but with high cheekbones, she was attractive in an austere kind of way. Earlier Tian Fei had boisterously stood up and shouted 'I want to manage a business!' Now she was at the podium while her classmates dawdled off to the next class.

'Do you like the Queen of England?' she asked

'Sometimes' I said

'We believe having a king, a queen, or an emperor, leads to oppression of the people' she said 'The Queen of England is socially backward'

'Some people in England think so too'

This answer seemed to satisfy her and she left.

A week later Tian Fei came back to the podium at the end of class. She was reading Mao. 'I'm studying the English translation' she stated proudly. She flashed a winning smile and pointed to a paragraph in a dog-eared red book.

'*A revolution is not a dinner party'* it stated '*or writing an essay, or painting a picture, or doing embroidery. It cannot be so refined, so leisurely and gentle, so temperate, kind, courteous, restrained and magnanimous. A revolution is an insurrection, an act of violence by which one class overthrows another.'* She turned and flew. It had been an odd outburst, but I was beginning to admire this girl's forwardness. It was opinionated and fearless, and apparently rare in this land of harmony.

And sure enough, the week after, she was at it again, at the front, ready to browbeat me with curiosity. This time she brought a friend. His name was Lei Shen, an athletic boy with an easy smile and swottish glasses. He insisted on sitting by himself so he could concentrate.

'Have you heard of former President Jiang Zemin's 'Three Represents'?' asked Tian Fei 'we are studying them'. Lei Shen shot Tian

Fei a look of contempt. I had heard of them, I said. After all, who could forget *'the requirements of the development of China's advanced productive forces, the orientation of the development of China's advanced culture, and the fundamental interests of the overwhelming majority of the people in China'*?

'We learn these things in class' said Lei Shen, mocking a yawn 'and catch up on sleep...In Westlife do you have to learn such things at university?'

'No' I said 'We don't'.

Lei Shen had many questions.

'Do Westlife children ignore their parents?'

'Do British students drink every day?'

'Do students in your country sleep with lots of women?'

He flicked a sideways glance at Tian Fei. Her brow was raised. She was not impressed. I kept the answers as grey as possible.

Next class, Tian Fei and Lei Shen brought back up.

'You live in China. Your parents must be worried. Do you ignore your parents?

'I saw you walking with a foreign girl - are you married to her?'

'Can you do your own washing?'

They all had many questions. But only Tian Fei asked political questions.

'Do Westlife countries hate China?' she asked.

'Who looks after the poor?'

'Does your Queen have to obey law?'

But even she listened rapt as the others received their answers.

Former generations of students had been idealists, a driving force for progressive political movements. They had been strong supporters of revolution, not dinner parties. After the communist 'liberation' of China in 1949, those former generations of radicals had become the new forces of conservatism. At least that was what Mao had claimed. So he relied upon the next generation of students to conduct his 'Great Cultural Revolution'. Mao set them against their institutions of learning, and any other pillar of authority until the urban centres slid into anarchy. While the Cultural Revolution unleashed chaos, hardship, and deprivation on many city dwellers, China's then students had fond memories of free-riding the rail system across the land and firing criticism at their teachers.

Such fun was not on offer to the modern generation. Higher education had expanded rapidly as the middle class flourished. Six million graduates had joined the job flood last year. It would be more this year. They would need all their wits just to find employment. There wouldn't be time for revolution, and only just enough time for the odd dinner party.

I was very curious to find out my students own opinions on the world. On the blackboard one class I scrawled *War never solves anything.*

'Do you agree or disagree?' I asked the forty two.

Chang Er stood up haltingly.

'All humans are the same' she said.

Fei Lian leapt up to shout (rather indignantly)

'But people like to fight!'

Tian Fei studiously ignored him.

'Sometimes war is necessary' she said 'If Taipei province becomes independence maybe China will have to fight'. China did not rule out military force to recover the rebel province of Taiwan.

'Someday soon, China will crush Taiwan' Li Xun volunteered 'Taiwan has always been part of China. Now the United States is trying to take it away from us'. Li Xun was a malnourished little fellow. His contribution to class usually involved reading military magazines under the table - brash, nationalistic publications filled with tanks and rockets, and oiled up heroic types modelling machine gun rounds. But this time around, he was interested. In fact everyone had something to say.

A lanky guy called Dong Jie jumped in with 'The Japanese killed thirty million Chinese people and never apologised' he reckoned 'Perhaps we need a war with them'. Then Wang De stood up. He was a buffalo sized fellow fresh from the countryside.

'Japan still wants to keep China weak and divided' he thundered. When it came to internal economic and social development, humans were strong and perfectible and would one day be fit to build the socialist paradise. But when it came to war and the outside world, humans were weak, goals still had to be achieved. I learned not to worry too deeply about the sentiments of boyish bravado.

'Japan may once have been our enemy' said Chang Er 'But now we have peace. We want trade' She had gotten rid of the pig tails since the last class. Now she had just a single pony tail which flicked about her like a horse's tail. Her neighbour stood up. This little lady was called Bai Nien. She clasped her hands together earnestly 'Japan is the home of shopping' she said, before adding less enthusiastically 'there should be no war - just a peaceful rise'. This mirrored the official line: China was 'peacefully rising'. It would come to power not with aggression, but gently, like yeast filled dough in a warm place.

I chalked *Men and women can never be equal*. Fei Lian marched to the front.

'The idea of women being equal sounds fair perhaps' he started 'But it is not the traditional Chinese way. I am a traditional man so my wife will have to obey me. She must stay at home to look after the house and raise the children'. The boys cheered and whistled 'and she must be a virgin...'

Tian Fei jumped up and climbed on a chair.

'Women must escape from the kitchen' she shouted, and turned to her friends for support 'Women, you have nothing to lose but your chains!' The girls applauded and the boys jeered and I slapped the board rubber on the table to get some order. Clouds of dust wafted over the students in my front row, the hardest working ones. They were all girls.

Each class at Educated People had a representative monitoring class communication, they reported to the Communist Party Secretary. I understood it was the class monitor in the expelled German teacher's class who had reported him for his verbal offences. In Tian Fei's class, Chang Xu was the monitor. She was a thick-set girl with a boxer's nose, heavy eyebrows, and an industrious demeanour. She was a member of the committee for the 'English Corner' after-class study group. She organised party workshops. In fact, she seemed to get everywhere. Often it was to Chang Xu's voice on University Radio that we awoke to in the morning. Last summer Chang Xu had volunteered to teach at an isolated country school down in Jiangxi province in the South.

'I just want to see China develop itself' she once explained to me with a sigh, for sacrificing oneself for the masses it seemed, was surely hard work.

Chang Xu's parents were involved in local communist party politics. Her father worked for the city government. Through him, Chang

Xu had plenty of *guanxi*. 'I help the assessors' she blandly admitted later. Tian Fei complained to me that Chang Xu was a snitch. She let them know which girls were of bad character; who was less likely to tow the party line. These girls were not invited to join the communist party.

Chang Xu, claimed Tian Fei, also gave the party secretary regular debriefs on what happened in class.

In a morning of dappled sunlight and frenetic deconstruction, Kristel and I had Lei Shen, Tian Fei, and Chang Er come over for lunch. They cooked for us on our gas stove: shrimp, bamboo shoot and preserved egg - the whites cultivated with mould, the yolks, black and delicate. For them we produced rare steak and cheese.

Lei Shen flapped about the cheese he had read about in books, and threw an ambitious chunk at his mouth. He chewed, gagged, doubled up, and spat.

'I thought it would taste sweet' he complained mournfully 'Neither is it anything like *Tou Dofu*'.

This was his revenge, this fermented bean curd, a speciality of Shaoxing city. At least I didn't spit it on the floor. Kristel managed to make some sort of gurgle which I presumed was supposed to convey appreciation. But *Tou Dofu*, it turned out, had the texture of fried egg and the hefty whiff of shit. Cheese and *Tou Dofu*, *Tou Dofu* and Cheese: both simple delicacies, protein and fat fermented, two food products evolved separately in isolated civilisations. We made several more attempts to swallow each others' food. Without alcohol it was a futile challenge. Yet our disgust at one another's awful food samples, the cheese and the *Tou Dofu*, was strangely unifying, a recognition of our similarities. We had each shared the sensation of learning, even if that learning involved the different tastes and experiences we had all accumulated since birth.

Dirty Hands

Chang Xu waited for me at the podia before the dust flew up from my chalk scribbles. It was an ominous sign.

'Its compulsory for you to attend English Corner' she said 'My form tutor says it is part of your contract'. This was not very amusing. Then Lou Da dropped by not only for a French lesson.

'There are the three emphases to university life' he said

'Educated People develops the students not only academically, but physically and morally as well. Students are taught to contribute to the country, to act selflessly and conduct themselves with integrity...' It was because of this I guessed, that the itinerants were stuffed into prefabs hidden behind all the construction.   After all you couldn't have uneducated ruffians polluting young minds with coarse country talk. Lou Da looked down the line of his forehead. 'And you must set an example of integrity and selflessness' he said 'You must go to English Corner'.

I pointedly ignored all further requests to attend English corner. But Kristel did begin to go.

'They bought me dinner' she admitted. The next week she was given a plastic statuette of David Beckham, then the following week she received a potted fern. Chang Xu tried her hardest to get me to go each lesson. 'It is your duty' she reckoned. I might have been having second thoughts, but it was the principle that counted. Then one fine Spring day when the students coaxed me along with the promise of ice cream I figured the principle didn't really count for much anymore. So we sat together outside in the school gardens - me and the educational terrorists - underneath the trellises of blossoming Wisteria. The sun beamed gently behind all the mist. Then the students began firing their questions.

A moonfaced boy asked 'How can we communicate with foreigners?' ('like you are now' said Kristel)

'How is Britain different from China?' asked a stocky lad carrying sweat patches and a basketball. Kristel and I began to develop stock answers to this question:

'In China you eat rice. In Britain we eat potatoes and bread' or

'In China the importance of the group is stressed over the importance of the individual.   This is not so true in my country'. Basketball boy was happy with this. These were the kind of answers that weren't necessarily even generally true but were the best we could come up with in two minutes. Fortunately these students were usually just grateful to have been understood by the foreigner without finding themselves publicly shamed.

A question that I always found very difficult was

'Do you like China?'

Because this too, was already far too broad a topic. Did I like green tea, steamed buns, dumplings, fresh vegetables, squabbling itinerants, curious students? Yes I did thanks. What about the endless jostling for space, pollution, English Corner, *Tou Dofu*? Perhaps marginally more than being poked in the eye with a chopstick. I would have liked to say that I did not like not being able to say what I wanted to say when I wanted to say it, because of the possibility of harming internal stability. But I couldn't explain that to them, because that might have harmed internal stability. And harming internal stability got people sent home if the last German teacher was anything to go by.

What was guaranteed, was that someone would ask 'Do you like China?' at English Corner. And I was surprised. The Chinese often seemed strangely interested in how foreigners like us might see their country. Was it a display of insecurity about the country's place in the world? With everything changing so fast it would be hard to blame anyone for feeling a little lost.

'Are you lonely?' was another difficult question. I never admitted to these students that not being able to communicate with most people meant that already sometimes, Kristel and I were lonely together. Perhaps I should have told them when they asked, for I was sure they would have understood. They had grown up a generation of loners. And in this society in which life was lived in public and little sheltered in private, there seemed nothing to fear more than loneliness.

Occasionally after English Corner, Kristel and I were invited out to dinner at a noodle house, or other roadside shack. Sometimes we brought the students back to the strip lighting of the apartment to drink Gin (popular) and taste cheese (not so popular). I'd have to watch the time to make sure they didn't go overboard and miss getting back into their dormitories before they were banged up for the night.

Now and then Lou Da joined English Corner, standing confidently on the sidelines with his hands behind his back, watching, scrutinising, always smiling.

'I have come to see how you are getting along' he claimed. But he also liked to show off his high standard of spoken English. He harangued the students in groups, and talked from the benches. He recounted legends, and lectured them on Chinese history. And on a lucky day, he would manage to corner one of the pretty girls.

Lou Da truly seemed to enjoy himself at English Corner. It allowed him to relax, even to let down his guard. Under the trellises one evening he turned to me and, with his chin lifted to the dusk.

'During the Cultural Revolution the party used to say 'the more knowledge one gains, the more anti-revolutionary one becomes'. Learning was the enemy of the People' he said 'Look at this' and his finger circled round all the chatters 'Now we have opened to the world it is an empowerment.'

With all the fireworks, the radio, and the smashed buildings, the students of Educated People suffered the awakening as we did. Only they woke in their single sex dorms as one of four or six. I got up to beat the unwanted alarms one day and walked across campus through the mist. I found the dorms and climbed stairs amongst huddles of smoking men to where I found Lei Shen in his room deep in a round of cards. Everything over here was public, the chatting, the computer game playing, washing in the bathhouse. The toilet doors did not close.

Lei Shen dropped his hand and showed me the midget turtles he kept in a bowl out on the balcony.

'The last ones died because so many people used to pass by the room and come play with them' he said 'Too many dirty hands'.

I hung out there with the boys playing cards and guitar while people passed all day, the milling single sex masses, dropping by to ogle the foreigner or fondle the turtles.

Later Kristel and the other girls joined us in the depths of the warren. It was Friday night, an end to the routine of the week. The place throbbed with young people, the kitsch urban girls scouring accessory shops for plastic jewellery and fake bags by 'Hello Kitty', gangs of ungainly men chewing squid amongst the buzzing crowds and the hot tang of cooking oil. They poured past the street stalls, and into the restaurants, the bars, the pool halls, internet cafes, karaoke parlours.

Lei Shen pointed to bar 'Zero Distance'.

'People take this pill' he said, and he rolled his head like some sort of zombie 'They do this'.

'Drugs?' said Chang Er rolling her head too 'We call the takers, *yaotou wan* - 'head shakers''. There had recently been a lot of talk in the local press about a rise in Ecstasy use. Now everybody knew about these people who found their necks twisting involuntarily after ingesting malign pills.

'Did you try any?' I asked. They shared a glance. Then Lei Shen broke into a very sheepish smile.

'Sure' he admitted.

From behind came a tut: Tian Fei it seemed, was not amused. I often wondered who was brave or foolish enough to sell such products here. On the Eastern seaboard of China, convicted drug traffickers took bullets in the neck.

We drank beer on the street and chatted to the hawkers frying bean sprouts amid drifts of plastic bags and discarded meals. Throughout the night the drinkers and *Yaotou Wan* poured out from the bars where they danced in the pink shadows cast by crowded brothels.

'In the North of China there would be trouble' said Lei Shen hopping out of the way - a squid seller had packed up for the night and was wheeling his cart home. Lei Shen regained his balance. 'They are China's drinkers up there in the cold' he said 'Drink, then fight. They think they have more *qi*. To them, we southern men are delicate, like women'

Tian Fei giggled behind

'We like you that way' she said 'better at other things'. Lei Shen did not have to say anything for his face was doing the talking - it had turned the colour of a brothel lantern. Tian Fei and Chang Er made to leave, for the girls' curfew at 22:30 was strictly enforced

'Don't want to be banned from leaving next time' said Tian Fei. Curfew for males apparently started a half hour later - and it did not sound too rigorously enforced.

'We jump over the fence and the guard pretends not to see' said Lei Shen apparently glad the subject had changed. Tian Fei pouted

'Just sexual discrimination' she said disgustedly. Kristel roundly agreed. Wisely, Lei Shen found himself with nothing to say.

We slept through the demolition and fireworks of the following morning. About lunchtime there was a knock on the door. It was Lou Da. By now he seemed to have gotten used to seeing me in my underwear, so I asked him in, sat him down, brewed green tea, and explained that Kristel was temporarily retiring from French class. Then I asked him why there were so many bordellos so close to the university.

'Sex is not conducive to the virtuous life' said Lou Da presenting his finger to the heavens 'At Educated People we teach the students should abstain from it. They should not take a girlfriend or boyfriend whilst trying to complete their studies'. To insure against this, in no case could a boy visit the girls' dorms. They could go to the brothels instead along with the merchants and itinerants.

Lou Da slurped tea. 'It is important for an educated woman to retain her virtue' he said.

And despite its moralising, the University of Educated People's hotel had decided not to miss out on any of this frustrated activity either. It had a special hourly rate pinned up on the entrance board.

'We call it the 'O'Clock' rate' said Lou Da. After all, you could try and keep people on the straight and narrow, but if they turned out to be all too human and failed, well there was no point in not profiting from it..

I still ran. Often I saw the girls who worked the brothels as I went. By day their gaudy sin houses reverted to lifeless prisons, with the girls sat outside doing the washing - like housewives. They usually looked unconvincing without their make up, tired, and a little gaunt.

Chang Wen came back to visit later. 'I've been trying to sell boxes after I've finished teaching class' he said

'How is it going?'

'Terribly' he admitted 'There is no money in paper boxes'. We took a stroll through the warren and he thumbed accusingly at the whores.

'All from Anhui' he said turning up his nose. 'They will go home when they have made enough money' he said, 'They will get married, visit the doctor. No one will ever know what they were doing here'. It was boom time for plastic surgeons. Theirs was an unlimited supply of customers, the country girls having their hymen re-stitched.

The Inspection

Over a number of days I began to be plagued by a man named Mr. Ji. He wore hair swept back with axel grease, thick rimmed glasses and a dirty leather jacket. He was an English teacher and I first met him when he jumped in front of me and blocked my path in the bottom of the stairwell leading to the foreign teachers' quarters.

'Speak the Queen's English' he requested. His favourite

student, a handsome boy stood beside him forlornly.

'Please say 'we are eating cream and strawberries''. I repeated the sentence. Mr. Ji clapped for joy and shouted 'Now say 'the tennis is fantastic in summer''. I uttered these words, and Mr. Ji poked the sad pretty boy with his skinny fingers.

'See. You must learn to speak like this!' he said.

Next day he was there again with the same boy in tow.

'Say 'dinner will be served in the garden''. I did. Mr. Ji shrieked orgasmically. 'Just the best' he said. He was there the next day too, waiting for me.

'Say...'

'I can't do this for you' I said 'I have other business'

Mr. Ji's face blackened.

'We need to improve English in this country' he said. The following day I looked out from my window before heading out. He was skulking down there by the bushes. So I stayed inside. After that I decided to avoid him by making my movements less predictable. In the streets outside of these times I panicked when I saw him coming, and dived behind any sort of cover - flower beds, building sites, Mr. Zhang's buffet, even Mr. Hong's refuse pile. But my unusual height and white face gave me no quarter amongst the street masses.

On one sighting, I ducked into the school athletics field. The students had colonised it to hear Mr. Yao the Vice President, who had just stood up to shout. I found Fei Lian.

'I am surprised to see you here' I said, groping for conversation. 'Really?'

'Yes. You are behaving obediently today'

'I am always obedient' he grinned 'Chinese students are more obedient than your Westlife ones. This is just our Chinese way'.

I asked him what was going on.

'People coming to judge the school. Vice President Yao says we will need to be very obedient during this time. But I just pricked my ear' He proudly rubbed the lobe, which was red and swollen. He had just had a stud put in, ready for the inspections that were about to come. It turned out that this year was the twentieth anniversary of Educated People. Twenty years since the school had begun an opt out from the rigid strictures, constrictive rules and low funding base of Chinese public education. The inspectors were coming to see whether it had all been worthwhile.

The authorities were taking no chances. There were rallies and study sessions, truck columns bringing in flowers, which were hauled away and sprinkled across the campus paths and gardens, around stairwells and entrances. Mr. Gong summoned us to his office.

'Here is the syllabus for the year' he said before ushering us out with a complementary box of tea. So there was a syllabus after all. Kristel had been pestering Lou Da and Mr. Gong about it at the beginning of term. Lucky it had come to light two weeks before the scheduled inspections. The syllabus was written in Chinese so we asked Lei Shen to help translate. He could not make out many of the characters.

'I think someone wrote this in a hurry' Lei Shen said 'Like how you eat' and he slapped me on my stomach, which rather depressingly, had recently expanded.

Then one morning I noticed a new pupil much older than the rest sitting next to Fei Lian and his proudly pierced ear. At the end of class she threw a brisk smile in my direction and left without a word. In the next class there was another older lady, a motherly type with glasses and a reassuring smile. This time the guest came to the podium before class began and whispered conspiratorially

'I'm inspecting your class'.

She sat down and observed while we played timed word games. The students hollered and screeched and a teacher from the next class down popped her head in. I expected she wanted the noise reduced, but on seeing a foreigner in the class, she thought better of asking for it. After class finished and the students had gone, my guest said

'Your western teaching methods are interesting. The lesson was very *lively*'. But this was an ambiguous compliment in China, with its suggestion of energy, assertiveness, the potential for loss of control.

'Bring the syllabus with you to class next time as the real inspectors are coming next week' she added.

The school authorities seemed to be panicking. University Radio started earlier, study sessions continued well into the evening. The students were working fourteen hour days. Students began to sleep in class, they were not in a fit state. Even Lei Shen fell asleep one morning and did not wake when Tian Fei indignantly prodded him the back.

In the English department, the faculty staff were presented with a four hundred page teaching and behavioural regulation manual which they been instructed to ingest in just one week.

'We want our foreign experts to have one too' said Mr. Gong. But fortunately there was no way around the obvious problem: who could translate four hundred pages in that small amount of time?

Four bus loads of the inspection team turned up the following Monday. They were men of slick silvery hair and prosperous bellies and the obligatory female battleaxe, all dignitaries from the city and provincial government. Betty greeted them proudly dressed in her platforms and pigtails, and some kind of blue suit. Even without the headset and roller blades, she looked like a messenger on some postmodern warehouse floor. She led the elders off at a speed beyond their capacity to see a show thrown in their honour. The rest of us were ushered in to the campus hall behind them. The show included Beijing opera, a rap act, and male students in leotards bouncing to Euro-dance. I began to suspect this process would be more traumatising for the inspectors than it was going to be for Educated People.

Over the next five days I saw gaggles of dignitaries shepherded through the grounds by entourages so large I wondered whether their real purpose was distraction. Then it was all over. Not a single inspector came to my class. Neither did they arrive in any of Kristel's. Instead they had declared themselves impressed enough with the foreign teachers after a handful of them observed Professor Darling's class for a few minutes: those *laowai* were probably after all, speaking any old gibberish.

At the end of the week, the four buses drove off at a stately pace, past the flowers and the crowds of adoring students appointed to wave. Mr. Gong flung out his arms and invited us to a banquet at the university hotel.

'We won't have to do that again for a while!' he shouted. Then he led his colleagues on their main mission - to get roaring drunk.

Teacher Xu soon seemed to be winning the proceedings. She was a solid old battleaxe from the North, and also happened to be the university's Communist Party Secretary. Teacher Xu led the toasts - '*Ganbei!*' which she targeted tactically at various dainty Southerners. Fortunately none came our way.

'She may punish her least favourite colleagues with toasts' whispered Lou Da 'But she hates foreigners even more. You do not even deserve a toast!'

Later I heard the inspection had been a success. Educated People provided a satisfactory standard of education. The inspection team was going to recommend that the university be granted the right to start offering four year bachelors programmes as well as three year diplomas.

By the following week the students' behaviour was back to normal. The radio wake up began later, synchronising once more with the demolition. Nobody fell asleep. My chalk flew, the dust multiplied. The only sign of slack behaviour came from Li Xun the military hawk, who read *Renmin Bao,* the People's Daily, under the desk. Later that day there was a knock on the door. Lou Da was back on form too.

'Can you write me a reference for a British University?' he asked. He was applying to study a masters degree in education. It would be sponsored by Educated People. I agreed to do it. He beamed primly and volunteered

'I know very much about your culture from books and television. Nothing is going to be a surprise'.

The only surprise it appeared, would be for me, when I discovered Da had already written my reference for him:

'*On top of teaching English he has also been awarded a high position in the foreign affairs department of Educated People University due to his excellent proficiency in English*' it said '*Mr. Lou Jie has taught us much about China and Chinese culture and has shown himself to be highly intelligent...We were most impressed by his diligence*'. Lou Da's work mainly seemed to be an inspired mix of net surfing and napping. But I signed it off. We might need the *guanxi*.

A couple of weeks after the inspections ended, the sledge hammering abruptly stopped. We overslept. Kristel got up and threw forks across the kitchen. An admin block had been razed and the acrobats were spent. Professor Darling's hairdresser was long gone. In its place a gatehouse had risen. The library had gone up four more floors, two new classroom wings were nearing completion, the surrounding wasteland of mud and building material had morphed miraculously into new garden, complete with replanted whole trees and reams of yellow turf.

I walked with Tian Fei and Chang Er. The perimeter fencing had recently been pulled back from the road where students and hawkers dawdled the gauntlet of taxis, bicycles, and three wheeled pedicabs.

'I heard they would make the land a path so students would be safe' said Tian Fei 'I am disappointed'. Just before the inspections, the freed land had been replanted with flowers. Barbed wire kept pedestrians on the road. I asked the girls how they felt about all this...all this progress.

'We know it is good for the country, improves people's lives' Tian Fei began 'but sometimes I feel...' She shrugged, allowed a vaguely lost look to creep across her face, and would not finish her sentence for any amount of prodding.

3. Business

Madame Xia was a wobbly-chinned matron who nested inside the water store. She spent her days tapping her fat fingers against a calculator or shouting at her scrawny chain-smoking husband. Sometimes she did both at once. The Xias operated inside a concrete box - a dank cavern of dust and must. Squashed into a small row between a flower shop and the *'hair consulrant'*, it was not far away at all from Mrs. Ping and her key making stall. The Xia's store was one of many scrabbling in the neighbourhood market for huge twenty litre bottles of drinking water. Capitalism in China seemed built on small stores like these that propped up the economy. They were prejudiced against by the state despite being treated like cows, milked for tax to keep in place what remained of the iron rice bowl - that state safety net of jobs and social care.

Kristel and I cut a deal. Kristel was to keep Lou Da sweet with French lessons and stop throwing things around when she got annoyed: I would ensure that our supply of drinking water did not dry up. So I began coming here to the Xias regularly, dropping by to pick up a bottle at the end of a run. It was safer to come to a bottle store like this than one of the boiler houses. In the boiler houses the paint flaked, and the cranky machinery carried the unmistakeable whiff of something unseemly - perhaps of a mouse that had taken a wrong turn a while back.

Madame Xia used to treat me as though I might unleash some sort of pox on her house, even letting money drop to the floor rather than allow the ghost to tarnish her palm with his hands. Yet it took only a couple of water-buying visits to establish the relationship, and once I had proved myself a regular, she didn't even glance up from her accounts anymore. Instead she yelled freely at Mr. Xia, kept poking the keypad and wrote more entries into the thick accounts ledger book sprawled in the dust of the table. Usually Mr. Xia responded with a string of grunts, plucked a barrel off the shelf, then shuffled over and dumped it at my feet; a lit Double Happiness hanging forlornly from his lips.

Refreshingly, the Xia elders now seemed to have forgotten that we were *laowai* and treated us like just a couple more ants. It was a form of embrace. We had merged with the one point three billion - if only briefly. If the treatment was down to apathy on Mr. Xia's part, and plain business sense on that of his wife, so what. Only the Xia's eldest son (only son) still had the curiosity to treat us differently. He was a starved man of thick rimmed glasses and a placeless age somewhere between twenty and forty. Often I caught him red-handedly gawping - usually when he thought I wasn't looking, but sometimes too when the excitement of dealing with a real live *laowai* simply got the better of him.

Like many in this new China of breakneck growth and fresh opportunity, the Xias had diversified. This family ran a profitable sideline in tickets for public transport, and sent eldest son downtown on the family moped to collect them from the various stations and ticket offices. They could get us on trains and buses, and even boat trips up the Grand Canal to Suzhou. Madame Xia's was formidable proletariat *guanxi*. Finally Chang Wen called one crisp late-Spring weekend. He lowered his voice and asked 'Would you like to help make a delivery?' We needed three tickets to Shanghai he said. Even the *laowai* knew where to begin looking for these.

Chang Wen was diversifying too - through his extended family. His family was from Shanghai, where he had been born. During the Cultural Revolution the family had splintered and two of his Shanghainese aunts had been exiled to the countryside for re-education. This re-education had been strenuous: both had learnt how to grow calluses and scratch a life from the soil. But then their lessons diverged. Aunt Zhu had been allowed back to Shanghai at the start of the eighties. She put the bitter lessons of the fields behind her, retrieved a material life in the city, threw herself at her work and became wealthy, a businesswoman working in murky export trades through connections in Guangdong, Hong Kong, California. More importantly perhaps, she had escaped the curse of a Chinese husband. Her sister, Aunt Mei, had married a farmer and could not return. She remained chained to the earth.

'Aunt Zhu is not educated' said Chang Wen 'but she has set a fine example. Today is a test. She told me 'Don't mess it up''. She wanted Wen to make a delivery of vitamin supplements. From Hangzhou to Shanghai, point A to point B, it was a simple request.

When I arrived at the water shop to enquire about train tickets, Mr. Xia was loitering in the corner.

'Come back in the afternoon' yapped his wife. So we did. And when we returned Mr. Xia was still standing in the same spot, hunched, and chain-smoking with an air of resignation. Eldest son looked us up and down, seemingly not worried that he was always being sent downtown to brave the queue jumpers rioting for tickets at Hangzhou central train station.

Eldest son always smiled when I purchased a new bottle of water. He knew I would save him some work and carry it myself. This had been the state of affairs ever since I once had to follow this little man back home while he huffed and furiously puffed at the pedals of his bicycle. Those melon-shaped calves of his looked close to bursting and I could not have felt better about flogging a donkey. From then onwards I insisted on carrying my own water.

But eldest son never took this opportunity to have a well-deserved rest. Instead he would follow me home, grinning inanely while I struggled off with the blue canister behind my head, attracting more than the usual curiosity from the neighbours.

On a weekday of frozen brows I tried so hurriedly to escape Xia junior's attention that I lost my balance on the curb and threw the water tank into the street right between Mr. Zhou's outdoor fast buffet and Mr. Hong's rubbish bins. It broke and drenched a couple of passing students. A little pig-tailed girl from a fruit stall broke into shocked laughter. And when I stumbled forward to pick up the remains, the locals whispered together in panic and judged the outside world. To smile, had been vain: those gibbering *laowai* were not only strange looking and unpredictable, but were obviously reckless, even downright dangerous. Mr. Hong at least, seemed to understand. But later, I realised he had just been greedily eyeing up the broken bottle. It had recycling value.

In the end I collected the tickets to Shanghai during the week. Next Saturday, a dull day of ragged clouds and heavy overcoats, we left. The three of us jumped a cab heading downtown, past the towers and the stained apartment blocks. This driver was just one more passionate maniac (flapping arms; '*laowai lai le*'; eyes glued to the foreigners not the road). Dumped under gigantic eaves, we arrived at the station, the new station - a monstrous conglomerate of smoked glass and concrete. A turd iced with blood red characters: *Hangzhou Huochezhan*.

This was our first Chinese station experience: a confusion of escalators and security guards, queues to throw baggage at the x-ray machines, tannoy announcements. To be confronted by a hangar of snack stalls with glass counters selling pot noodle, vacuum packed chicken legs, dried squid. It was like a brutal sort of airport: sterile waiting room coloured only by the movement of people. The guests were itinerant workers carting their possessions around in sinewy bags of wicker, unsealing nuts and gabbing together. A gaggle flicked tea, one picked his nose. There were day tripping middle class girls in low cut tops and heels, pouting. The power clothes set - impatient looking businessmen in suits or leather jackets clutching their briefcases furtively, as if they were off to make an urgent deposit somewhere out on Hainan island. And because the long rows of seats were full of this human medley we sat on the floor amongst the plastic wrappers and cigarette butts. Wen said

'Not long to wait. But don't sit in farmer spit' and then he squatted and squinted at a newspaper, rolled back on his haunches like a straining frog - the typical pose of the waiting Chinese male.

Platforms were off limits, and the passengers struggled safely at bay behind metal turnstiles. It was no use letting the hordes anywhere near the tracks while the trains were not stationary. I heard a train grind underneath. Then the turnstiles were open, the passengers surged down the steps, carrying us past an attendant standing to attention in the military uniform of the People's Railways, and onto the carriage.

This beast spewed plumes of fluid smoke and dated to the early 50s communist honeymoon period. It was a clean antique headed by a battered diesel. Two yokels sat in our designated seats, but they moved away nervously when they saw the foreigners coming. A tankard of steaming water located at the carriage end had been poached by a gang of noodle eaters, and the tea drinkers were just behind them, pushing impatiently to get at it. My stomach was angry. We had eaten nothing apart from exhaust fumes, smog, and tankard steam destined to fog up the windows. Kristel bought pot noodle from a train attendant. She opened the lid, gave the dried noodle and plastic packets of chilli and beef a thoughtful look, then turned to me.

'You're in charge of water' she said. I got up and walked the length of the carriage to jostle with the crowds by the boiler. And when the conductor gave the all clear and the train wheezed out from beneath the concrete shed, it was 08:26. Which is exactly what it said on the ticket.

This express train was travelling north, moving away from the hill-lined caldron of central Hangzhou and towards the plains, the

37

'countryside'. A jumble of steam, rusting pipes and machinery passed by - these were the city outskirts where construction dust drifted.

'All new' said Chang Wen, pointing proudly at rows of whitewashed towers. This was progress, humans at war with the farmland. But a few miles out of town the heavy plants and manufacturing assemblies tailed off and the tower blocks were left behind. The detached dwellings became less gaudy, more functional, poorer. This flat country stretching almost three provinces north had been one of the cradles of Chinese civilisation. It was also flood country, a melding of plenty and sorrow stretching the millennia. Industrial decrepitude obscured the low horizon giving off the air of some Dystopian Norfolk.

And in this countryside that had been scraped and worked for thousands of years there were few fences and even fewer trees. But amongst all this, the signs of human habitation were never far away, concrete bunkers and grey-washed walls conquered only by a dull blanket of sky above. A few of these homes were mounted by stairs to nowhere - primed for a second storey annexe for a married son. But the annexe was unlikely to be built in this China of uprooted existences and city migration.

After the first twenty minutes we passed the same dilapidated houses, the same small vegetable plots, the occasional peasant and the odd tree, dishevelled and lonesome: a looped videotape. Only the taller, but equally dreary buildings of the city of Jiaxing broke the monotony of the countryside. The Chinese Communist Party held its formative session on a boat in the middle of a lake here. It was a meeting that destroyed most of its participants within twenty years. Outmanoeuvred by pragmatic political players like Mao, the young idealists had been replaced by cynics.

And Chang Wen shifted in his seat, leaned into my ear, and whispered

'Communism eats its own children'.

For a few minutes, we sat in silence. The videotape looped some more. Chang Wen looked behind him and leaned over again.

'They say China is a democracy because the communist party rules in the interests of everybody. Other times they say that democracy is no good for China, that the peasants are not educated enough...'

'But the peasants are the source of the party's power' I said.

'Yes. Yet in China now, it is the cities who reap the benefits'

All farmland here was under siege from the rich city - from the greedy tentacles of rigid planning and the speculative developments that exploited the system.

Shanghai was swallowing every urban area within three provincial boundaries, devouring the peasant plots in between. All the cities within the range of one hundred million speakers of the Wu dialects of the delta were being soldered together into one seamless citadel of concrete and steel. First came the roads, then the factories, apartment blocks, malls, motorways, supermarkets, warehouses, and all the other haphazard business of modernisation. Caught inside this event horizon were Jiaxing, Shaoxing, Yangzhou - all cities a million strong. And Hangzhou too.

'Perhaps the Communist Party will only fall if they lose a war' said Wen.

'In Taiwan?' interrupted Kristel.

He nodded. I asked him if that's what he wanted, to see China lose a war in the Taiwan Strait.

'Of course not!' he exploded. 'It should be invaded and conquered! But it needs to be done quickly, before the United States or anyone else intervenes. The head of the snake must be cut off. Then its body must be destroyed'

'But Taiwan is a democracy' I said, playing on Chang Wen's sympathies. He fidgeted and shifted.

'Just a joke...' he said, and settled back into his seat, laughing his embarrassed laugh. The loop continued, field, bunker, peasant; field, bunker, tree...Two attendants breezed through the carriage, carrying baskets and hollering. They shook pairs of black socks under the passengers' noses and shouted

'Not Expensive!'

With the audience held captive for hours, the canny train attendants knew how to make the most of their time in the new China.

Kristel snorted. Wen sat with his arms folded.

'I used to support the China Democracy Party' he said 'They would have cared for the farmers. Then they were banned. One day I went down to join the protest against this decision outside Hangzhou Number One People's Court. But there were policemen waiting for us, recording our faces on video. So I decided to go home'.

I sat there wondering what I would have done. But it was an impossible question. Pragmatism, obedience, and consensus were pedalled here as the height of virtue, expressions of discord were damned simply as selfishness. But not everyone in China went home though. A few days later I read on an international news website about the fate of a true Chinese rebel, the dissident Wang Youcai. He had been a student leader during the 1989 protests in Tiananmen Square, and later a founding member of the China Democracy Party. Sentenced to eleven years for subversion, after six years inside, he had been released from Hangzhou Number One prison into exile abroad. Wang Youcai was one of the luckier ones. His cause had been celebrated and the United States had pushed for his release. A round of trade negotiations had been coming and it seemed a good time for China to show some goodwill. Dissidents were useful enough when it came to bargaining.

Field, bunker, factory, tower...the real suburbs of the megalopolis were beginning to rise from this landscape of vegetables and mud. We were arriving in the city once known as the Paris of the East, the Pearl of the Orient, the Whore of Asia. Now it preferred 'head of the dragon', 'the window on the world'. Other Chinese said Shanghai was a city of materialistic pretentious folk, disdainful of provincials; a city of henpecked men and ruthlessly ambitious women. Yet the hangars and tunnels of Shanghai's central station belonged to commuters and migrants, an odd mix of suited cosmopolitan slickers and bewildered bumpkins in patched jackets who sat on cabbage sacks, ready to start life on the city streets.

Amongst the tumbling passengers we bundled off the train and pushed towards the exit, a wall of glass sharpened under the harsh midday light.

'100 % From Anhui' said Chang Wen, 'All of them', and he gestured disdainfully at the itinerants. They were drawn from every nook and cranny of the country - not only from the poor hills of Anhui province, but from the small towns and villages of Zhejiang, and the plains of Jiangsu too. Three million of them arrived in this window on the world every year without residence permits, looking for work in a city hosting one fifth of the world's construction cranes. They found discrimination. Blamed for rising crime and stealing urbanite jobs, they were illegal migrants in their own land. We descended into the subway amongst the activity and litter and Chang Wen sighed.

'It's a bit of a mess' he said.

He was right.

Respect

Jabbering travellers and Chinese queuing - every man for himself. This was the Shanghai subway. At a station in a faceless suburb, Chang Wen ushered us off. There, we waited on a windswept platform while Wen tapped his fingers nervously.

'I was very young when my Aunt came back to the city' he said 'She lived with us. We still had food stamps for rationing. Every day we ate rice and cabbage. Rice and cabbage. Rice and cabbage...' But just after Wen's first birthday the Great Helmsman, Chairman Mao, had died and everything had begun to change.

A middle aged lady strode on to the platform. She was handsome, with silvered hair. Chang Wen stood up.

'You brought the vitamins?' she asked.

Wen nodded and passed over the case.

Aunty checked inside. *'Hao de'* - good - she said. All present and correct. She threw a stream of words at Wen, then turned and walked away leaving him frowning. The deal had been done.

'She says that I am an intellectual' he said, as though this were some kind of blight 'But she will try hard to help make me a businessman. I am lucky. She learned to fight in the fields. She always knows what she wants. She is a better teacher than she admits'. There would be no time for small talk or matters of philosophy he reckoned, only time to campaign.

We travelled back to the core of the city. The sun made a rare victory over east coast smog, glancing off the canyons of gleaming offices in People's Square. Thickets of skyscrapers had bloomed all over the place and hurried business men ruled the pavements. This could have been almost any international node in the cities network. The only sign of China were the gawping itinerants. For despite their numbers they were somehow unnoticeable as they sat against the walls or slunk along like doped ferrets. Opposite City Hall was the museum. It hovered in a square of grass, fenced off from the public, a lawn to be admired from a respectful distance, not walked on. At least that way it would not become a camping ground for the itinerants. If you wanted to preserve anything in China, it wouldn't do to let the people near it.

Near the shops of *Nanjing Lu*, gangs of seedy hawkers huddled in the shadows of side streets, emerging coyly to whisper *'buy not buy watch?'* Inside Starbucks turtle necked men and furred women sipped cafe lattes. Itinerants outside checked the bins for plastic bottles under street signs sponsored by Pepsi. Down the road a half-naked boy no older than ten and a girl of even fewer years shouted at the anonymous pedestrians.

'They say they are orphans' said Wen knitting his brows together 'I don't believe it. Perhaps their parents are close by, watching the children making money. Probably children and parents are from Anhui'. The girl wrapped a steel rod around the boy's neck. He tensed and grimaced. It was a school day. Then the show was over, rewarded with gentle patter and change thrown to a hat. Above soared one of Puxi district's trade mark skyscrapers - crowned with a revolving restaurant in a Shanghai take on 1950s futurism. I wondered if any of the office workers had seen this little show from behind their desks on the eightieth floor. The children must have looked like specks of dust; dancing, and insignificant.

'Never pity them. Everyone is trying to make money' said Wen. He put his finger and thumb up to his ear and began to rub them together. It was a clumsy gesture, and I guessed it was the first time he had made it.

The West had once built an outpost of itself here down beside the sluggish Huangpu river. Our civilisational clutter still stood opposite the sampans and coal barges, a profusion of American and European architectural heritage - Romanesque, Gothic, Renaissance, Baroque, Neo-Classical, Beaux-Arts, Art Deco. Collectively, these old granite vaults were known as 'the Bund'.

'None of them Chinese. All of them foreign. Foreign architecture built to house foreign organisations' said Wen with his brow lowered 'I often wonder, why don't we knock them down?' *Big Ching*, the old clock face dominating Customs House, was modelled on Big Ben. There had been jazz houses, gentleman's clubs, insurance companies and banks; the China headquarters of traders Jardines and Matthewson, a company that had once helped instigate the opium wars. Jardines and

Matthewson still traded in London, and on corporate induction days for new recruits they smiled over tea and biscuits, and said light-heartedly

'We started off in life as drug dealers!'

Chang Wen looked at me sideways.

'These buildings remind me only of weakness'.

Remarkably, almost a century earlier the scholars of the May Fourth movement had called for China to feel this shame in the face of foreign encroachment. The peasants they said, were not politically mobilised and had no sense of belonging to a country under threat. In a strong China, the collective consciousness of the people would feel the sting of humiliation and be spurred on to renewal. But now the red standards of the People's Republic of China hung from all of those imperial rooftops.

During the Cultural Revolution, red guards had named this street 'Revolutionary Boulevard'. But 'Bund', or embankment, was a Hindi word derived from Persian and brought to China by British imperialists.

Kristel had skipped ahead. We found her on a promontory overlooking the thicket of towers on the other side of the treacle. Liujiazui was its name, the office district whose skyscrapers had all risen from the marshes of Pudong in less than twenty years.

Wen gestured hazily.

'That one is being built by the Japanese' he said.

'Which one?'

'That one' he said 'with the cranes'

'There are cranes everywhere'

'By the tower that looks like a flower'

'I see' I said. But I didn't.

'When it is built it will be the tallest. But it is not influenced by traditional architecture. Many Chinese are angry'

'None of these towers look traditional'

He waved this away.

'There was a circle supposed to be cut from the top' he claimed 'they had to change it'. The pile of cranes was building the redesign - the construction of this building, the Shanghai World Trade Centre, had been delayed.

'Always trying to demonstrate their superiority' said Wen despondently 'That is the Japanese. They will not apologise for what they did but they still want to dominate'. The mayor of Shanghai and half of his citizens had complained. They didn't want the rising sun falling on Shanghai again even if it this time it would only be seen through shadows cast by a hole in a tower. Later the building was approved with design modifications and here it was, rising out of Pudong. Teetering behind it far into the distance were the endless regiments of luxury blocks for the urban middle class.

'I'd live on this side' said Chang Wen as if he were actually about to make the purchase. Then he squinted at the cluster over the river. 'Better a box over here in Puxi than a flat over there in Pudong' he said 'that's what we say. Those developments over there do not have good *Feng Shui*'. With its wealth, its muscle, its exhibitionism, Pudong's Liujiazui was supposed to epitomise the new China. It seemed impolite to point out that much of Liujiazui smacked of blandness and conformity.

I heard shouting. I looked down and found a tiny old man in Mao suit and Russian bear hat clinging to my coat. It seemed he had a problem: it was me.

'He says this is his' Chang Wen said, gesturing at where I was standing.

'Mine!' he cried, with Wen translating.

'What's yours?' I asked.

'This' he said. 'My photo taking spot. If you want to stand here you will have to pay me'. But he had no tripod or camera. He had nothing but the clothes on his body. He was just another homeless itinerant trying to make money, like many in this city. I declined to pay the old man and instead shook off his arm to take pictures of the busy river. All the while he screamed impotently in my ear, and Chang Wen vacantly translated.

'He is saying something about children… foreigners… *disrespect…*'

But it was a desperate position, to be elderly and lost in the new China's Shanghai, a city in which permanent revolution seemed to have gained a new meaning and constants always passed away.

Developments

There were still pockets of older architecture around Puxi. In the old town they were being picked off piecemeal, those single storey whitewashed terraces. They were dirtied by fog and demolition dust, the roofs of terracotta often broken. Wen led us through back streets where a pack of housewives gossiped. All were enjoying the last of the day's sun, washing clothes in outdoor basins, stringing t-shirts between the blocks. A dog sniffed around in the guttering. A teenage girl with a wide face and plaited pony tail fried noodles in an oversized wok. I pointed my camera at her and smiled. But she frowned and raised her palm: no photo.

Wen raised his big head and said 'She is a good girl. A modest girl'. At this I sensed at least one of Kristel's brows rising.

'I grew up here' Wen interrupted himself in a merciful changing of the topic. He swept his arm around three hundred and sixty degrees 'but they knocked down the old house some time ago and built this...' A white tower sprouted at the end of his finger, interrupting the flow of the old streets. Wen flicked to the next street along where the traditional patterns began once more.

'Maybe they will do the same next door'. These narrow streets seemed like some kind of larder from which the cranes and towers behind them might one day take their fill. Watching your home get built over was apparently a routine event in the new China.

There were more washer women there in the next streets, scrubbing casually. Chang Wen approached a small huddle beside a stone doorstep. One of them had just stamped on a cockroach. Kristel and I caught up and Wen turned in triumph.

'I am correct' he said 'they all have to move out by the end of the year'

'Where to?' I asked. Wen turned to them.

'To a tower she says' he thumbed towards the squattest of these matriarchs 'Maybe like the one built where I lived. But out of town. The city government is paying to move them'

The sledgehammer crews were coming. In the new China, new was always better. Shanghai's *Shikumen* town houses had been built around compressed courtyards. They were terraces that had housed the generations. They had survived looting by bandits in the Taiping rebellion, world war, civil war, even Mao and his cultural revolution. Surviving an economic boom was a different proposition.

'Are these people happy about moving?' I asked Wen. The huddle turned and debated. Then the faces pulled away and the most walnut faced emerged. She broke into a stream of speech which Wen had trouble keeping up with.

'She was born in this house' he translated 'But prefers to live in something modern. This place is hot inside during summer, and too cold in winter. Too cramped as well and the rooms are dark'. She didn't say anything about the blatant lack of privacy. I suspected that this was no real problem in this country of most social beings.

'This was her parents' house?' I asked. Wen passed the question on. Spittle flew from her mouth as she gunned back an answer once more.

'Yes' he said 'And their parents lived here. And the parents of her parents' parents'. But if the old doesn't go she says' Wen paused - the old woman shrugged '...then the new won't come''. He ended with a cryptic flourish

'She has to like what fate gives' he said.

And we moved from the disappearing alleys, past the park where a sign possibly stated *'No dogs, No Chinese'*, and found ourselves in the Yu Gardens Bazaar. It was a theme park of stores, restaurants and tea houses cluttered with fish ponds and flying eaves, hawkers and stalls flogging Buddhist figurines, plastic swords, Mao watches.

'Knocked down the old blocks to make way for it' said Wen 'Much better now with all the shops'. This attitude was so different from that found in Europe where buildings from the older world were venerated and preserved.

'Aunt said she wants to move into property development' said Chang Wen with a lick of his lips 'She sees towers all over Shanghai. Let more people move from the country. Make Shanghai the greatest city in the world'. But Aunt's vision did not seem to be waiting for her: it was already here in the subway, the towers she had not built, the sprawl. It was here in the Yu Gardens Bazaar where the fake Qing buildings had replaced the original Qing buildings. And it looked far from over. In the yellow skies stalked the cranes busy building the future. They were multiplying.

Back at Shanghai station the passageways had fallen dark and foreboding. But the itinerants and their sacks still flooded the forecourts.

'All arriving at once' sniffed Wen 'they should stay in Anhui until we are ready'. It was meant to have been a foreign town. But the first refugees had come seeking safety almost immediately as the Taiping Rebels burst from the South and put eastern China to the sword. Waves of the shelter-seeking arrived during times of famine, while the warlords connived to carve up the people outside. In time Shanghai had become not only a refuge. Instead it had become expected to export stability and prosperity to the provinces. This dream had ended. Led by the communists the seething multitudes had arisen in the hinterland and swallowed the city, both its squalor and its riches, imperialism and shame.

But today once more new life began here. There were livings to be had in construction sites and back alleys. And when we arrived in the final shadows of afternoon the modern refugees still packed the station, overflowing the platforms, and squatting in front of the carriage doors until shunted along by the conductors. We passed them all in the race to find seats on our train home. And then very slowly passed the city of these Chinese dreams: the belching plants, the warehouses and estates of towers. Dusk fell. The suburbs rolled on.

Kristel fell asleep, pressed against my shoulder.

'Shanghainese are proud people. Aunt Zhu is typical Shanghainese' whispered Wen 'she is too optimistic. Always sees the better future. The communists promise a better future. Maybe just this once, their beliefs are similar'

Ink slowly blotted the clouds.

'Civilisation grew powerful. Then it collapsed. It grew again. And collapsed again...' He illustrated this using his head as a lumpen pendulum and said 'in China history is circular'.

Fields disappeared altogether in the dusk. We were faced with our own reflections in the windows.

'Now in China, people do not care for books. Only for money. This we call a rise!' he coughed.

'You want to make money too' I said.

Wen winced.

'In China we *must* make money' he said 'But education was more important before, and studying for exams was the way to wealth. I am a good student'. Wen studied himself in the window 'my girl does not want to marry a poor teacher' he said. So Chang Wen it seemed, would have to try his hand in the commerce that the old order had deemed so grubby and low.

47

'The imperial officials would have laughed…my example for a successful future comes from a woman' he said, and he coughed in some sort of humour.

A big-eyed girl was watching. She was a pretty thing with unusually short hair.

'I heard you speak English' she said 'Can I practice?' In the seat next door her boyfriend squirmed uncomfortably. He had big spiky hair and a particularly boyish face. He pretended to be too cool to acknowledge the foreigners. It turned out that was because he didn't speak English and didn't want to lose face.

They were both university students.

'My parents do not know about him' said the girl, nodding at spiky. 'They told me to stay away from boys while I finished my studies'.

'What have you been doing in Shanghai?' asked Kristel, waking in time to join in. The girl blushed.

'We just spent our first weekend together' she said. It was a confession freely given. And the dream city had released them from the strict codes of a more traditional China.

Chang Wen leant over and cupped a paw so that Big Eyes could not hear.

'Lots of love affairs in modern China. Aunt says she wants to get into the hotel business. Make money from lovers. Much easier than making money from boxes'

I pressed my head against the filthy window. In the blackness of the countryside, the bunkers had vanished.

'How will you make your money then?' I asked. The train hiccoughed. Wen looked at his shoes and grunted.

'Maybe from kitchenware?' he said without conviction. 'It is easy to get rich now in China. Lots of opportunities. I need ideas. I need connections' he said. Then he turned to the window doubtfully.

'I do not know where to begin' he said.

4. Mi Jin and Han Jie

People and traffic, students and chalk, radio, fireworks, dust...two months had passed in China. By the end of March dead heads of lotus swayed by West Lake's shore while cherry trees on the White causeway spilled pink petals. Ferries tilled to the three mid-lake islands. Lovers paddled in shallow row boats against the hazy backdrop of the southern hills. As I sat there one morning contemplating this scene from a bench lakeside a group gathered to watch. What was this? A foreigner...a *writing* foreigner!

Suddenly the student hammer murderer from Yunnan province was captured hiding out on tropical Hainan Island. Then two brothers from Henan province were arrested for robbing, killing and dismembering at least eleven women over fifteen months. The futures of these suspects did not seem to be in doubt, because according to Chinese Central Television and the rest of the national press they were guilty. After trial, the penalty would be death, a bullet to the back of the neck. *'Choke the chicken to scare the monkey'* they said in China. Yet it took a lot of choking to put these monkeys in their place, more than three thousand a year claimed Amnesty - two thirds of the world's total.

Very Good

Today was to be the first day of Chinese class. I switched on the television. The Communist Party was congratulating itself over the fortieth anniversary of its diplomatic relations with Ghana. *'China is friendly and peace loving'* said the news anchor. I poured milk on my cereal. *'Fresh, delicious, tasted of first love'* it said on the carton. A new round of construction and demolition was underway outside and the itinerants were battering fanatically. Kristel and I picked up pens and paper and left. Mrs. Ho was busy mopping the stairs, humming to herself. British Dave we discovered halfway down, stooped against the wall.

'How is your seeds-only diet going?'

'Not well - been feeling a bit ill' he said. Kristel pulled me onwards into the rampaging street where we jumped a cab, which flew downtown amongst the thousand other nut jobs jack-knifing the lanes and braking furiously. The cabbies of Hangzhou had all fitted their vehicles with seatbelts - for decoration presumably.

By the lake we were dropped. From there we strolled to class via flowering plum where a sign stated *'Nature is our Friend Forever'*.

Teacher Nan cycled from a lakeside apartment to an unlit building in the city's heart with stairs that reeked of stale urine. She bowed little red ribbons were in her hair which contrasted curiously with her large teeth. Teacher Nan hopped around with the excitement of a child, teaching Chinese during the day to Chinese students, and Chinese at night to foreigners. She was the wife of a son of an important provincial official. She was one of the new middle class, with her fingers in more than a few pies, lots of *guanxi*.

'You need to think as a Chinese' she said 'that means you get Chinese names'. So Teacher Nan gave us Chinese names. Kristel became *Mi Jin*.

'It means Shiny Rice. Shiny, like a *crystal*' said Teacher Nan giggling. She caught herself and had a go at regaining her composure 'To be named after food is an honour in China' she said. I knew it.

'You be Han' she said It is a Chinese name like your *Hempson*. This name is common. You are one of the 'old hundred names''.

Teacher Nan asked what I would like as a first name.

'Something good' I said.

'Very Good' she said. This then, became my name: Jie, or 'very good'. Teacher Nan also taught us some of the simplest characters. In *putonghua*, Ma, or 'Mother' was a combination of the characters for female and horse. The characters for 'male' and 'difficult' were different, but they were pronounced the same (nán). Thus the Chinese were not as patriarchal as they may have seemed.

There were a few dialogues to read in the textbook. One of them was this:

A: 'Ni qu nar?' *Where are you going?*
B: 'Wo qu Tiananmen. Ni qu bu qu?' *Im going to Tiananmen. Are you coming?*

'Have you heard of this square?' asked Teacher Nan with a casual flick of the hair 'It is a famous parade ground for festivities' she added.

'Yes' I said. I did not tell her that where I was from it was better known for slaughter.

Little Emperors

Often when I ventured into the street the young pig-tailed girl from the fruit stall who had laughed at me as I smashed a water canister in the street was out there too, usually idling on the curb. She would giggle when she saw me, then run off to hide. I pretended not to notice. She was one of China's *xiao huangdi*, the spoiled little emperors.

We were to meet many more of them when we fell into teaching English at a local language school. The cogs of such a venture had fallen into place because someone knew someone who knew someone. And that someone worked at a university where he knew of a couple of foreigners. Information had been exchanged, palms greased. And suddenly, we had extra-curricular jobs. Ten minutes before lessons were due to begin the director of the school swung by to pick us up. Xu Ping was her name, a short little creature with hair drawn back so tightly it looked like it might snap, like over-tuned guitar strings. She had just started the business. We stepped into her four wheel drive. Its windows were blacked out.

'Do you want textbooks and teaching materials?' she asked. Yes we did.

They were provided eight minutes later: *'Good times are for sharing with friends!'*

'Do you want a teaching assistant?' asked Xu Ping.

'Here you are' she added, forgetting she had presented the idea as a question. She thrust a couple of delicate looking teenagers our way. Kristel was hustled off to another room. The assistant trailed behind.

Xu Ping soon came back for me.

'New blackboard' she said, pulling me around the corner with the girl in tow, a dainty one with a tiny nose and slight build who appeared to float as she walked, like a ghost. 'Assistant is called Zhao Jung' said Xu Ping 'Welcome you to Babel language school!' and she shoved me and this girl into a room. It was brimming with kids. They were amusing themselves tearing at each other's hair and throwing chalk.

'Hello' I said, taking my position on the podium. For a moment I held their attention. The little faces turned towards me, and a lone voice whispered

'Waiguorren'

Then a pig-tailed girl threw paper at a frail looking boy and the class fell once more into anarchy. In vain I slapped a board rubber on the desk. It smothered me in powder. Zhao Jung intervened, stepping in front of the dais as if to protect me. She screamed. The kids sat to attention. This was an impressive result.

I took the register. The kids had been granted English names in the same way we had acquired Chinese ones. One boy had been called 'Big Hammer'. A girl went by the name of 'Commie'.

'*Commie*?' I asked Xu Ping 'Are you sure it's not *Connie*?'

'No' she said. It was definitely Commie.

We played pass the chalk, and counted in English. At intervals I threw simple questions at whoever held the chalk - name the colour, name the numbers, name that letter... And whenever this chalk was thrown too wildly, or the naughty boys became excitable and climbed on top of their desks, Zhao Jung might open her mouth and calm us all down with a little song of Heads, Shoulders, Knees and Toes. Afterwards, when the kids had left and the chalk begun to settle, I turned to her.

'Thank you' I said.

She attempted a smile.

'The kids are difficult' she said 'All spoiled. In my hometown the children have respect'. These city kids were also little emperors, the *xiao huangdi*, not wanting for material but lost without siblings, a world revolved around each of them. Perhaps it really was different still out in the countryside. Amongst the poverty of the farmland the one child policy was not so strictly enforced.

Zhao Jung was from out there in the countryside. Or sort of. Really she was from a factory town in the heart of the province which produced copper pipes, one of those places mainly bypassed so far by the economic revolution. The motorway was supposed to have come, but the authorities found a cheaper route back to the coast that did not have to cut through the hills. The town sounded as if it was looking to become a relic of central planning.

'No new jobs at the factory' she said, biting her lip 'Young people are leaving'. The elders would have to retire first she said. Output was static and the books were filled only by orders from the government. The state at least, could not afford to see such a place fail.

Each week Kristel and I turned up for duty. Each week we were saved by our assistants. A few weeks into term the parents were invited to watch in some kind of snap inspection. We knew because the phone had rung late in the previous evening. It was Zhao Jung.

'Tomorrow, can you not play games in class?' she asked.

'Why?' I said.

She paused in some kind of sigh.

'The parents will be angry' she claimed. I could tell she wanted to say the parents didn't pay substantial sums just so their adorable little offspring could play games.

'Games are good for learning' I claimed. But Zhao Jung was insistent.

'In China this is not a traditional method'

Once she had secured agreement from me that I would not let the side down with games, Zhao Jung excused herself and hung up. Immediately the phone rang again. It was Zhao Jung.

'Can I speak to Kristel please?' she asked. I passed the phone to Kristel and left them to it. I came back later once it was over to ask.

'What was that about?'

Kristel laughed. 'I'm sure you can guess' she said. There would be no games for anyone tomorrow.

Instead on the big day, mothers, grandmothers, fathers, other assorted relatives and well-meaning neighbours crowded into my classroom ready to watch me fight their kids and the blackboard. The stragglers jostled outside, twisting their necks curiously through the open windows like battery chickens. Zhao Jung stood on the periphery with her lips clenched. But there was no chalk throwing. No table dancing. There was however plenty of reciting, mainly of lists of fruit. Because under the low ceilings I taught by rote. It was a method that helped China lag in international education league tables. And I wondered whether the Chinese could ever turn their backs on this method of drudgery. How else would these kids learn at least five thousand Chinese characters off by heart except one by one, again, and again, and again…

At the end of class the guests filed out and Zhao Jung broke into smile: I knew this because her hand now covered her mouth.

'Thank you' she said.

Xu Ping was out there chatting to the parents. And after they finally left she strutted into the classroom to deliver the verdict.

'Satisfactory' she said and her mouth flinched, threatening to smile 'They like you. They like *Mi Jin*. You are responsible foreign guests' She raised her head victoriously.

'And we are all still in business' she said.

Anhui People

Spring matured. The sun began to battle cloud and 'mist'. We pretended not to be at home when Lou Da or British Dave knocked, and ran when necessary from Mr.Ji and his hunt for the Queen's English. Kristel drank tea with Mr. Gong and spoke French. I drank beer with Lei Shen and spoke English and rudimentary Chinese. Mrs. Ho swept in the stairwell and spoke to herself. Steadily our Chinese improved. Then one morning I saw Mrs. Ho once more on the stairs. Before she could open her mouth I was in front of her.

'Where are you from?' I asked.

'*Aiah!*' she shouted, almost dropping the broom. 'You can speak'.

Finally we were able to convince Chang Wen we did not need collecting from the school gates anymore, because even without the address paper we had been here far too long not to be able to find our way to the city centre by bus. It left after all, from right at the end of the road.

'It will be dangerous for you to travel alone' Wen said.

But it would not be we explained. Because it was far more dangerous here on campus with all the traffic, the open manholes, the live electric wiring sticking out from all the unfinished construction work.

The bus avoided the new overhead expressway bisecting the city, the one that was so new it did not feature on city maps. It meandered instead the older route where trucks and bicycles slugged it out, and shabby workhouses counted down the ends of their useful lives. Occasionally it stopped at the new traffic lights with their LED screens...30, 29, 28, counting down to green as taxis shoved in and the three-wheelers pulled u-turns.

Hefang Jie...the end of the line. This length of terracotta roofs and whitewashed walls was one more mock up of a traditional Song street. It ran between the museum of tax and an Irish bar, a gaggle of shops and stalls built to snare domestic tourists. They roved in packs, they had come to smoke cigarettes through a two-storey pipe, watch an old fashioned peepshow run by a man in Manchu robes and a false *queue*, to eat skewers of roast mutton sold by Han Chinese - who in their white flat caps, pretended to look like Muslim *Hui* people. Most visitors successfully ignored the hideously burned young man who flapped helplessly on the roadside, pawing a small keyboard. Hefang Jie was again an idealised version of the old China, Disneyland via the Song dynasty. Just to think, a few hundred metres away near the replica Song city gate hid real buildings from the Qing era - dirty, unkempt, and pondering a date with a sledgehammer crew.

With its pebbles and pot plants, the tang of star anise and pickling herbs, the evocation if not the substance of endurance, I liked the *Huqingyu Tang* Chinese medicine store. It was popular with Western medical teams sent over to investigate the science behind the medicine. Here they might find dried sea dragon, snake, ginseng and deer's penis ('…if you have trouble with your wife' suggested the assistant). Chinese medicine treated the body as a universe with its organs indivisible from the whole. It was a system of sophisticated systems working in balance to maintain a healthy functioning human. This seemed a uniquely Chinese set of ideals, this hope that a system's components should work together for the greater good and the obsession with balance which did not appear to be playing out so well on the city's streets.

In the hills above posed a restored fort. It contained a Confucian temple. Inside languished ornate scenes from the mythical Song: the bald but bearded sage; the yellow-robed emperor on the royal throne, plump and haughty; a court of stern officials; and pale faced females - their cheeks blushed red - all set against a background of flying cranes, opaque clouds, craggy peaks. This was supposed to have been a scene from the city about which the Chinese said 'In heaven there is paradise. On earth there is Hangzhou…'. It seemed far removed from the office towers, the spillage of fast food joints and downtown department stores where round eyed models graced huge posters for Lancôme and L'Oréal.

There was always the lake. Today the lovers were out there, skating the shimmering surface. The hordes remained on shore, snaffling ice cream and sticks of tofu beside the rubbish bins that proclaimed *'Love our homeland'*. There were shouts of 'hullo!' and excited finger waving.

We aliens were being pointed out to the children, because in the inland provinces where the domestics came from they didn't have as many real live *laowai* like they had here.

The willow budded and broke into luxuriant fronds, the cherry flower was fading. Elderly folk congregated in the pavilions to sing as *Erhu* were strung, or hung out by the flower beds to listen to Chinese classical music blaring from hidden speakers. Police officers drove golf carts on the pedestrian boulevards and beggars scoured for plastic bottles. Often Chang Wen joined us to pass comment on the citizens of the lakeside.

'We didn't have beggars before the economic reforms' he said one bright morning. The lake's waters were static, a sheet of dappled glass.

'No?'

'No' he reckoned 'Now people put their parents out to beg and their children out to beg. There are also lazy peasants and disabled people. All from Anhui'. Another one passed. Wen wrinkled his nose as subtly as he could manage and added

'I don't think these people can be helped'.

And from that point on, whenever a beggar of any category got remotely close, Chang Wen shifted towards me in telegraphed secrecy, put his hand to his mouth, and whispered

'From Anhui province'.

A few days later an aroma of fresh lily conquered the streets. A new flower stall had opened across the way and there had been fireworks that morning. We met Wen downtown again, and caught another bus, which wound away from the city centre, up the back country hills, past plantations of tea, bamboo groves, fish ponds. It led to the tea houses of Dragon Well - *Longjing* - Village, where grew the best tea in all of China. Mao, Deng, Jiang Zemin had all stopped by for a sampling. The great emperor Qianlong too had visited Dragon Well in the late eighteenth century at the pinnacle of Qing power. As his empire creaked, and rotted from within, he planted here eighteen seedlings. They had since sprouted, flourished, gently relaxed into old age and twisted into knots that no longer produced. For two hundred annual cycles new plants grew here on the slopes and valleys, nurtured in rolling cloud. They matured, produced, grew gangly and useless. But still Qianlong's tea lived here amongst the new season's plantings. They had stood here as the Taiping ransacked Hangzhou, during the fall of the emperor and the Japanese invasion. They had outlived Mao and his ridiculous schemes. They seemed less likely to see out the hawkers who nowadays sloped in the shadows ready to ambush tourists with counterfeit tea.

'From Anhui too' Wen said of them, squeezing his eyes together in the forlorn hope that they might just disappear.

We wandered up the 'nine creaks meandering through the misty forest', a grand title for a pathway that tracked a dribble through valleys of bamboo and scrubland, up a dusty trail and across redundant stepping stones: Hangzhou did not come more remote than this. The path zig zagged up to tea fields which had once been hewn from the woods. Here lampshade wearers plucked and tossed leaves into wicker baskets carried on back. I wondered whether they agreed with the sign at the edge of the rows that stated *'Protecting birds is protecting human beings themselves'*. As we passed the workers raised themselves and stared slack-jawed at the *laowai* and their Chinese friend.

'The peasants come from...' said Wen.

I guessed.

'Correct' he said 'These *Anhuiren* will overrun us. And you knew this already!' he looked at me with what I took to be paternal pride. But many tea pickers were from the local Zhejiang countryside too, escaping the interior villages.

'You begin talking in Chinese' reckoned Chang Wen 'You begin thinking in Chinese. You are becoming a *Hangzhouren* Han Jie'.

Little Dog from the Desert

A week later we met Chang Wen amidst the fumes and litter of a downtown bus stop. He had brought a girl, one shrouded in a coat of heavy make-up who clutched forcefully at Wen's arm, as though it were the lever by which he could be manoeuvred. This girl had also brought a male colleague whose job it soon became apparent, was that of chaperone. For this girl was Wen's fiancée, Cheng Hualing.

'Her colleague memorises everything I say' stated Wen miserably. But on the positive side he pointed out, Cheng Hualing would surely need someone to talk to while Wen made the talk with the foreigners.

'I had marriage negotiations last night' he admitted 'Her father said I must provide Cheng Hualing with a house and a car. He wants a new van for himself too'

'Sounds expensive' I said 'how you will afford it all?'

'I need a new job' he said, pursing his lips and trying to touch his nose with them. 'Her father told me if I want to make it I must become a businessman and forget about teaching. But how can he ask me to do this? He is just a delivery driver!'

We dawdled up the North Hill, past the noodle shop where the owners had recently become angered when I left a tip, chasing us up the road. The chef had caught up with me where the woods began and insisted I take my money back. Now we were entering those same woods. We wandered through the glade where just last week a gang of elders had been listening to captive songbirds. Kristel had taken a photo and disturbed them all. The elders shook their fists and growled 'The birds have stopped singing' But there were no old men here today.

'Even her mother has something to say. Says I cannot buy jewellery or a German car on a teacher's salary. I said we don't need jewellery or a German car. She told me maybe I don't need her daughter'

'See how easy you have it' whispered Kristel with an impish pinch of my arm.

Cheng Hualing and her colleague strolled ahead, she was coyly laughing at something he had just said. Wen didn't seem to notice.

'We have different expectations' he said 'Maybe this is the problem. I was born five years before her; before the reforms. But the psychological gap is greater. We were the last generation of idealists. The next generation are materialists'. It was becoming harder for men to find a suitable partner, he reckoned. The patriarchal values of the old China had met the one child policy. There was gender imbalance and the tables had turned. In the new China, women of marriageable age held a stronger suit.

Up we passed, through newly prosperous suburbs, and a village of large tiled peasant houses where the stench of burnt plastic belched from household waste burning out in the backyards. It was a stiff climb up stone steps, through pine groves and the odd bamboo, then we were at the summit where incense floated dreamily above the city. Here squatted a Buddhist temple. A large television aerial had been plonked into its forecourt, dwarfing the buildings and outhouses. Perhaps those superstitious monks would be converted by the civilising power of TV.

'It is the new dream' said Wen 'the dream is that we can do whatever we want. Cheng Hualing tells me that anything is possible. I think she is mistaken'.

Cheng Hualing burst in, grasping Wen's hand and chattering energetically. He turned to us.

'Cheng Hualing wants to take us to market…Everything has to be done immediately' he said, and he shook his head. I nodded too, pretending out of laziness, that I empathised.

It was only a short ride by cable car down towards the city, and from there, a bus trip. It led to the Hangzhou flower and bird market, a new block of glass and terracotta: five storeys of orchid and bonzai tree, fish and pygmy turtle, yapping puppies in large pens served up and sold off in plastic bags - like heads of broccoli - and teeming boxes of tiny mice, which spilled from their containers to be crushed carelessly into the floor. There were squirrels and rabbits, little dogs in large cages, large dogs in little cages, and parrots clamped to metal posts that squawked and pecked at their chains. The dangerously *bourgeois* habit of owning pets was becoming fashionable amongst the middle classes.

Amongst all the yelping and squealing, Cheng Hualing and the chaperone went missing. We searched around, and eventually found them. Hualing was looking very pleased with herself.

'Look!' she shouted, pulling an arm from behind her back which carried a pink cage. It contained something down-like and very shy; a tiny ball no bigger than the palm of my hand, with long ears curled tightly down over its eyes, a head, buried deep in fur, whiskers, and nervous nostrils.

'For you' squealed Cheng Hualing, her legs crossed in mock bashfulness. She thrust the cage into Kristel's hands. It contained a desert rabbit, a female from the wilds of north-western China. Cheng Hualing grinned expectantly, like a cat that needed stroking. Kristel's mouth dropped open. I felt sure it reflected my own. What would we do with a rabbit? Animals were not just for the year of the dog and we were not staying forever.

We tried to get the money back: ten yuan for the cage, five for the rabbit.

'Not have money' said the seller grumpily. It was already too late.

'If you don't like the rabbit you can eat it' suggested Wen helpfully: it was an experience that would have been over in two mouthfuls.

Kristel removed the tiny rabbit from its prison, and replanted it in my coat pocket. Its velvet ears flopped over the sides. We all ate lunch in a hotpot restaurant - a mess of steam and chatter. And when the waiters weren't looking, I fed the rabbit lettuce meant for the boiling pots.

Then she came home with us, where we named her 'Little Dog' because she was attention seeking, like a puppy. Kristel began conducting toilet conditioning. Later she attempted to claim success. But the best Little Dog ever seemed to do was run to her designated toilet spot after she had released herself elsewhere - on the pillows, on Kristel's trousers, on my chest. She did though busy herself at home, eating the flowers and a pot plant Kristel had received as a gift from her students. She jumped out of the box that had become her night pen. She defecated all over the vinyl floors and cold bathroom tile. She galloped to greet us whenever we arrived home from classes, standing on her hind legs, with her paws out and her nose dancing. Whenever I moved her from my palm to my chest, she scrabbled violently, the burrowing instinct untamed.

I even took her outside to get exercise. She bounced on the short grass - the itinerants had freshly mown the lawns. Betty walked by when she saw us playing.

'Ai' she exclaimed 'so beautiful!' and she dashed forward to pick the thing up. I did not notice the approach of Mr. Ji and his increasingly neglected teeth until it was too late.

He saw the rabbit.

'Eeah!' he screamed excitedly. Betty placed Little Dog back in the grass and we all stood there watching as Little Dog scampered backwards and forwards, a sniff here, a scratch there.

'Rabbits are delicious' said Mr. Ji finally, his eyes fixed. I decided to pick the rabbit up and take her indoors. Once inside she hid for some time in the liner that we used as a bin.

Studying

The blossom faltered. Willow burst into fronds which fluttered on the breeze. Recently the communist national leadership had been busy with the important business of criticising Chinese celebrities for their wayward hair styles. Under Teacher Nan's patient eye, Mi Jin and Han Jie had been improving their Chinese. They practised on the taxi lunatics who chauffeured them to class, and experimented inanely with last lesson's words.

'What is your favourite country?' (it was China!)

'Do you prefer vegetables or fruit?' (...)

'Recently I have been suffering diarrhoea...'

Usually these drivers played along good-naturedly, listening casually, grinning at our mistakes. Even whilst gabbing, both Han Jie and Mi Jin could now keep half an eye on the route taken and politely request a change of direction if any cabbie tried to take the scenic route.

I loved this language, with the added interest of mastering the four tones; the logical grammar disdainful of tense; the simplicity of description - the use of 'da', meaning 'big': skyscrapers - big buildings (*dalou*), universities - big schools (*daxue*), biggest little brother (*dadi*). And I enjoyed practicing my character strokes, locked up in our room, sat at my creaking desk with a flask of green tea to hand. Sometimes I began in the early hours and finished long after the afternoon session of Chariots of Fire had piped up on University Radio.

Then the May Day public holiday was upon us all. The one point three billion were released upon the roads and railways; about to stretch the infrastructure of China to breaking point. Itinerants flooded across the country to their ancestral family homes, and the middle class sneaked away breaks. From across the plains, the mountains, the freezing wastes of the North, the baking sands of the Western deserts, from towns and cities all over the Wu heartlands and inland provinces, came the domestic tourists - all converging on the city by the lake.

'Don't go down there' warned Chang Wen by telephone 'It is dangerous of course. For the next week I will not leave my home. I will not see Cheng Hualing'. For Chang Wen, this was a time of rest. But we went anyway without him to take a stroll beside the lake of the city of heaven.

Down by the lake there was little moving through the crowds, the traffic, the congestion. The playful elders were gone, the police golf carts nowhere to be seen. The masses had arrived, finally overcoming even the urban landscape. Around the pavilions and stone causeways of the shore, many were knocked into the waters. It seemed prudent to retreat.

Back on campus we ran into Lou Da, who had come by the foreign teacher's block to steal books from Professor Darling.

'All of China is here' he said, trying to stop the spoils from sliding away from under his coat where he held them fast 'So I stay on campus and send Zhou Mei-xie out for food'. And when he added

'Tourists regularly drown in the lake over the holiday', for once, I believed him. For the rest of the holiday Kristel and I holed up in our room, brewed the pot, and practiced Chinese.

Tyranny

Zhao Jung called a few days after May Day had ended and the hordes returned from whence they came.

'I will no longer be your assistant' she said. Babel had cut her salary. It seemed this kind of classroom assistance was not the once in a lifetime opportunity for work experience that Xu Ping kept claiming. Yet Zhao Jung was to my classes what the communist party claimed to be for all of China: the only force capable of upholding order in the face of chaos.

'Babel knows this' she said 'But Xu Ping is very stubborn. She thinks if she gives in now, then we shall keep taking'

'What will you do?' I asked.

'Go back to my hometown' she said 'I'm almost a qualified teacher. My parents tell me I must find a husband'.

'Do you want to find a husband?'

'They want me to meet the son of the factory manager. He is a very good marriage prospect'.

'Have you met him before?' I pried.

'He went to my school' she said 'I remember that once he pulled my hair in the classroom'. Her currency was surely strong out in the languishing countryside. So Zhao Jung left Hangzhou for good, heading headed back south to live a quiet life in the valley town which the motorway had failed to connect to the world. I did not see her again.

So it was just me versus the terrors. The *xiao huangdi* too, seemed to understand that I was doomed. It was impossible to stop eight year old girls from throwing paper across the classroom, or six year old boys from fighting. They would point out that they needed to use the toilet by grabbing their crotches and gyrating. Never had anything made me feel quite so powerless and out of control as this one small class of renegade infants.

I ran my final lessons as a form of tyranny - books slammed on tables; banishments to naughty corner. There would be no more Mr. Nice Foreigner. Under the new regime, correct answers to questions gained the children pole position to exit class. Bad behaviour earned five minutes detention. Over the course of the lessons I tweaked punishment and reward, and chalked many angry records on the board. Strong willed authority was what these kids needed, otherwise we would have chaos and anarchy. The justification was an old one. The Chinese had been repeating the same mantra to themselves for centuries. Whoever held the mandate of heaven held the right to lead forward all the children, the good people of China. And in this classroom, the mandate was surely mine.

But when Kristel's assistant quit, her classes collapsed too. So we sacked ourselves. I had learned only how to bully children. The students had learned only how to fear the foreigner, and would likely never forget this *Gweize*, the foreigner who had barged into their lives, garbled incoherently, shrieked, screamed and tore out his hair, and then vanished mysteriously half way through term.

We heard only once more from Xu Ping, that stiff-haired entrepreneur of the new China. She called us out of the blue one evening early next term.

'Babel needs you. We are making good business' she said 'Please will you teach for us?'

The Rabbit

Meanwhile the rabbit continued messing all over the floor. And too many people still knocked on the door, all wanting something. University Radio seeped through the windows. My student Chang Xu caught me walking to class one bleary morning. Her morning show had just finished.

'I have explained to the students we must all strive harder to

63

build our China' she said.

As if this all wasn't enough, outside the acrobats were still having fun bludgeoning buildings. Kristel and I began to fight. We sniped at one another as we passed Mrs. Ho on the stairs, and bickered on the way to collect water from the Xias. It was time for some space. We requested another room from Lou Da. We were entitled to it under the terms of the teaching contract. Lou Da made the arrangements. Mrs. Ho hummed loudly and dusted down the empty room above. Kristel moved upstairs.

Little Dog became subdued, hair started falling from around one of her eyes - she had spent too much time with her nose in the rubbish and gotten ill. One evening in Chinese class, Kristel mentioned the rabbit's poor health. Teacher Nan smiled sweetly

'My daughter had a rabbit' she said 'But unfortunately it died'

'How did it die?' asked Kristel.

'We forgot to feed it' she said.

Only a generation ago humans had died in their millions out in the starving villages. No wonder most Chinese did not seem to consider animals worth the attachment.

Tian Fei and Chang Er dropped by. Tian Fei was more darker skinned than ever. She let it slip that Chang Er had a new boyfriend. He was studying engineering here at Educated People.

'He does not care for money' Er said, flopping down at the table 'he wants to build things'. Tian Fei beamed brightly in a show of sisterly affection. And when she saw the rabbit, she did not even lecture me on the decadence of pet keeping. Instead she knelt down and teased its chin.

'Beautiful...' she said 'I will make it better. Can I borrow it?'

'He is very clever too' continued Chang Er, her pony tail jerking around excitedly 'he reads old books. Daoist books and Confucian books'

Tian Fei screwed up her face.

'He gave me this book' Er said and she pushed her head against her chest and held it up. *My Country and My People* it was called, by Lin Yutang. 'It is about China. Famous in the West' she said 'I finished it already'. Er placed it with both hands on the table.

'You can read it'

Later that evening I found in it the following quote.

'*We do not teach our young to become like the sons of God*' it stated *'but we teach them to behave like sane, normal human beings'*. And on the same page: *'we have no use for impracticable idealism, as we have no patience for doctrinaire theology'*. Clearly Lin Yutang had written these sentences before the Chinese Communist Party had become a force to reckon with.

The next day I surprised Lou Da on the stairs - he was on his way back down. I assumed he had been on a washing expedition with Zhou Mei-xie.

'The rabbit is ill' I said.

'It will certainly die' Lou Da replied, his eyebrow raised at seeing my legs trouser less.

'Why do you say that?' I asked.

'All these rabbits die' he said 'Mei-xie had one. It lived four weeks. Then it died. She got another. Lived four weeks. Then died. She didn't buy any more rabbits' he leaned closer towards me 'some people say the pet store injects them with a chemical to make them die. They do this so you will have to go buy another one' he said 'call it good business'.

I headed back inside and called Chang Wen. Outside, the acrobats were still swinging.

'If you are sick of it, you should release it into the wilds' Chang Wen reckoned 'Cheng Hualing says she is surprised it is still alive at all'. I did not point out to him that the wilds were far from China's east coast.

Then to make matters worse, Little Dog fell from my shoulder and crawled into a corner. She hid there for two days. When she emerged we took her to the vet where an X-Ray enlargement showed her little rabbit leg broken. Then every day for a week we raced across the vastness of town by taxi to get our rabbit expensive injections from the vet.

I called Chang Wen again.

'We didn't release the rabbit' I said 'we are getting her treated instead' I told him about our trips to the vet, the x-rays, and injections. Chang Wen remained silent.

'Most peasants in China do not get that kind of healthcare' he said finally. These trips were the self-indulgence of foreigners too foolish to deserve their money.

We continued with our visits. Then on our last trip across town, I called Lou Da for a translation of the vet's final diagnosis.

'Its leg is broken' Da said gravely. 'It will never be able to walk again'. He paused for a second. Then asked brightly 'How are you getting on with Kristel?'

'Fine' I said. It might not have been any of his business, but since he had just done me a favour it was no time to be telling him so.

'That's good' Da continued, adopting a sagely tone 'we say arguing is like cutting water with a sword'.

But our rabbit had been permanently crippled. Next week on the way to class Professor Darling stepped out of his flat and caught me as I did Lou Da.

'My condolences' he said.

'Thanks' I said.

As usual I passed Mrs. Ho on the stairwell. This time she remained silent, donating instead a bony hand with which she patted me on the shoulder. Even Mr. Gong, Head of Languages, seemed to have heard. Over the usual French and tea session with Kristel he tapped her arm and said

'I am so sorry. Let me know if you need anything'.

Little Dog recovered only very slowly. She no longer scrabbled on my chest or ran out to greet us when we returned from class. Instead she limped about the kitchen and hid under the bathroom sink. From around her eye, hair continued to fall. Then it came from her chin too, then her legs and back. Eventually it fell in clumps from every part of her until she was spotted in bald patches.

Then I met British Dave on the stairs before I had a chance to hear him coming and close the door.

'I am sorry to hear about it' he said 'Lou Da told all of us that Kristel split with you'. And like that everybody's true concern became transparent.

Setting Dave straight seemed to dishearten him. His face sagged.

'I split with the girl I was seeing' he explained 'I thought maybe we were in the same boat'. He had met her near the market when she had laughed affectionately at his clumsy attempts to buy steamed buns in the common language.

British Dave sat down while I made tea.

'I told her I would stay here and live with her. Set up a teahouse together' he said 'but the week after I told her, she said she didn't love me. She likes some boy she met in a bar. He told her he has a car and might buy a house...imagine, I can't even compete with a peasant's son'   He groped his mug and looked inside. He had thought there was a niche for him here, in this town where the locals called him 'foreigner'.

'There is nothing left for me here anymore' he said 'So much for running'.

He grinned, a big sad one that seemed to tickle his eyes.

Water

Towards the end of term, the heavens opened. The rainy season had arrived. Mrs. Ping gathered up her son, pulled her key making machine up against the nearest wall and sat under a flimsy parasol that sagged as the water fell. The rubbish bins spilled themselves across the streets and rotting vegetables were dashed into the tarmac. Mr. Hong had acquired a panama hat. He stood there unbothered by the rain, chain-smoking whilst it ran off his hat. The creaks at nine streams began to gush. The drains overflowed. Chinese bicyclists pedalled above them, all alike in their multicoloured plastic overalls. In her yellow one, Teacher Nan looked like a misplaced fisherman as she cycled to class.

And I continued to run. Usually, amongst traffic and exhaust fumes, I was not sure whether I was actually healthier before or after I went out. But with the coming of rain, running became cleansing - just like it was for the streets of the city, where the stench of fumes and rotting fruit dissipated into the drains.

As the water fell, the roadside eateries offered shelter above tile floors splattered in rice and mud. Sat at the plastic tables and using the disposable chopsticks, the labourer clientele spat gristle on the floor and watched as Yao Ming carried the Houston Rockets to victory.

Most meals I felt, were a success. And even if I never would develop a taste for the slow roasted fish heads with brains of mucous, I did became fond of Hangzhou specialities like the Dong Po braised pork in Shaoxing wine, or the West Lake Vinegar fish. I never could tire of watching Chinese street life as we ate - the peasants on their tricycles, the cocky chickens and the lazy dogs, the pedalling students sometimes balancing a lover on the handlebars. And as it rained, I watched the fruit sellers retreating under tarpaulins, the rainbow of commuters cycling home in their waterproofs.

One evening Kristel and I headed over towards the boys dorms to eat fried noodle in a hawker area protected from the weather by a high tin roofed canopy. While the rain clattered above a couple of women found a black rat hiding behind a stack of firewood. Both women shrieked, and so did the rat. The women pulled loose bricks from the roadside and hurled them at the rat. Most of them missed and skidded across wet tarmac. But a lucky shot had hit the mark. The rat limped over towards a wall where it was cornered and one of the women stamped on its head. Once the fun was over, everyone returned to their food. The rat, it seemed, had made a big mistake coming near these people.

Another evening a bedraggled Lei Shen turned up at our door dripping all over the place. He wore the kind of grin that might pull facial muscles.

'I have a surprise for you!' he said. He led us deep into the warren, where rain rattled on tin roofs. Housewives queued at the boiler houses. Prostitutes enjoyed cigarettes before the evening shift began. Somewhere amidst this sprawl, Shen brought us to a dim little eating house.

Grimy fish tanks lined the corridors. A glass bowl of shrimp occupied a table. The dish had soaked in herbs, chilli and the stiff rice spirit known as *Baijiu*. This was the surprise: the shrimp were still alive. Straight from the tanks the critters had been hauled. Now all they could do was vainly flick themselves from the toxic brew. Out there around the table were three hungry diners.

'My grandmother loves these' said Lei Shen 'she pretends not. She is a Buddhist. Not supposed to eat animals. But she has a drink and then everything tastes good'. He unleashed a hefty laugh and pushed my head towards the bowl.

I plucked out a victim and stuck it in my mouth. Since the idea of eating live animals seemed more than a little freakish, I chewed quickly so I would not have to feel it wriggling. Twitching on the plate, shifting chilli oil around like windscreen wipers were the antennae of the severed head. In China, it was not to be the last time I would empathise with a prawn.

Hand waving, protests, backslapping, perhaps a few toasts - this was the art of settling a bill at the end of a meal. All parties might demand to pay, but one by one, each was supposed to duck out until one party remained to claim the prize. It was a peculiarly Chinese game. Whoever extended the invite was responsible for payment. That was unless he or she was owed a particular favour. Whichever the case, whoever was to fit the bill was supposed to allow everyone else to give way first.

Chang Wen played this game most rigidly. He also had plenty of home grown advice to give during any meal during which he expected to pay at the end.

He nodded towards those soy braised fish and said

'Eat the eyes. They are good for your eyes'.

He eyed the chicken thighs and said

'Chew the bones. They are good for your bones'

Wen leaned down beside the fish heads and pulled out a straw through which he was going to do some sucking.

'Eat the brains. They are good for your...'

'I can't'

'No? Why?'

'I have allergies'

'What allergies?'

'Yes. What allergies?' asked Kristel. I trod on her foot.

'Ouch!' she said 'Why did you tread on my foot?'

'Is the waiter talking to you Wen?' I asked in a cunning bid at distraction.

We all looked.

'No. He is facing the other way' Wen concluded unhelpfully. So I gave up and tried the brains, sucking them up with a straw. Whenever it was our turn to take control of the bill, there were no fish eyes, chicken bones, or slow roast fish heads whose brain you were supposed to suck through a straw.

It rained continuously. Finally I came to the feeling that for some time living here in China, I had become more fully present. An unlikely kind of mental clarity had swapped itself for routine and sleeplessness. I no longer seemed to be spending time divining the future or replaying the past. It had something to do with the constant stimulation. All that noise, all that dirt and disorder - the endless patter of rain, digging, and the stench of wet, decaying fruit.

The weather had other advantages though, holding Mr. Ji at bay for instance. And Lou Da stopped by only once in search of French class.

'Don't you think it is about time you took me to dinner?' he asked, shaking his umbrella. For some inexplicable reason, I agreed that it was.

Next week Kristel and I took him downtown, to a colourful little barbeque restaurant with a view over the rain sodden lake. Zhou Mei-xie came too, her eyes always fixed on the table cloth. And as we sat there looking out upon belligerent clouds and drooping willow, Da switched on the broad grin and said

'Mei-xie doesn't talk much'.

She blushed violently. He flicked her ear 'but at least she is obedient. A real Chinese girlfriend'. Kristel changed the topic.

'Are you looking forward to studying abroad next year?'

Lou Da kept his eyes locked firmly on me.

'It will be no different from here' he said 'Globalisation is making everywhere the same. Your Britain is the same as our China'.

'I think you might still be surprised' I suggested. At that moment I couldn't think of anything stranger than this effete individual wandering the estates of Bradford.

'Don't you think Kristel would make a good mother' he interrupted, frowning.

'So would you Lou Da' Kristel replied.

Later I paid the bill at the front of the restaurant. And Lou Da did not argue with me as I felt sure he had been brought up to. Instead he called the waiter and harangued him for a while.

'What did you tell the waiter?' I asked Da on our way out.

'I told him I have eaten at several places like this one, and this one was very average' Lou Da said, flapping his arm contemptuously 'But then I told him you two come from Britain where the food is terrible. So of course to you the food tastes delicious'.

I decided I did not owe Lou Da any more dinners.

At the Café

Over the course of the endless downpour, our rabbit sat in the corner moulting everything. But it was only a rabbit...an animal doted on by men. In China, an irrelevance. Pierced eared Fei Lian dropped by our flat while I was out and convinced Kristel I had agreed to lend him my umbrella. British Dave popped by for more tea. He now preached the virtues of a watermelon-only diet. Professor Darling invited his favourite students out of the rain while his wife was out. They were girls who watched over him as he too practiced his characters.

Kristel and I trudged daily through the water. We visited the internet café, searching for websites we were unable to access (amnesty international, human rights watch, Falun Dafa). And I was sitting there doing just this one day when a big hand gripped my shoulder. It was Mr. Zhang, the place's greying manager.

'*lai, lai, lai!*' he whispered excitedly. We followed him past the rows of smelly gamers and out to the back door. Here he shoved us unceremoniously into the rain and locked the door behind us. We walked back to the front entrance to see what was going on. The police were there. Two smoked underneath the gold characters, attempting fruitlessly to avoid getting wet. A few others were inside the glass doors, slouching on the counter and intimidating Mr. Zhang, who grinned and bowed, suddenly the old stereotype of the sly Eastern sycophant. There was no explanation as to why these men had come, or why they might care about *laowai* in particular. But then, somebody had been accessing internet sites that they were not supposed to, the type of internet sites that might damage internal stability. And with those implications of devious individualism and wilful contrariness, in all probability, that somebody was a foreigner.

We still returned to Mr. Zhang's. But he was not so friendly anymore. He took to forcing his smile, and made us to leave our passports at the counter. One typically wet day some time later, I noticed the internet connection begin to limp. So we moved from Mr. Zhang's and scoured the warren in search of a faster connection. It was to no avail. Over the next few days, internet speeds became slower and slower, then dwindled to a complete halt. For almost two weeks the internet furred up completely across North Hangzhou, and we were thrown back to a stone age of telephones and posted mail.

When eventually the internet did perk up, I came across some interesting news on the overseas media. Over the previous two weeks, protestors had been arrested in Beijing; some political activists had gone missing; a large rally had been held in Hong Kong. Across the world, memorials had taken place in remembrance of June 6th, the anniversary of the bloodshed around Tiananmen Square. It had come, and then gone, just like that. No mention of it in the local press, television, or in school. Teacher Nan had not mentioned the square in Chinese class since lesson one. The only sign that anyone in the mainland remembered was the mysterious internet slow down.

Chang Wen popped by the University of Educated People a few days later, his great bulk sodden from head to toe. And when I asked him about this missed anniversary he narrowed his eyes darkly.

'Many in this country have not forgotten' he said 'you will discover this if you keep studying'. And whenever I became bored of drinking tea and writing characters, I remembered these words.

I wrote and read and copied and memorised. Outside it rained. Clouds stampeded down from the hills to lash the West Lake with lightning. Metal row boats huddled together underneath willow, which flailed madly in the wind. Traffic tail backs multiplied and scooter riders balanced themselves in knee deep water at the junctions. And always standing out in it, the formidable constant: Mr. Hong breathing smoke over the sodden garbage.

Then finally one day, after the long weeks of rain, a chink opened in the black lid of the sky and the lake waters sparkled darkly. Summer was on its way.

5. Unloosed

Little Dog hobbled for relief under water that leaked from a pipe. In class light bounced against the white walls and fans blew the notes off my lectern. Out on the street, vendors fanned themselves under umbrellas and the demolition acrobats cowered under their half-finished works. Dogs hid again, the beggars fled. Beside the lake clumps of hawkers shielded themselves behind wilting willow, and tourists herded to the safety of tea houses. Even their guides were intimidated, removing caps and wiping brows, consoling themselves with ice cream and giving the megaphones a few hours rest. Out on the water there were far fewer boats, and those that dared duel with the blazing heat rowed a little desperately - as if attempting to escape a desert island.

Then buses began rolling into town. They came from all over the provinces and special administrative districts. They clogged the city's arteries and spewed domestic tourists into its heart. These tourists arrived with cameras and guidebooks and colour-coded tour caps to make sure they did not get lost or separated from the group. But more importantly, they arrived with each other. They jabbered, teased, posed, and snapped. Nowhere was going to be safe anymore.

One of China's legendary romances had unfolded on West Lake's Broken Bridge, when Xu Xian had given the beauty Bai Su Zheng the cover of his umbrella during a rainstorm. The two had courted and were married, but a blissful life together had been spoiled by a scheming abbot from a temple on Golden Mountain. This abbot had been hunting the White Snake - the true identity of Bai Su Zheng. He now discovered Bai, capturing and imprisoning her under Thunder Peak Pagoda. There she languished for years until her sister, the immortal Black Snake finally arrived to rescue her, and reunite her with Xu Xian. The abbot meanwhile, was thrown to an ignominious end at the hands of a crab.

The Broken Bridge still spanned a corner of the lake. It was difficult to miss with all the tourists crawling on it. They bulldozed over its graceful stone arch, then stormed past the willow on the White and Su causeways. They trampled over the plant beds of Flowers harbour and hurled whole loaves of bread to the goldfish of the viewing ponds. At Thunder Peak, the former prison of the White Snake, the tourists raced up escalators and glass panelled lifts to the top of the pagoda. Here they snapped struggling boats and purple sunsets that slid behind the western hills. This Thunder Peak Pagoda had needed neither public consultation nor legal wrangling. It was newly risen, a monument to a new age.

At the zoo the hordes watched boxing matches between sun bears dressed in ballerinas' dresses. They laughed loudly at this spectacle - *these bears were in dresses, boxing each other's lights out!* The same crowds could muster only a few titters for the bicycling monkeys, but they were back on form again outside by the panda house where they pointed, jeered, and snapped whilst their kids attacked the windows with fists. There was only a single subdued panda in there and it didn't seem to like the attention. Animals were cared for, it seemed, only if they were dressed up or dancing or doing something else that put them in their place.

Amongst the shrubs of Manjuelong park, to the south of the lake, the hordes mobbed the Log Flume. There was a sign there written in English which stated:

Amusement rules for drifting:
1. Submitting yourself to working personnel's direction
2. One ticket each person, marching into the ground in a queue
3. Children below 1.2m height must be accompanied by adult for amusing

But no-one seemed to be following any of these, or any other instructions.

The city soon became thoroughly overrun. Tourists rushed the viewing platforms near the three pools that mirrored the moon and infiltrated the woods around Baochu stone pagoda. They burnt incense at the cleft in a cliff known as Yellow Dragon Cave and crowded to opera performances amongst the bamboo groves. They swamped the usually sedate Baobu Daoist temple and forced the monks to butt them out of the way with black hats like bishops' mitres. Pacified by music that blared from the flowerbeds, they waited by the sign that stated 'West Lake'. In no particular order each took the same shot: centred sign, two fingered V for Victory, snap; Centred sign, two fingered V for Victory, snap...Here was proof for the tourist. This was the true West Lake and no fake. This was the West Lake at which the chairman had rested whilst his political campaigns unfolded; the lake in which more than a thousand years ago the Song poet Su Dongpo had built his causeway, planted the cherries, and written 'West Lake is always alluring'; the lake which the provincial tourist board listed as *'Hangzhou No 1 tourist attraction!'* It was also the lake about which Chang Wen said

'It is highly polluted. Fall in and you will become very ill'. Thus this lake epitomised the story of the new China: there was myth, hype, clamour, and crowds - the masses were being unleashed.

An Intriguing Landscape

The Chinese authorities seemed to enjoy categorising. Everything needed to be ordered and slotted into some kind of hierarchy. It was a masculine sort of obsession and it seemed to me the inevitable fixation of a patriarchal society. Another obsession was the relentless hyping of scenic spots which often just appeared an extension of the kind of propaganda that the communists had long excelled at. With words you could create your own reality.

Nowhere were these Chinese infatuations better illustrated than in the marketing of tourism. Shaoxing for example, was Lou Da's hometown. It was *'One of the first 24 historical and cultural cities in China'* according to the city government. It was described as *'like a pearl with simple but elegant light'* and native guide literature reckoned *'the natural scenery in Shaoxing is totally charming and varied with an intriguing landscape of numerous green hills and clean waters'*.

Long before tour season began in earnest, we had taken Lou Da up on his offer of a tour. It did not start off intriguingly, but then Shaoxing's suburbs reared from the usual peasant plots and bunkhouses as a mirage of balconied apartments and blackened factories. A mock European castle stuck rudely out of the industrial district, and the bus station was new, a ziggurat stolen from Babylon and updated to keep the local glass manufacturers in business.

The city was also the richest in Zhejiang.

'Famous for beautiful women' claimed Da apparently bored of himself 'Like delicate pottery they are. They have good manners and make good wives' then in a sudden burst of energy, he cupped his hand to my ear 'We can find you a wife Justin' he said 'no need to tell Kristel'. Kristel looked as though she had just swallowed a mouthful of fermented bean curd.

'I don't know what you are saying but I'm sure it is nothing useful' she said. This was fair enough. I felt that Shaoxing's prodigal son, Lu Xun, would have agreed for he had once written '*To be suspicious is not a fault*'.

'I was saying Shaoxing is as beautiful as its women' reckoned Da wearing the iron smile of defence 'But first I must take you to the East Lake, where waterfalls glance from the heavens'. It turned out that the waterfalls of East Lake had dried up in the winter and were not glancing from anything. The ponds were dehydrated and cluttered with plastic bottles and food wrappings. A lone boatman plied the waters, staring gaunt and pleadingly, while the industrial plants next door belched insensitively.

Unfortunately the place did not get better elsewhere for the stench of *Tou Dofu* rose too from the steaming woks of surrounding streets - it was a speciality of this town,

'The best in China!' boasted Lou Da, by which I was sure he really meant it was the worst in China. 'It is the smell of my home!' he said. We trawled through these stinky streets to a streetside restaurant where customers were being harassed by a gang in military clothes - black overcoats, polished boots, a red pinstripe down the trouser leg. There we ordered green tea eggs, which were salty and fragrant. We tucked in. Then without warning the military clothes gang whipped out instruments with which they began to pound out martial tune. Up pulled a car. A short bridegroom stepped out of it, a porcelain bride hanging off his arm. Behind them wheeled the wedding party. The military gang, it turned out, also doubled as a brass band. They kept this appearance up until all of the guests had moved safely through the revolving doors. Then they disintegrated to a rabble once more, laying down the trombones and lighting cigarettes.

We were still there tucking in (preserved fish this time) when the next bride and groom arrived followed by their entourage. The gang jumped straight back to attention, and pumped out another tune. It turned out we were witnessing some kind of wedding conveyor belt - for even marriage could be an activity for multiple groups of strangers in the middle kingdom. The band followed this routine a couple more times: stand up, stand down, stand up, stand down. Then finally they belted out a last number before piling into the back of an open topped van, which sped off in a spatter of gravel.

The sky was already darkening by the time we arrived amongst the incense caldrons of King Wu's mausoleum. Wu had been an early crusader in China's war against nature, building a huge network of dykes with which he attempted to shackle the waters of these parts. Now he was remembered through this compound nestled in the woods where in an outer courtyard an exhibition had been set up as part of a modern war against drugs. A charred body, an amputee, and a sallow looking girl with a hypodermic sticking out of an elbow were amongst these charming exhibits. The dealers were on display too. They were prisoners bent double at a sentencing rally, their arms wrenched behind them. Lou Da ducked and put a finger to the captions.

'All shot' he said.

No Spitting

Chang Wen scratched his head one Spring Saturday.

'Can we find peace in Hangzhou?' he asked. The question was as rhetorical as it was absurd. But in answer to it he decided to take us to the mausoleum of the great General Yue which was separated from the West Lake by pastel walls, a screen of parkland, intermittent traffic jams, and a modest army of hawkers who prowled near its entrance like hungry cats. One of these cats leapt out at me from behind a clump of reeds. He was wearing a plastic face disguise kit - glasses and nose with party whistles attached to the nostrils, and he now blew the whistles as hard as he could, making them flutter out sideways.

I did my best to hide my surprise, and asked

'What are you doing?'

'I'm selling these' he said, pointing to his face disguise. He did this casually, as though he hadn't just jumped out of the bushes at me blowing party whistles from under a false nose. 'Do you want to buy one?'

It was an odd sort of advertisement. But it did have stopping power. Maybe this was the only way to sell plastic facial disguises.

But I told this man No, I didn't need one. I didn't have the heart to tell him I would not even have taken one home to my brother as some sort of joke.

In the main hall stood a sculptured image of General Yue Fei. The man had beaten back mounted hordes bursting from the northern steppes and saved the Song imperial court. Now the final image of remembrance had been carefully cultivated: *'he wears colourful [sic] apparel and is found sitting on a cushion that is beautifully embroidered'* stated the literature *'There is a majestic expression on the face of the general. He seems to be courageous and with a sword in his hand he displays a solemn readiness to protect his country from the hands of enemies or invaders.'*

But it seemed to me that the general spent most of his energy studiously ignoring the hordes here, who were busy poking the goldfish, trampling the reeds, and snapping each other standing next to the wooden statue - *V for Victory!* They did not seem to have noticed the sign that stated *'Visit politely, please'*.

Yue was buried at the back of the compound - or at least his helmet had been, for his body had never been recovered. Cast in iron close to the burial mound knelt two statues. These represented the General's nemesis, Prime Minister Qin and his wife Lady Wang. Jealous of the General's standing at court Qin had fabricated a plot to overthrow the emperor, implicated the General, and later had him executed by sending a presiding judge an execution notice hidden within the skin of an orange.

Tourists had once been encouraged to spit or even urinate upon these statues. But the authorities had since decided that this was not an entirely social activity and had had them cordoned off. A sign had been put up to hammer this home: *'No Spitting'*. There I was joined by an old man in an immaculate blue Mao suit. He bent over innocently and took a loud gob at the two condemned by history. Then as the light faded the tourists left and the hawkers packed up, and the reeds and ponds of the tomb began to sparkle.

Fiction

Chang Wen wanted to visit the hometown of Chiang Kai Shek, the nationalist General who had lost the civil war to the communists. Wen's grandfather had fought and died for the nationalists and this uncomfortable fact had later caused Wen's father to suffer during the Cultural Revolution. I wondered if there was still a residual element of nationalist loyalty still hiding inside Wen.

'The General lived in Xikou' Wen said 'hidden in the hills which he thought would be safe. But his first wife was killed. By the Japanese of course'. The tourist board called the town *'A fictitious land of peace away from the turmoil of the world'*. We reached it one cloudy morning through the port of Ningbo. There we waited in a bus station of beggars: old, malformed ones who pleaded at passengers' feet, and energetic young ones, with forlorn mouths and puppy eyes. We boarded a tattered local bus that rocked up the hillsides all the way to the hometown of the Generalissimo.

Xikou hung with the faeces of caged geese and the strange scent of sweet spinach biscuits that baked in great iron ovens. Unwieldy flocks of hawkers stalked the bus station, all flogging the same wares. In one hand they carried brass hammers, and in the other, plastic binoculars. These were the produce of Xikou. It was the same all over Zhejiang, where little backwoods towns monopolised production of the oddest niche products. Tour leaders and their cap wearing minions had already overrun the place. They seemed to coagulate especially down by the river which had been strangled by weeds - where on the same banks the town's housewives scrubbed washing and some of its kids hurled stones at drifting polystyrene.

Chiang had lived in a waterfront villa here with his second wife, the beautiful diva Soong Mei-Ling. His was a flat roofed structure labelled 'European' by the communists because it was big, made of concrete, and had once had running water. Chiang had long ago broken the brotherly love between the communists and nationalists who had been joined under the umbrella of the First United Front against the Japanese. Chiang had shot all suspected reds in nationalist areas and then focused on cleansing them from their bases in the wild hills of Hunan. But later Chiang found he had exhausted his resources against the Japanese. He had lost the civil war and fled to Taiwan. The Communists had liberated the General's house: now tourists filled the stairs, the bathrooms and the landings ogling the sepia photos and the wooden furnishings that lent the place a sparse elegance. Guides skipped through hollering over the megaphones and no one removed their shoes anymore. It seemed the ultimate humiliation.

Tourists jabbered that night out in the car park of our hotel, and through the flimsy walls of the rooms on either side of ours. At 3am, the phone rang. A woman was at the other end.

'Do you want a friend?' she asked.

'I already have a friend'

'Another friend?'

'No thanks'

She hung up.

Some way outside of town the next morning we visited a limestone waterfall where blood red characters had been etched into the limestone and clambered down a concrete tower to the bamboo forests below. We passed hawkers selling paper umbrellas and lurid blue pylons that rose incongruously from the forest. Finally we arrived at a parched crevice deep in the hills that bore the label '*where Chiang Kai Shek fished*'. It was a desolate place, a puddle suspended half way down a ravine. And in any case the concrete dam behind which this feeble pond collected was still setting and the workmen were only just finished.

But even if the place had suspect authenticity it did not stop the tour groups. They were being farmed through the entrance kiosks and marched down the hillsides in a blaze of bobbing caps. Beside the pond the cap wearers busied themselves reeling off snaps. Then they were off again, rounded back up the hill to the waiting coaches.

Attachment Thinking

One morning after class, Chang Er became insistent that we visit Tiantai Mountain. Tiantai was home to the Tiantai sect of Buddhists. It was listed as a 'world famous national scenic place of interest'. It also happened to be Chang Er's home town.

'The best time is the spring, when the peach flowers' she added.

'Come with us then' I said. After all, it was spring and the peach was probably in flower. She shook her head.

'Too much study' she said. The only thing I imagined she would be studying would be her new boyfriend. But Kristel and I took her up on the recommendation.

After the familiar journey to Ningbo we joined a peasant bus. Old and wizened country folk, they were all travelling home from market. They were toothless and coarse; they giggled, spat, and shrieked merrily. We sat and nodded politely amongst their sacks of cabbage while the bus wound higher into hills past the homes of these people, wooden shacks teetering above the paddies.

The Tiantai sect lived in a yellow walled compound carved from pine forest which had been founded by a wandering monk, Zhiyi, who had here collated the contradictory texts that circled the land and preached the attainment of enlightenment through reflection. He had taught:

- *Phenomena are empty of self-nature*
- *Phenomena exist from a worldly perspective*
- *Phenomena are both empty of existence and exist provisionally at once*

The first of these rules applied directly to the proliferation of featureless hotels which had recently bloomed along the newly arrived surfaced road. For in the language of the local authority, Tiantai Mountain was '*rich in tourist resources*'.

So we chose a hotel at random. Random however, turned out a poor method of choice. For backing onto a marsh the place had become a strategic intersection of man and mosquito. We did not endure it for long but got out early the following morning. We fastened ourselves to the back of motorbike taxis and wound up looping road right to the summit of this place, not so much a mountain as an overgrown hill whose plant life had grown wild and spilled over like a mad scientist's hair. There were fields of tea up there, and plantations of arrow bamboo. The peach was in flower as Chang Er had predicted, providing colour with which to show up the ominously low-flying cloud. Also hidden up there just badly enough that it perhaps wanted to be found, sat a small temple. We sniffed around the incense barrels and a monk slid open a door disguised by wood panelling.

'*Lai!*' he said (come). We followed him into the room, which was furnished very simply with a single bed and a bookcase that smelled of damp.

> 'What do you do as a monk?' I asked
> 'Study' he said
> 'All the time?'
> 'Yes'
> 'Just study?'
> 'Yes'

I continued on a line not too dissimilar. The monk listened compassionately as I continued to ramble, and answered monosyllabically at all of the appropriate intervals. He was a gangly man but he had refined the art of deliberate movement. And once I had exhausted my stock of questions, with a loll of the head he gestured to a book from the shelf. It was titled *'Just Doing It!'* an English language book written by a Korean Zen master who had once lived barefoot in the mountains eating crushed pine needles and experiencing 'visions'. He bid me open the book, so I did so, and found the following passage:

> *'Most people live in a dream, their 'like and dislike thinking' dream. They are always thinking about the past and the future. But the past and the future do not exist! All we ever have is 'right now.' We live in a 'moment world,' but we 'think' that we live somewhere else. The only place that you can become you is right now. Thinking itself is not good or bad, but our attachment to thinking creates suffering. Zen means wake up from your dream, your attachment thinking.'*

'For you' he said smiling – a good natured but absent one of the type given by those who in the final conclusion, have defined life as an endless comedy. With his head shaven the eyes seemed to have grown to such importance that every flicker had meaning. So when after a few minutes I caught his eyes resting on the door through which we had come, the message was clear. We thanked him and continued on our way, and I wondered how this monk could ever be able to wake up from his attachment thinking with all the tourists rambling through his back yard.

As we began our descent a van flew past and screeched to a halt in front of us. The occupants of the vehicle were students - two boys and two girls, all city dwellers from Ningbo, who insisted we ride with them. All the way to Tiantai down the mountain bends the driver grinned at us through the rearview mirror: this journey was definitely veering towards the dislike end of my thinking dream. So I was relieved when we arrived in town - which it became painfully obvious, was just another inland place of smoked glass and burning rubber. We thanked the driver and he asked rather hopefully

'Photo?'

But it seemed the least we could do, so Kristel and I climbed out to the side of the road where a truck had been run into a ditch and abandoned. The four students followed and for a full minute snapped with a fury which was more usually in China, reserved only for mealtimes.

Once they were done we waved them off and caught a public bus back to Tiantai's main coach depot. A group of schoolgirls followed us on, sat at the back of the vehicle, and engaged in a hushed debate. Then after we had travelled a few more of the town's shambolic streets, the bravest - a feisty little creature with a sharp fringe - broke away from the group and piped out

'Nice to meet you. How are you!'

'I am fine' I said 'and you?'

And with this brave one turned to her giggling friends and asked

'What did he say?'

But no-one knew. And because no-one knew, they all laughed until they were all spent of energy and a period of reflection fell upon them.

'We should have brought a camera' said the brave one, sadly.

Sadness

The Temple of the Soul's Retreat (*Lingyin Si*) was one of Hangzhou's greatest draws. It was described in the tourist guides as *'without doubt a premier showpiece in the West Lake environs'* and *'The loveliest sight of the city'*. The place found itself doing very well in the classifications league too as *'One of the ten most famous Buddhist temples of China'* and *'Number 1 Hill in the Southeast'*.

Lingyin Temple was also one of the richest in all China. It slumped in the folds of a lush river valley, where it was protected against lightning by the water dragons mounted on the edges of its eaves, and more recently, by earthed metal rods. Guarded by a ticket kiosk and an automated ticketing system complete with electronic barriers, these temple grounds were taking on the feel of some kind of forest subway. Tourists moved through the tunnels and escalators of the gargantuan new bus station and bought the tickets with which they would slot themselves into the scenic spot.

Beyond the barriers were pathways that meandered a dried up creak were the tangled roots of the 'Peak Flying From Afar', where Buddhist carvings dating back to the Song hid amongst the tourists - those lower on the hill decapitated or maimed (the carvings unfortunately, not the tour guides). They were victims of red guard excesses. Those further up the hillsides had remained unscathed however: a monument to the laziness of students.

Most visitors marched straight up the riverbed to the gates of the compound, where incense drifted from great copper caldrons. In their red and yellow tour caps the hordes of domestic tourists had been highly visible amongst the foliage on Peak Flying From Afar. Now they were bundling through the gates and reeling off shots while their tour guides screeched in front, and an entourage of hawkers scavenged behind. With all the smoke and camera flashes and hollering, this was some kind of battle re-enactment.

But this time, the tourists had competition. The peasants were here as pilgrims, standing out in their rude country clothes and yellow prayer satchels. They hobbled past the laughing Buddha where the couplet stated *'His belly swallows all the sadness of the world; His mouth mocks all cruelty under heaven.'* The villagers had brought with them their ailments - their broken legs, their deformities. One woman had an eye that appeared to have collapsed. She wobbled over to a prayer box and slid coins through a slot. Then she leered over Chang Wen as he bowed. He was praying before the stupendous camphor wood Buddha. Zhou Enlai had personally intervened to save this one during the Cultural Revolution.

'I have cancer' she told him 'So I have come to pray'.

An entrepreneur from Shanghai was

'Praying for good business!' His offerings were conspicuous: incense sticks a metre tall, splashed yellow and red like the caps of the tourists.

A woodblock sounded. Drums thudded. Chanting monks in robes of saffron marched slowly in to seat themselves under curtains of red cloth. They were skinny beasts with outsize heads who moved only one foot at a time, apparently multitasking with their meditations. The herds watched and snapped. Elsewhere on the mountainside there was a pearly *Maitreya* future Buddha to behold, the bronze figures of the five hundred *Arhats* - saints - to gawp at. There were bamboo strands and fountains, four heavenly kings looking violent in face paint, and sutras carved in stone. Truly the temple was an enchanting place even while the frenzy of tourists and pilgrims ran amok.

But Lingyin Si's different visitors led segregated lives. These began outside the gates, where these tribes waited for separate buses. Onto their coaches piled the businessmen in suits and leather and the restless tourists of t-shirts and trainers. And the old China lay across the road where threadbare brown jackets hung on the pilgrims. They were wearing plimsolls and weathered trousers. They squabbled incessantly. Lumped into their groups at their separate bus stops outside the *loveliest sight of the city* were cracks in the new China - the chasm between the city and its countryside spelled out in an apartheid of clothing and colour.

Silence

'It ranks second on the list of newly developed natural scenic sports among the Forty Best Tourist Resorts in China. It was also awarded the title of one of the Ten Best Tourist Resorts in Zhejiang Province.' This was what the China Daily had to say about the caves of Yaolin.

'We call it a wonderland' boasted Chang Wen on the bus. He had convinced us to take the short trip there with him towards the end of Spring. At a kiosk we paid the steep entrance fee - it was after all one of the ten best tourist resorts in Zhejiang province, the higher the ranking the higher the charge - and climbed down into a series of caverns and underground halls. There were flowing rivers and pretty ponds, and stalagmites and stalactites facing each other off against neon backlighting: mauves, turquoises, reds. These lights sprayed the wonderland with colour and showed up an elaborate decoration of food wrappers, bottles, and cans...It also teemed with tourists, who were herded around the dark and slippery pathways by the usual screaming guides. The route was fixed and the way congested not only by people, but by hawkers, their souvenir stalls, and plastic statuettes carefully positioned in the pinch points that many of our comrades had assumed for some reason, provided some kind of photo opportunity.

Through alternating bouts of murk and swirling colour we passed in the damp and the heat, with the echo of a hundred voices. The environment did not entirely overcome my instinctive fear of the dark and it was not too soon when the currents dragged us back out where we re-emerged squinting into the light. The crowd raced along until slowed through a filter of hawker stalls. Here there were tables and plastic awnings, and the sun streaming through them across all the sales clutter. I heard a cry

'Listen!' it went. For there on a wooden bench stood a plump policeman. He wore sunglasses. The policeman produced a megaphone and began shouting. I leant over to Wen.

'What is he saying?' I asked.

'He wants us all to visit his friend's stall. He wants us to buy Buddhist carvings'. Everyone had become a businessman.

Traffic began to back up into the caves. I pitied those inside, jammed amongst more people, noise and darkness. The policeman's skinny friend gave him a toothless smile and the thumbs up. Encouraged, the policeman began shouting more loudly and swinging his arms like a conductor on crack.

It was almost as frustrating being stuck here as it had been down in the caves. So I made to leave. Wen grabbed my shoulder.

'It is not a very good idea' he said 'to make a policeman lose face'.

'Doesn't this kind of abuse annoy people?' I interrupted. Wen responded by pinching my arm. I took his silent request and waited there until the policeman was done selling. Light flickered lower now through the awnings flushing the carvings for sale with contrast.

'Silence is a protest' whispered Wen as the traffic began to flow once more. He lifted his hand as though a moment were about to transpire 'Lao Tzu said 'We turn clay to make a vessel, but it is on the space where there is nothing that the usefulness of the vessel depends'' and then 'it is not what people say, but what they do not say that is important.' In China especially, he might have added.

Good Business

Around the time of the May Day holiday when China's transport was stretched to breaking point, Lei Shen lead Tian Fei and Chang Er up the steps of the Jade Emperor Hill. Kristel and I clattered after them watching legs patter in and out of the mist banks. These clouds scurrying over Jade Emperor Hill were one of the *'classic top ten scenes of the West Lake'*.

Towards the summit we met buses and tourists. Up here the gloom seemed to have wilted the cherry. Eight Diagrams field should have lain below, planted in halves of yin and yang. The personal farm of the emperor had been established there during the glorious days of the Song. Eunuchs had busied themselves all year ensuring the field overflowed with ripe crops - rice and maize - symbols of the emperor's own fertility. Even in times of famine this field had still been maintained. This had sometimes meant crops forcibly appropriated from local peasants to keep it going. But there was no field today. Just a blank wall of cloud.

The tourists did not seem too disappointed. Instead they trotted off to the local temple - *'one of the critical Daoist temples of West Lake'* - where they lit prayer sticks and chattered. Despite the weather there was no stopping the buses and the cargoes which spilled from them. The tourists poured in. And as each wave receded, a little old man bent with arthritis and sporting whiskers of silver moved around the incense stands to extinguish the prayers of those who had left. He dropped these sticks to the side in case tourists from the last batch were still lingering, and then with the next wave, moved them from the side back to the sales stand.

Shen noticed this too. But when he saw that I had been watching he laughed uncertainly.

'How do you call this in English?' he asked.

'Recycling' interrupted Tian Fei, showing off.

'This temple makes good business' said Shen breaking a smile. 'If I cannot find a job in a foreign export company maybe I can sell incense'. The old man wobbled back to the stands and began plucking out the last lot of smoking sticks.

Watertown

Along the borders of Jiangsu and Zhejiang, hidden amongst the tributaries and lakes that fed from China's great man-made artery - the Hangzhou to Beijing Grand Canal - sprawled the watertowns of the Middle Kingdom. Their fortune as hubs of commerce had followed that of the canal. In times of strong governance they were bustling places, wealthy and full of traffic. But in times of war and administrative decline these places prone to silting had usually been among the first to collapse. China being once more in a vigorous phase of expansion, the watertowns were again coming to life.

'Not so much trade on the water these days' said Chang Wen as we sat by the lake one day 'now they are important for tourism. I have friends who have been to many' he said, folding his arms 'so I must visit at least one'. Wen especially liked the idea of visiting Xitang watertown, partly because it had been heavily marketed on billboards downtown. Normal superlatives apparently did the place no justice: *'exquisite bridges dot the mirror-like rivers …like flaring clusters of diamonds on the neck of the old town'*

So one weekend somewhere between seasons we travelled across the plains in a tin of small business people stuck to mobile phones, and a few spitting itinerants. The watertown of Xitang first arrived as another set of treeless suburbs, then the platoons of commie blocks standard to urban China. But these outskirts soon proved to serve a purpose - they were simply a protective curtain that kept the New Chinese mess away from a core of preserved brick and whitewash handed down from the days of the inward Ming. Here the roads scraped to cobble and the shops advertised only with flags of cloth. Red lanterns hung from the eaves of whitewashed terrace. The steep arched bridges that crossed the waterways themselves were…well, exquisite.

The herds were here too of course. They clambered around snapping the proprietors of restaurants fishing for their customers' dinners. They snapped the stonework of the bridges and the ferry boats that slid underneath them. They poured past the gauntlet of hawkers flogging Chinese ink scrolls and steamed pork in lotus leaf from open fronted stores. And their guides steamed merrily in front, cackling from one canal to the next. These hordes were daytrippers from Shanghai and Hangzhou, from Suzhou and Nanjing, the middle class Wu speakers come out to play. And apart from flaring pearls, willow and mud and cobblestone, another attraction had emerged: it was us. The tourists approached in groups. They wanted photographs; they shouted 'hello'; they waved brightly, and pointed and laughed. I scowled, Kristel gnashed her teeth. We both pretended to be deaf. But the requests for photos kept coming.

Later I found a secluded spot a slumped willow, pulled out my notebook and began to write. It was no use. A small posse formed to find out what I was doing. Suddenly we had ourselves a circular situation. I wrote *'the more I write about the crowd…the greater the crowd becomes'*.

Then the ferryman passing below pulled on a khaki poncho and moored to the side. The heavens heaved open and the bridges emptied.

There was a flurry of colour as the tour cap doffers bobbed to the shelter of terraces. The rain dropped like pins on the canal surface and I angled my camera to capture the roofs, the lanterns, the bridges, the water. This high-arched bridge was ours. All ours. I captured Xitang as I wanted it to be. It was finally the glorious and long gone China of the Song where the skiffs had loaded up with grain from the bountiful harvests, and sauntered downstream to the capital. We were the only tourists in this China.

Observe Social Ethics

It was a coastal city of palm lined promenades and shoe factories. Not only shoe factories, but clothes, electrical goods, and auto parts too, for Wenzhou was another of China's richest cities. A few decades back fearing an attack from across the Taiwan Strait, Mao had moved much of the nation's industry deep within the inland provinces and starved the coast of investment. Plundering the inefficient state industries for tax had never been an option here. To keep itself in business, local government had been forced instead to support the city's proud mercantilist tradition. The entrepreneurs and emigrants who had once left for Italy began to stay put and build successful enterprises. Lei Shen's father had been one of them.

'His factory builds key rings' Lei Shen claimed

'Is there much money in key rings?'

'Yes' he said 'much'.

At the end of the May holiday we escaped the crowding beside the lake and travelled to the coast of southern Zhejiang through the sultry hills and forgotten towns of the province's interior. In the south of the province where the foliage had become the scrub of North Africa, the weather also had reconfigured. Gone was the humid blankness of Hangzhou, in the city of Wenzhou it was dry and the clouds were strangely bright.

Shen waited at the station, squinting amongst the spanking towers and hawkers trying to flog cigarette lighters - of which this town apparently made more than anywhere else in the world.

'Welcome!' he shouted while standing in the middle. He flagged down a taxi, which we clambered into. Shen then engaged in frantic banter with the cabbie. The local dialect was a speech so gutteral and strange it made both of them bob heads as they spoke, like a couple of

feeding pigeons. *Wenzhouhua* was incomprehensible for speakers of *Putonghua*, the common tongue. Even other Wu speakers were said to find *Wenzhouhua* notoriously eccentric.

'He sounds like a chicken...' Chang Er had teased 'making eggs'. The city's isolation on the coast behind the hills ensured this distinction. *Wenzhouhua* was so unique that during World War II, soldiers of this city had been recruited as Chinese wind talkers, speaking their tongue in encrypted military communications. The Japanese had floundered where the mandarin speakers had and did not manage to penetrate it.

Suddenly our cabbie was gone. We had stopped at a red traffic light and now he seemed to have bailed out. Then I caught him in the wing mirror. He was conversing with a colleague about a hundred metres back. The lights turned green, so Kristel leant over the driver's seat and hit the horn. The driver walked back and climbed in. Before driving off he flashed me a stern look and pointed at the steering wheel.

'No need!' he said. Clearly he had gotten this wrong.

In the afternoon we boarded a ferry and spent the afternoon on *Jiangxin* island. There was a fairground there, and a rusty spinning star: *'decline the mental patient, the excessive drunk, the hypertensive and the cardiac'* stated the rules. We lounged in this park and threw pebbles into the bay.

'Wenzhou people always look to the ocean' said Lei Shen. The sea stretched out to the horizon - it had been pocked with container ships and fishing vessels.

'It is very busy out there'

'Yes' he said 'The outside makes us rich'. This seemed a very un-Chinese sentiment. In such a huge land it was natural that most looked inwards. But Wenzhou had thrived on trade with foreigners. Deng Xiaoping had been defending this city in particular when he said *'When you open a window you let in flies'.*

That evening Lei Shen's father drove us to share a banquet he had thrown in honour of some business clients. He was an energetic type who used his hands a lot when he talked - which was worrying when he took them off the wheel to expound on a point.

'My father says he ran from the country' translated Lei Shen. The table was laid out with the specialities of the coast: blood clam and skewered prawns, raw crab and deep fried lobster.

'Then he made cigarette lighters. He lived in one room with five others for many years'.

Mr. Shen had saved, rented a small building in the outskirts, and bought some basic machine tools. His first customers had been made through an old mate who had moved to France. Now he owned a factory and a man with a total three years of schooling had ended up sending his son to university. Mr. Shen dined next door with his business partners leaving us with Lei Shen, his cousins, and his friends. He wobbled in slightly later, his cheeks red. He uttered something in Wenzhouhua.

'He says welcome you. This city has always liked foreigners' translated Shen 'In fact he says in Wenzhou people like foreigners almost as much as they like business'.

We were off again next morning. Yandang mountain was *'one of the China's top ten must-see mountains'*. It was composed of *'eight scenic areas'* which included the *'Three Best Wonders'*. These were the magic sounding 'Spiritual Peaks', the 'Big Dragon Waterfall' and the 'Spiritual Rocks'. As we approached from the east the following day, the Spiritual Peaks loomed in layers of bare rock - they were iced with moss. The tourists were here, the liberated classes once more on the rampage. This time they were upwardly mobile citizens from Wenzhou wearing the same coloured tour caps and cameras as anyone and led by the same megaphone abusers from everywhere.

Darkness fell. We followed the tour groups. The first we tacked to the back of was led by a pixie with vocal chords obviously larger than she was. Her charges lit up the night with the musical glow-sticks they had just bought from the musical glow-stick stall. The pixie meanwhile shone torchlight at a piece of rock and shouted.

'Bird wings' whispered Shen.

We turned a corner and she flashed another rock.

'Wife and husband peak' said Shen.

Then she threw torchlight to the side and illuminated something else - another rock perhaps? She screeched and Shen was once more provoked.

'A girl in love' he said, nodding into the black.

By the light of the next day we found the woodland passages cluttered. At one junction I slipped in mud causing several friendly hands in the vicinity to reach out and save me. A little girl looked up to her mother and asked

'So foreigners can fall too?'

I wiped mud from my bottom and trundled with everyone else past a sign that said *'Observe social ethics and pay attention to public hygiene'*. Then we arrived at the waterfall at Big Dragon Pool where the guides competed to be heard over their megaphones. They had stiff competition from the hawkers selling bird whistles, the painters flogging name cards, and the tourists who bought it all. Another sign here said *'Please treasure the pleasure brought by the sun, grass and forest in the scenic area and use clean and discipline to repay them'*. As if that was going to happen. Only some kind of catastrophic economic collapse was likely to bring clean and discipline to this place. Still, it was nice to see that the authorities had such a sense of humour.

Promotion

On a fine morning at the end of term the foreign teachers of Educated People crowded into a white minibus for the 'foreign teachers excursion'. Betty had organised the whole thing, it was all on the university - a reward for coming so kindly to help China develop itself. Last year the foreign teachers had been to Zhouzhuang watertown. It had received mixed reviews.

'A great trip it was' said Professor Darling contemptuously 'apart from Lou Da's karaoke'.

'Come on now' scolded Emma 'it was just fine Frank. You said you liked canals dear'

'I remember...'

'I remember I had poisoning from seafood' interrupted British Dave.

It began in a flotilla of vehicles carrying us the foreign teachers and a host of administrators and school officials. Out crawled the cavalcade, through the dirty suburbs and the countryside, treading the well worn route to Shaoxing and on to Ningbo.

'I just know Lou Da is going to sing' claimed the Professor.

Lou Da ignored him, and instead turned to me to make polite conversation.

'Homosexuals are tolerated in Britain?' he asked.

On the edge of a turnpike road where the hills met the coast, a contingent of the local police rolled up. The local police chief had come in his chauffeur driven car. He was escorted by motorcycle outriders.

'My friends!' squealed Betty. It turned out she knew them already. Indeed the police were coming with us. Chief was almost as short as Betty – he had swapped length instead, for width. He waddled over and introduced himself while his escorts looked on with self-importance.

The police paid our entry fees to visit a local reservoir, which for some reason the usual herds were avoiding. Kristel and I busied ourselves paddling in a stream while our Chinese colleagues shrieked and pointed.

Lou Da walked on the path above calling out questions.

'Where do homosexuals meet in Britain?' he asked.

The police arranged for us to stay at a hot springs hotel. On the journey over, Da asked

'What age can they have sex?'

It was chief who paid for the evening feast of sea slugs and sea cucumbers. Afterwards I sat in a hot pool with all of my male colleagues. Darling was there. So were Mr. Gong and British Dave. The teachers and administrators were all there, along with businessmen from Ningbo, who jabbered uncontrollably on mobile phones wrapped in plastic bags. Chief plopped into a corner and began joking with his men, who shifted over to give him some space. From the television blared the China India football match (end result 1-0 to India) and Lou Da did not ask any questions about homosexuals. In nakedness everyone was equal.

The next day after the final banquet, the old battleaxe Teacher Xu, got up to make a toast in honour of the chief - after all the alcohol was on him too. The chief of police threw his shots down with bravado and his neck shook like turkey wattle. Teacher Xu punished him for his pride and continued the toasts. But the Chief held himself well and even managed afterwards to lever himself out of the chair with only the minimum of assistance. He staggered to Educated People's white minibus and climbed up front with Betty and the driver. His motorcycle outriders raced ahead and Lou whispered over the back of the seat

'In Britain what are the rules about marriage for homosexuals?'

Then as the minibus picked up speed, Chief lurched towards the window and hurled vomit down the sides of the vehicle.

'Go-faster stripes!' shouted Darling with glee. We stopped at the county border and allowed Chief into the custody of his men. We continued without escort past Ningbo, then Shaoxing once more. Our van became tediously bogged in traffic.

'The policemen really like Betty' offered Da helpfully from the back 'perhaps it is because her uncle is Vice-Governor of Zhejiang province'.

6. Summits

Still the sun bore down on the city by the lake. The ring of hills circling the water created a natural caldron and guarded against such a thing as a breeze to temper the heat. In the classrooms the foreign teachers wilted despite fans on full power and windows that let in dust and the pollen of flowering grass. Out on the desolation of the summer streets the locals pointed and laughed - they could see the sweat leeching into my clothes. Neither did my students believe that the patches appearing on me within five minutes of a shower were the result of anything, but the bad hygiene of a Caucasian caveman. The chairman once said '*to be hygienic is glorious, to be unhygienic is a shame*'. Like many of his slogans, however, it did not apply to himself: Mao followed the peasant method of rinsing his teeth with tea. Consequently they were usually covered in sticky film. He did not clean them properly once in his entire life.

The Chinese never seemed to sweat, even in this sun. Only excitable computer gamers and battered old peasants gave off whiffs of lax hygiene. Deodorant could not be found anywhere in this city despite its growing consumerism. So I carefully hoarded supplies from home. And when I accosted Lei Shen about male use of this precious substance, he laughed heartily and said

'Only girls use such things'.

But it turned out he didn't really know what deodorant was. He had mistaken it for perfume, which most female students could not afford in any case. I changed shirts at least twice a day and took long, cool showers. I wrote frantic messages home asking for urgent deliveries of body care products. My prayers were occasionally answered. These came with computer disks in which parts of personal messages had been blanked out and chocolate bars ripped open. I constantly collected bottles of water from the water house. Madame Xia's fingers still tapped furiously and Mr. Xia would give his customary grunt - that greeting of sorts.

Mosquito season had begun and clouds of the beasts started collecting in the stairwell. No matter how often the stairs and corridors were fumigated, the flying awfulnesses were always back the following night waiting to slip through the doors, the air vents and through draughty gaps in the windows. Those scouts that made it through the outer perimeter were attacked with electric tennis rackets. We wheeled out incense and powders, creams and sprays. Yet still each morning, a quick survey of limbs suggested that the enemy was winning.

The students dosed in class, they yawned, and they itched too. They complained of open windows and the mosquito terror - it was even worse for them, defenceless in their open dorms. Attention spans dwindled even when classes moved out to the lawns and underneath the groves of hyacinth, where the scent of nectar hung sweet and sickly.

The streets burned. Even the little pig-tailed fruit stall girl stayed indoors. Mr. Ji caught me one day when I was off my guard and accosted me with a bag of plums

'Say to me 'the football season will begin this winter'' and he thrust his neck forward and flashed a smile of receding gums. Little Dog moped around the house while her leg slowly mended. Students from English Corner came knocking on the door to practice English. Sam came knocking on the door in the hope of a French lesson and to pass comment on our pet ('I am very surprised it has not died yet'). Oversexed cicadas rasped from the trees. It was all becoming a bit trying.

And the chances of this unending summer dying early seemed about as likely as Madame Xia treating her customers with any respect. With all the questions, the heat, sweat, smell of rotting fruit, rabbit droppings, copulating flowers, mosquito spray, itchy arms and irritable moods, it was time to escape.

To the mirror image of this lowland crucible and the heat of the plains: a cool sea breeze, mountain streams, and most alluring of all, escape from the multitudes, from the citizens and the tourists; from hawkers and students; cab drivers and pedi-carts; from university authorities and noisy construction workers. We needed an absence of *people*.

So we pored over maps and reference books in air conditioned safety while CCTV droned…*'17 teenage boys murdered by a migrant worker in Henan province keeping their belts as souvenirs'* We finalised our travelling plans to include heights and thinner air. Our targets lay in an enticing line across the south of the country: the Buddhist island of Putuo Mountain off the eastern shores, then west to the Yellow Mountain of Anhui, and finally, the great Buddhist mountain, Emei Shan, brooding further west, deep in the Chinese interior. Protected by the air-conditioner of the bedroom, Kristel, Little Dog, and I hid from the outside world as far as was possible, and counted down the days until the end of term.

Putuo Mountain

Little Dog was deposited with Chang Er and her fussing dorm sisters. Down at the station, People's Liberation Army soldiers jumped the queue for tickets. We arrived at the front an hour later. Then the kiosk attendant shut up for lunch. Still, we were in good spirits given that there would be no chalk or dozing students for the rest of the summer. And after rushing to join another haphazard line, we had our tickets. By the time the final bell of the last day of term sounded, Kristel and I were already on the afternoon train to Ningbo.

At Ningbo station a small beggar child dived towards me and attached herself to my leg. I shook her loose. Instead she grabbed the next best option - a leather jacketed man with a mobile phone on his waistband - a trader, a representative of the petit bourgeoisie, a man who did not acknowledge an urchin stuck to a thigh. Instead he lumbered across the waiting area while the girl giggled and clung on for the ride. From here it was a short bus ride out of the city to the harbour, past drab districts of factories and housing blocks, then wasteland, where the only colour was on an advert that heralded the coming of a new development: *'man and nature living together in harmony'* it said. The bus pulled up beside a dirty wharf, and then we boarded a boat - the fast ferry to Putuo Mountain - which skimmed low on the water line and out on the grey seas, which glittered in bouts of light. Out here on the ocean, the sun continued the struggle, warring against the clouds and pollution. Buddhist songs - choral sea-shanty like chants - played on a loop over the boat radio. Most of the passengers fell asleep in the stagnant heat, covering their faces with the red or yellow caps their tour group leader had given them.

I fell asleep too, propped up against Kristel. In turn a pot-bellied little man fell on me, snoring in snorted fits and leaving a little trail of drool on my shoulder. Then the hum of the motor dropped several tones until the boat simply drifted. Through the porthole the giant bronzed statue of Guanyin – goddess of mercy, the bodhisattva of compassion, the patron of this island – came into view. She stood on a promontory like a lighthouse, at the southernmost end of the island giving

97

no welcome, for she gazed back inland, with her back towards the sea.

Putuo island was the fabled home of Guanyin for the Chinese. But the original deity was born deep in the Himalaya, where Guanyin was male and had devoted his life to hearing the cries of the many wretched beings of the earth. It was a story of sorrow and loss. The celestial Buddha blessed Guanyin with eleven heads so he could hear the cries of the suffering. But then his arms shattered as he tried to aid these suffering multitudes. The lost arms, in their turn were replaced by a thousand arms. Guanyin was released from the eternal cycle of pain, elevated to god hood, a *bodhisattva*, pathfinder for the rest of humanity.

But this was not the Guanyin of Putuo Mountain. Putuo's Guanyin had found his way down to the Chinese lowlands and undergone a sex change. Chinese Guanyin had been executed by her father after refusing to marry. Her soul rode to hell on the back of a supernatural tiger where she played music and caused flowers to blossom. Her beauty was so stunningly radiant that hell bloomed as paradise. This caused the Lord of Hell to fall into a desperate rage. He sent Guanyin back to the world of the living - to this slumbering island, the isle of Putuo Mountain. Here in her final refuge she devoted her days to healing the sick and rescuing mariners from these grey waters.

The boat moored outside entrance kiosks with a hefty fee for tourists - paradise was expensive. A fresh breeze rolled off the sea. Out in the dusty car park at the island entrance, taxi sharks waited to swallow this new intake ('are you my friend *laowai*?') We picked a van, and jumped aboard. It rolled through Mediterranean scrub, up narrow lanes and past sandy coves. Past one hundred step beach, then one thousand step - raiders from the East had once landed on the white sands. They too had worshipped the goddess. But it had not stopped them stealing from the temples or raping the nuns.

At Fayu temple in the island's centre, afternoon was departing. Shadows were emerging on the flagstones, blurred by smoke from great stone offering bins. Across the courtyard cried a peasant woman, prostrated, at the foot of a monk. With the pressed yellow tunic and shaved head, he was one of those curiously ageless Chinese men. The monk turned to us and said in English

'She did not bring her identity card. The government says all who stay must carry a card. It is illegal for her to spend the night with us' he put his hands behind his back and dropped his head, muttering to himself. 'I think I will let her stay' he said finally.

'Won't that cause trouble?' I asked.

He laughed.

Many of the cloisters and hermitages on Putuoshan had closed after liberation. Two thousand monks and nuns had lived here around 1929. Most of the clergy had been kicked out during the massive land redistribution programmes of the fifties. The Communists then had the popular support of the peasants in confiscating the huge landholdings of the Buddhist church on this island and in the adjacent provinces.

Red guards visited the island of Putuo Mountain during the Cultural Revolution. They made little impact. They had found only the barest skeleton crews manning the temples and considered their destruction not worth the hassle. Perhaps the young Maoists who had made it this far forgot about destroying the 'four olds' (old customs, old culture, old habits, and old ideas), tossed their little red books into the sea and gone skinny dipping off one hundred-step beach. I imagined some of them had even converted and were still living in the temples amongst the camphor trees and incense, converting youthful fire into a kind of serenity.

The nuns had never come back. But a few hundred monks now lived here once more.

'Come' said the monk. And we followed him into the private chambers. He donated peaches. They were green and ripe and sumptuous.

'Grown on the island' he said 'we don't take much from the mainland. Instead, the Government takes money from us, from the entrance fees from tourists like you'

Fayu temple was in good repair. The guardian statues at the front held their sticks upright, which meant 'rich temple, visiting monks may stay the night'. Putuo Mountain made a decent cash cow.

'But now the old days are gone' he said 'when I was growing up, our family had to keep the shrine to the goddess of mercy hidden in a secret room. It was banned, following any of the 'four olds'. One day our neighbour told students about the shrine. Many came to the house. They looked for the gap in the wall. But they couldn't find it!' he smiled wanly 'Said they would come back because they knew it was there. They knew nothing. My father said Guanyin had protected us'

'Is that why you became a monk?' asked Kristel.

'My parents wanted it' he said 'and it has served me well. I travel. Last year I was in Singapore. Some time ago I lived one year in Sri Lanka'. Applications to enrol in the monasteries were booming. Many families wanted to attain this slice of the good life for their children.

We sat there eating peach. The monk received a phone call on his mobile phone.

'Its New' he said, tapping it. He took the call. Then 'I have to leave' he said '…more peasants, without papers'.

Outside in the night, the scent of joss hung pungent. And with the hum of cicadas and the soft swell of the ocean a few metres away behind the low dunes, sleep came swiftly to our hotel room. There were no women phoning for friendship. The next day a deep fog rolled in. We retraced our footsteps back to Fayu temple. Further on, the path led past sleepy restaurants where dying fish flapped inside polystyrene boxes. Dopey hawkers sold jade pendants, wooden gourds, incense sticks. They seemed loaded on valium, these sales folk, with their half-hearted sales pitch and useless patter. They even neglected to chase us some way up the path as they might have done back on the mainland. Instead they slouched back down beside their stalls, ready to doze.

The path began to steepen, and we ascended stone steps towards the summit. There were few tourists treading the path that day, but to keep us from feeling lonely, there were speakers cunningly hidden in the undergrowth peddling the same Buddhist shanties we had heard on the boat.

Off the path where began the bamboo forest, a sign read *'you can make thousands of matches from one tree but one match will destroy thousands of trees'*. A lone pilgrim prayed on each step. He stepped, stopped, placed a piece of thinning cardboard in front of his knees, knelt, bowed, touched his forehead and hands on the stone: there were two thousand steps up to the Huiji temple, just below the summit.

On a corner of the mountain a monk sat on a bench.

'Take a photograph' he said, pointing at himself. He was dressed neatly with socks tucked tightly into trousers and saffron tunic slightly starched, as though it had just come off the shelf. This man was too proud of his uniform to be a real monk and I suspected he had bought it from one of the tailors hidden away amongst the craft stores at the other end of the island. Furthermore, didn't monks usually have a place to be? Have a meal to cook, a book to study, a sutra to chant? Apparently this one was content to hang around in the woods on his own. And when he demanded money, I was convinced. He was no follower of Guanyin. He was a faker, a con-artist, one of the caste of free-riders taking advantage in the new China.

Above the Huiji temple, a place terrorised by tourists strenuously avoiding the short climb and running themselves up and down by cable car, stood the highest point of the island. Just another hundred metres further up we lost the tourists again. It seemed it was too far for them to walk. We stood outside an old property with whitewashed walls against which rubbish had piled. Its windows were smashed, the place had been abandoned. It may have been ex-military. The view was uninterrupted: the length of Putuoshan sprawled below. Scrubby hills slanted gently toward the sea. Near the temples of the South they finally burrowed under the water. To the North, the ground plunged more precipitously, broken only by the perilously perched temple at Fanyin Cave, which straddled a break in the cliff. To the East, the ocean stretched dull and unobstructed, until it merged with the sky somewhere out in the distance.

And I noticed a sound I had not heard before in China. Silence. The tourists were gone. The Buddhist music playing in the undergrowth was gone. There were no car horns, bird whistles, loudhailers or hollering; no fireworks; no demolition; no construction; no University Radio. Even the sound of the white-topped breakers against one thousand-step beach had disappeared, but they could still be seen halfway down the island's length, surging into the bay. Kristel and I stood there on the edge of the Middle Country where sound had been swallowed in the ether, and for most of the afternoon stared out over the greying east to the lands from which pirates had made their sallies: the Ryukyu islands and Japan. They were places far out there in the mist. Places where the people knew Guanyin only as Kannon, but still prayed to her and requested her blessings.

Yellow Mountain
Not long after we arrived back from Putuo Island, Chang Wen

called round.

'Are you 100% sure you can climb Yellow Mountain?' he asked, scratching his head. Wen was still surprised to discover that we were able to get around in his China. During our early days of travelling this country he had rarely left our side. He was finding it difficult to leave behind the mothering instinct he had acquired.

'I find my own country difficult to understand' he said 'so how will you manage?' With all the chaos and vanishing reference points it was no wonder anyone was confused. So how in the hell were aliens supposed to fend for themselves?

'My uncle says you have to walk for two days and it is easy to fall off the cliffs' he said, adding hopefully 'perhaps you can get carried around the mountain on a bamboo seat?'

The students came round to pick up Little Dog once more. Chang Er frowned

'It's such a long way up!' she said. Lei Shen cocked his head and asked

'Are you sure you can do it?'

Almost everybody seemed to fret about the foreigners' trip to the yellow mountain. None of our friends or acquaintances had visited the place, but they had all heard the warnings: the paths were steep; the guard rails too low and not well maintained; there were too many people; the bamboo rickshaw carriers would shove you off the side of the mountain without even noticing. Their suspicions were honed on old wives tales, exaggerations, the hubris of eager tourists passed through the personal networks.

Only Lou Da thought differently.

'The mountain is not that high' he said with a disparaging flick of the hand. But of course, he hadn't been there either.

Yellow Mountain – *Huang Shan* – inspired an entire school of painting in the Qing dynasty. It had provided inspirational material for painters and poets for millenia. It had been the favourite place of one of China's most popular characters, the Tang poet Li Bai, who had drowned in a river trying to embrace a reflection of the moon.

There was no railway to the Yellow Mountain or anywhere close by. It was buried deep in the wilds of Anhui province - amongst poor and remote villages hidden amongst the hills and forgotten in this age of rising skylines and conspicuous consumption. So we caught the bus from Hangzhou West bus station, a sort of pressure chamber between the prosperous life of the city and the productive grind of the countryside.

This was another brand new node in the travel network - more smoked glass and the name of the station sketched in giant gold characters. It was staffed by lonely city women selling pot noodles and shrink wrapped chicken claws from behind the usual glass kiosks. But the passengers who passed through here were not businessmen or students, the merchants or work seekers who plied the express routes to Shanghai and along the east coast, but rough peasants in plimsolls and old suit jackets. They scurried between buses and concourse ferrying sacks of rice and cabbage through the exhaust choked air.

These buses looked like hand me downs from the coastal routes - they were mud spattered, the seats that had been ripped had been thrown back together with masking tape and sticky plastic. The whole set up seemed a generation behind. It made sense. There were motorways leading North and East and even South out of Hangzhou, but not yet West into the untamed hinterland. There was no point wrecking decent buses on primitive roads.

The bus filled with raucous travellers. A tense verbal exchange broke out between the conductor and a male passenger at the door of the bus. There were more seats than passengers and this man had paid for a seat that no longer seemed to exist.

The conductor suddenly turned around and pointed at someone more pliant.

'*You* have to go' he said. The unfortunate passenger ejected himself. But this did not stop the peasants continuing to load the vehicle with rice and cabbage. And when the driver finally tested the accelerator, the ancient beast wheezed out of the bus park bouncing wildly on shot suspension, while cabbages rolled across the aisles. The passengers seemed to be holding some kind of spitting convention, hoiking between the vegetables, and pointing at each other. Someone filled the vehicle with smoke from a strong cigarette. It swamped the windows and obscured the view. But we were not missing much - just suburbs. And after the civilised city streets abruptly gave way to pot-holed single track it was just industrial countryside and the odd broken down vehicle that passed.

An hour or two west of the city the plains ran into steeper

gradients, the scrub of the coast melted into impenetrable bamboo. On a sharp bend in the centre of a ramshackle village of whitewashed bunkhouses spilling down a hillside, a coach had collided with a truck. No one had been hurt, but the road was blocked and traffic had backed up for a couple of miles in both directions. The local police came to work out how to disentangle the wreckage and stop it constricting the road. Most of the village turned out to watch, including a housewife carrying a live chicken by the neck, a group of kids wielding plastic swords. In front of them the cops swapped cigarettes with the local menfolk and bantered about how they might sort out the mess.

There were two other non-Chinese travellers on the bus. They were an Indian couple who were also heading to the same destination: from Hyderabad she said, but studying architecture in the United States. They had been in the country for five days. And the girl pouted, flicked her hair and said:

'It disgusts me when they spit'. She had a hook nose adorned with a little mole that looked strangely like a stud. The boy nodded in a half-hearted show of solidarity. He didn't really care about spitting.

There was a shallow river tracing the valley floor below, and cut into the steep gradient on the other side of the water - in parallel to the blocked track - a new dual carriageway was being constructed, its foundations bulldozed from the orange underbelly of the hillside. The dual carriageway would leapfrog a generation of road building and become the new passage through this valley. It would bypass the problem of vehicle collisions on blind turns, and probably this village altogether. What would become of such a place once its main artery had been made redundant? The villagers would have to watch as the goods lorries hurtled away on the other side of the river. Unless something radical was done, they would be left to scrape these hillsides while their children fled to the cities.

Kristel and I strode down to the river winding in the base of the valley where the late sunlight sprinkled the water with gold. I sat down behind a concrete wall to read 'My Country and My People' by Lin Yutang, the book that Chang Er had given me. In it I read *'The Chinese are a nation of individualists. They are family-minded, not social-minded, and the family mind is only a form of magnified selfishness...'*

This did not seem to have stopped the locals solving the

problem of the crashed vehicles. By the time we left the riverbank, it was dusk. The police had come up with the idea of pulling the two apart with a steel hook attached to a well-wisher's van. Rather amazingly, a form of queuing had been arranged to allow traffic to take it in turns to pass through the small opening created, and then it was just another few hours of winding forward in the dark before the bus stopped deep inside Anhui at the town of Tangkou, the staging post for the Yellow Mountain. Here, elderly peasant women sold cartons of Yellow Mountain tea, a tea that was held in modest esteem across China. They congregated on the pavements and under the high road bridge that bypassed the town and its valley. The industrial centres of the coast were now far away, and without the light pollution, the stars had lost their shyness, twinkling against the mountain that loomed ahead.

We walked up the road past a couple of chickens and dirty children with the couple from Hyderabad.

'…and the smells…' she said 'terrible!'

She hadn't been impressed by the food, the manners, the queuing, or Shanghai. In fact she didn't like China at all. As she spoke I caught myself thinking surely she must be used to spitting and smells seeing as she came from Asia's other giant state, another place where human life crawled in all its guises.

We found a little hotel in the shadows of the bridge. We decided to stay. So did the Indians. After washing up and relaxing, I wondered if I had judged them rashly. They had only just arrived. China could be a pretty odd place for the uninitiated, to put it mildly. For some reason I found myself wanting to make sure they had a good time in the middle country, hoping that they too would learn to like the place - this hag with gold teeth. I knocked on the door. The boy answered it. He looked sullen.

'Will you join us for dinner?' I asked. In the background I heard the girl.

'The beds haven't been made properly' she said.

Not long afterwards we all trooped downstairs to eat chicken and rice. Afterwards I called for the bill and arranged to pay. But the girl from Hyderabad pulled half the money from the table and threw it back to me. She said

'Don't be funny' she said 'I pay for myself always'. But she was breaking the rules. We split the bill. I left as soon as I could - the Chinese would have understood why. As an example of losing face it was from the textbook.

Our ascent started early next morning. The Indians caught the same bus as us. She sat cross armed at the back, looking down her nose. He sat resting his arm gingerly around her shoulders – in the case he needed to restrain her should she lash out and bite without warning. This ferry bus to the foot of the Eastern steps wound around hairpin bends and mountain fissures as the sun flitted through pockets of yellow mist to illuminate the forests. Above towered the peaks of which Li Bai wrote:

> *Thousands of feet high towers the Yellow Mountain*
> *With its thirty-two magnificent peaks*
> *Blooming like golden lotus flowers*
> *Amidst red crags and rock columns*

It was of course, all impossibly beautiful, a scene straight from a traditional scroll painting. Instead I was thinking about how we might escape our companions. We were dropped off at the start of the long path upwards and it was not long before we ran into congestion.

'Too many people' she said.

The four of us walked in silence until at a bend overlooked by a crooked pine

'Could fall off at any minute' she reckoned. We continued. After another half an hour the girl said

'I need the bathroom' and she stepped off the path and into the pines.

'Quick!' hissed Kristel, quickening her pace. This was our moment. Before we rounded the corner I took a last look back at the boy. He had been watching us, resigned. I pitied him. His was quite a burden, to suffer such a neurotic partner, to endure such confident negativity.

'You guys go on ahead...' he called. But I didn't catch the end of the sentence, because we were already around the corner.

The Eastern steps crawled with porters carrying whole pigs and crates of beer to the hotels and amenities of the peaks, trinket sellers had dug themselves in on the corners. The rest of us - tourists - toiled upwards past the greedy eyes of people carriers, observing who was faltering so they could try to seduce them into bamboo chairs.

Upwards we continued in single file up the twisting steps, through forests and clouds and bursts of sunlight. At intermittent intervals lay hawkers who screeched into the fog. It would have been possible to tell how far up the mountain you had come by charting the price rises they quoted for water. We continued. Up and over, around one corner and the next, until we began to near the roof of the mountain where the people carriers ceased to volunteer unsolicited quotes. By now the bamboo forests of the base had long disappeared into the sunny mists below.

The congestion worsened as the path met the entrance to the cable car station. Up here the eastern steps split off in several directions funnelling tour groups fresh from the cable car into streams headed to different hotels located up on the steamy plateau. Pinnacles of stone piled above us. Gnarled little pines clung to them. This all was the very stuff of Chinese dreams, the inspiration behind a whole school of Chinese painting and more than 20,000 celebrated poems dating at least back to the Tang.

There were no speakers in the undergrowth up here, but some of the tour members made up for this by shouting messages at strangers across the troughs while mist rolled through in thick banks. In the heart of the plateau, the fog disappeared and the sky turned a dark navy blue. Clear skies! It was the first time I remembered seeing the sun unobstructed since our arrival in China. On the rare days in Hangzhou that were not cloudy, the sun glowered off-white even at midday, its strength defeated by pollution. In four months the sun had been sickly. Its unusual brightness up here in the plateau of the Yellow Mountain hurt my eyes. Only the concrete path was immediately visible to me.

All over the heat of these swarming peaks, brass and steel padlocks had been attached to the safety railings; couples had their names inscribed into them and by locking them to the mountainside they bound themselves together for eternity, up here where the mist and the sunlight merged. The people carriers rested at various intervals on the path, hidden in the shade - men small but sinewy to a man, with calves hewn out of the very granite of the landscape; their shoulders often rubbed raw and bloody by the constant carrying of weights heavier than they were.

We shared a stuffy double bunked room up there with an

American girl and a British man. They were in an advanced state of courtship, her bra was already on the floor.

'Turn over' I heard him say as we entered. We dumped our stuff and left them to it. Instead we explored some of the lesser trodden regions of the plateau. We found a chasm, a stone bridge, and a flight of steps leading to nowhere. When we returned the other couple had gone out for the night. They woke us later stumbling in drunkenly through the door and rummaging around for their gear.

Our alarm clock blew an hour before dawn. We packed up, and we left this cell and its occupants behind in the dark. I was really starting to dislike the foreigner in China: indiscreet, rude, engaged in their own selfish personal adventure. They had big noses too.

Fortunately the heat of the previous evening had dissipated under the cloudless skies of the plateau. We hiked past the refreshing terrace, a natural stone balcony above the valley floor, and climbed to a pine-camouflaged piece of granite several hundred metres further up. The tour groups would soon be out in force, hoping to watch the sun rise over *Beihai*, the North Sea, called so because of the cloud layers hanging below the ridge, layers that blanketed the valley in the coolness of a Yellow Mountain morning. By the time the first strands of colour appeared on the horizon, this tree lined ridge - two kilometres long - had been entirely occupied. People hung from trees and sat on the rocky ledges, a sea of bright tour caps commandeering every available spot so that the beauty of the ridge had become nothing more than a human swarm, a watercolour overrun by the masses. Down on the terrace itself, the crowds had jammed themselves in so tightly that only the safety fence prevented people from being flung into the cloud sea below.

The chatter soundtrack rose as the sun threatened to appear. But after first light bronzed the tallest of rock pinnacles, it fled instead behind a thick shield of cloud. The hum of humanity dominated the terrace and the valleys, overpowering them, the mark of the people stamped on the sublime landscape. It seemed a deliberate act. In this civilisation nursed on flooding and tears, nature was always to be subdued. Together we vanquished the cloud sea.

It didn't really seem to matter that the miracle sunrise had not been performed in any case, for the tour group members were already thinking about more important things - like breakfast. A burst of congestion materialised on the paths surrounding the North Cloud Sea, the tourists all filed off back to their hotels. It was not long before the mountain was quiet again, and back down on the refreshing terrace, the silhouettes of ragged peaks across the valley faded in and out as cloud squadrons moved against them. Only wind filled the void.

Nothing is more important to the average Chinese tourist than the filling of his stomach. We took advantage of the breakfast rush and headed straight down - we would get a lead on the crowds rushing the mountain today. This route ran the longer, more precarious Western steps. Past Bright Summit peak we dropped, past Lotus Flower Peak, where the steps were narrow and the railings low - just as my students had feared. We cut around the base of Heavenly Capital Peak, where a single staircase headed directly up hundreds of metres of smooth granite straight into the cloud. In the more safety conscious climate of the new China, visitors were prevented from traversing this pathway. It was cut off by iron chains - the steps apparently closed for 'maintenance reasons'. But these chains were well rusted and no maintenance work seemed to have been done in years.

Park rubbish collectors ambled past us on their own long journey upwards. Prices for water fell steadily as the peaks fell away and we descended through the disparate clouds. When the sun came out, we were low enough that the people carriers gave up soliciting altogether. Instead they squatted, smoked, chatted and slept in the shade like Chinese Huckleberry Finns. And when the bamboo and the elderly hawkers of tea reappeared, we knew the bottom was close by. The Yellow Mountain was a joyous carnival of tourists, hawkers, maintenance workers, all undertaking a similarly strenuous task - a very Chinese democracy.

Delicate Eyebrow Mountain

In Hangzhou, we prepared for the third peak. *Emei Shan*, or Delicate Eyebrow Mountain, lay in Sichuan province. Sichuan was the province of 'Four Rivers', the most populous of them all. Over a hundred million people made their home in the fertile river basin. Back home Little Dog's leg had been improving in Chang Er's hands. And this time Chang Wen came all the way to Hangzhou station, along with Cheng Hualing and her parents who Mr. Xu had driven here in the bread van. They all stood around gingerly in the vaulted waiting hall, not knowing what to say, perhaps expecting not see us again. After all there were corrupt officials and begging monkeys out in Sichuan.

Wen said

'Next time I see you, you will have lost some weight', then the gate to the platform steps screeched open, and we were off, caught in the crowds that always accompanied the boarding of a train in a Chinese city, down the steps, past the carriage attendants in their smart military style uniforms and onto a well painted, tidy train and the 'hard sleeper' beds that would become our temporary home. This was a 49 hour train journey, two days and two nights. I hoped we would like our travelling comrades, because we were all going to have to get very intimate. There was no first or second-class on the trains. This was, even after everything, still communist China. Instead there were 'soft sleeper', private cabins with personal reading lights and more comfortable beds. They cost double the price of the 'hard sleeper' bunks which were stacked three to a column, six to a bay and close to a hundred a carriage, all open to the connecting corridor. It wasn't that there was anything 'hard' about hard sleeper; it was just that 'soft' sleepers were more luxurious. On the People's railway some passengers were more equal than others.

The other citizens of hard sleeper class dug in like ticks, crunching sunflower seeds and throwing the husks on the floor, breaking out bottles of beer and packs of cards and occasionally shouting '*Ganbei!*' in raucous toasts. The carriage took on the atmosphere of a roadside restaurant, a lively Chinese village. A food trolley appeared every couple of hours so the beer, nuts, dried squid and packaged tofu did not run out until lights out. At 22:00 exactly the carriage attendants moved through the train closing the curtains and switching out the lights. The garish families and drunken men grudgingly climbed into bed. Drinking time had been called. In another land perhaps the passengers would have rioted. But this was China, where the individual perhaps often allowed himself to be coerced by the group.

I moved to the space in between cars, but soon got frustrated trying to read under the harsh glare of the lights out there - the floor was hard, my only companions smokers

'What are you doing?' they asked

'Reading' I said. They shook their heads at such deranged behaviour. I went back to the compartment and lay down in my middle bunk, where I found Kristel arguing with the neighbours because she had tried to turn the lights back on. We soon learned to avoid the bottom bunks on Chinese trains, which became communal seating areas in the day. Two middle aged women had drawn the short straw in our compartment, but they didn't seem to mind gabbing with the strangers who stopped to prop their feet up on these ladies' beds. Our new comrades didn't even seem too bothered later in the dark by more visitors inviting themselves for a sit down and a chat while they waited to get off at one of the halts stopped at in Jiangxi and Hunan provinces throughout the early hours.

Next morning the carriage radio network set off at precisely 06:30. The attendants marched through, flinging the curtains open. The breakfast trolley followed not far behind. The rest of this village were already awake, chattering and picking at the nuts left over from last night. The top bunks in our compartment had been empty at lights out, but now they were occupied by passengers. They must have gotten on during the night.

Outside, the brash forms of Zhejiang dwellings - the concrete and smoked glass - had disappeared. Now there were concrete tumbledown shacks with tiled roofs instead. They stood in fields of rice and maize. For the rest of the day while Kristel dozed the train chugged through shabby industrial towns and green hill country, past the crumbling tenements and wet grime of Nanchang, where the Chairman had once lived. Then deeper, into the bowels of China over flooded rivers and drowning paddies.

By mid afternoon one of the passengers had been brave enough to start a conversation with me. A participating audience assembled to watch the small talk and clog up the passageway. Then a balding man with squinting eyes burst forward to take charge. He shouted

'Come to *Jiuzhaigou*'. It was a famous national park in Sichuan province. 'Come with us' he said 'It's the most beautiful place in China. At *Emei* you will only find Buddhists and monkeys'

Buddhists and monkeys sounded just fine, I said.

He asked me how much money I earned. I told him. He invited us to eat with him in the dining carriage. His name was Mr. Li and he was staying in soft sleeper with his mistress, who looked much younger than him. Mr. Li was a businessman from Guangzhou, with a wife and two

111

kids back home. His mistress was pretty, but wore her looks with such bad
grace - all scowls and bad posture - that this observation was merely
academic. Instantly it became clear why the foreigners had been brought
here.

And Mr.Li's face fell. His mistress had seen foreigners before -
and maybe even spoken to them. These ones rustled up here on a train to
the interior were nothing new, and they certainly did not impress her.

'I'm hungry' she whined 'When will the food get here?'

Kristel eyed the mistress, perhaps working out how to go about
imposing a gag. Mr. Li's face meanwhile had creased in deep thought.
Then his little eyes widened.

'Let's drink beer! Can you drink beer?' he exclaimed

'Oh yes!' shouted mistress 'Lets drink' and she brightened
further when Mr. Li challenged us to a couples' drinking competition.

'Waiter bring us beers' he shouted. They arrived immediately.

'*Ganbei!*' screamed mistress and we all slapped our cups
together. But Mr. Li quickly began to suffer. After two bottles of beer his
cheeks were slapped pink, and after three they had turned to rose petal.
His eyelids started to sag but I decided not to give him face by giving up
this game because I noticed that whenever he was sure his mistress wasn't
looking he filled his cup only halfway for each whole cup he poured me.
After another bottle, he cried

'Enough!' For a while we played cards instead. But not for
long: he was too drunk to follow the rules - and she, too bored.

Night Two: the train rumbled through mountainous Guizhou,
approaching Sichuan from the South on tracks the heroic People's
Liberation Army had carved through the hills with the sweat and blood of
fifties idealism. One of the women on the bottom bunk was sick. She left
a small pool of vomit on the floor mat of the compartment. It laid there for
the rest of the journey, winking lazily. We crossed swollen rivers and
chugged past more rice and more maize. Children stick fought beside the
track and an old peasant lady plucked the corn from a cob with her fingers
- she had no teeth. In the dense thickets of maize around here, the train
tracks served as a sort of road for pedestrians, and the life of the village
surrounded this thundering vehicle and its rails like the insulating plastic
of an electrical wire. It struck me too that our integration into the life of
the train was as close as we might come to living as the Chinese, with its

community and inescapable bustle, the petty interferences that had to be accepted with good grace.

By the time the train pulled underneath a concrete block adorned with the characters for 'Chengdu station', the skies had been smothered in rug. The city lay at the centre of the fertile Sichuan bowl, in this province ringed with mountains. Not long ago Sichuan had been particularly hard to access. Weather conditions were forever cloudy and wet. Taxi hustlers were abusing the fact that the pavement outside had been closed by road works and they harassed the new arrivals merrily. A stench of exhaust fumes and factory pollution had conquered the air, the trademarks of a generic Chinese city. So we decided to leave on the short journey south to the nearby town of Le Shan, which, it turned out, did not seem a whole lot different.

But here we found *Da Fo*, a statue of the Buddha carved out of a sandstone cliff. He was now officially the tallest in the world since the extremists of the Taliban had blown up the Buddhist carvings of Bamiyan in Afghanistan. We approached him from the cliff side, passing close to the sign that said *'Nice to Live!'* Da Fo himself sat below, staring out over the water just as he had for the last 1300 years. He had been hewn from the sandstone as a kind of lighthouse, warning passing vessels of the treacherous sandbanks here in the murky confluence of the Dadu and Min rivers. Now it attracted tour boats instead, fighting to maintain stationary camera stops for the tourists whilst the currents raged against them. Many smaller sculptures in this area had been decapitated during the Cultural Revolution. But the stone giant himself remained unscathed. Those puny red guards had come with hammers and chisels, not explosives.

On the slippery steps leading to Da Fo's feet, I met a sweaty East Asian resting on his climb upwards. We exchanged greetings and he said proudly

'I am not Chinese. I am Singaporean'

'How are you finding China?' I asked

'The dragon is finally awakening. It's going to mould the world' he reckoned. Then

'This is the land of his ancestors'. And with this, he seemed to grant himself a licence to lecture.

'Your forefathers tried to make us buy opium' he said 'we don't want any of that stuff. You can keep your crack, your cocaine, we don't want any of it'. He chopped the air with his hand as if to show what would happen to me if I personally tried to throw drugs at him. I sat on slimy sandstone and listened, somewhat amazed, to this unexpected rant. He seemed to have internalised the century of shame as part of his identity. And he lived in a land made prosperous by colonialists.

'The dragon is awake!' he exclaimed. Then I realised he was starting to repeat himself, making me suddenly bored. So I left and searched for Kristel. She was down on the riverbank with the sandstone giant, who sat with his hands clamped firmly on the knees, gazing at the smokestacks on the other side of the water. Da Fo was oblivious to imperialism, revolution, and communist initiative. Hopefully he might also manage to outlast China's greatest cultural threat: the continuing economic boom.

Emei town was hidden under a screen of fog when we arrived on the bus from Le Shan early next morning. It had been a typical interior bus - rickety, containing a smattering of peasants, a few businessmen, some urban dwellers visiting family in the country. The TV blared out violent Chinese sitcoms involving historic figures and plenty of martial arts and the driver liked to scream. The road into the village could not have filled anyone with hope for tranquillity, lined as it was with hotels, guesthouses, restaurants - and shops of mass-produced ink scrolls and wooden Buddhist statuettes all fighting for attention like spoiled kids.

We chose a restaurant on the main drag - a row of kitsch whitewashed blocks adorned with flying eaves. Inside, dined a Frenchman.

'Why doesn't the menu come in French?' he complained to his guide, a Nepali. The Frenchman had spent six months on the Tibetan plateau and the grasslands of Qinghai and had come to Emei for rest and recreation. He was a middle-aged man helping to set up a trekking company out here that would lead Westerners through the wilds. He had complaints about the yaks which were used for carrying provisions - their behaviour was terrible, they needed a strong hand - and he was having difficulties finding a suitable herder. He took particular interest in Kristel, leaning forward with big eyes and touching her shoulders over lunch, and he became particularly excitable when he discovered we would be staying at the same hotel.

Later Kristel saw him alone in the lounge where he had raised his eyebrows and said

'I've something in my room for you'

I persuaded her not to go find out what that might be.

This town was the gateway to Delicate Eyebrow - named after two facing peaks. It was tallest of the *Ssu-ta Ming Shan,* the holy Buddhist mountains. It was a United Nations world heritage site and one of the mightiest pilgrimage destinations in China. A journey to the top of Mount Emei passed through 'Four Seasons'. At the summit was a 'One Thousand Buddha summit' and a 'Ten Thousand Buddha summit' and in total, there were 'Four wonders' to see, including the spectacular 'Buddha's Halo', the phenomenon of a rainbow forming around the shadows of people cast against the clouds. These had once caused the faithful to leap off the mountain in fits of ecstasy, believing that they were about to enter the pure land, the realm of ultimate bliss. There didn't seem any point in leaping anymore though, since science had shown that this halo was simply a light trick, caused by its reflection off water droplets.

Emei was the first place Buddhism established itself in China - at least a hundred years before the birth of Christ. The oldest monastery was a thousand years old. Inaccurately, it was known as 'Ten thousand year monastery'. These places had all been patronised by Puxian, the lord of truth, the Buddhist representative of practice and meditation. He had once flown to the mountain from India on the back of a white elephant. Since then the mountain had transmitted the faith. From here on Eyebrow Mountain, Buddhism had fanned out into the Chinese lowlands, arriving in the heart of the imperial city where during its glorious peak in the Tang dynasty, the faith had been patronised by the emperor.

Regiments of elderly folk climbed the steep paths of concrete step all twenty-two kilometres to the top: they were peasants on pilgrimage. Some of these white haired sprites wore Mao suits, but others had on flowery blouses, combat fatigues or old leather jackets. They skipped upwards through the pine trees keeping up a constant stream of chatter and when overtaking us, the old women asked us mockingly

'*Lei bu lei?*' – are you tired? Because the Chinese never grew old. Those in the city often began second childhoods, spending their days drinking tea and playing *mahjong* in the park with their friends, and if they were lucky enough to have pious children, they were tended to the end of their days. These folk on the mountain went beyond that. They climbed the thirty thousand steps to the Golden temple while youngsters took the cable car. People of this age in China had lived through the warlord era, the anti-Japanese war, the civil war, land reform and the Great Leap Forward. As they were mostly former farmers, the Cultural Revolution - which afflicted the cities - may have passed them by. To watch them play made the present seem a hopeful place.

Wannian Temple hummed with flies and blue butterflies the size of outstretched palms flapping about in the scrub. There were, of course, hawkers and melon-calved people carriers cleverly positioned at the strategic choke points, awaiting the hungry, tired or weak. But then these other travellers disappeared - and further up the vastness of the mountain only the occasional peel of floating laughter reminded me that we were not alone.

A gang of monkeys sat lazily on the terrace below the temple at Elephant Bathing Pool - at this, the exact the point at which Puxian had finally landed with his white mammal friend. The monkeys had set up a checkpoint to harass tourists with bureaucratic efficiency. They barred the steps, and standing on two legs, solemnly checked bags for food.

I walked onwards until I heard anger erupt from behind.

'Merde! Merde! Merde!'

It seemed Kristel had been ambushed by one of the more aggressive males. He had approached from the back and stolen our biscuits while his mother distracted Kristel from the front. When this evil one came back posturing aggressively for more, I struck him with a walking stick I had purchased in Emei Town. The only thing we had left to eat after that was a packet of peanuts, but when I pulled them out of the bag and into the open, I had a fleeting glimpse of fur moving in the bushes and thought better of it.

Above the terrace, ten labourers were painstakingly chiselling grooves into the paving slabs to improve shoe grip in the rain.

'How many have you finished?' I asked

'Two a day' said the roughest looking. At that rate they could be working there forever. But that was the nature of work in China - the labour pool was so vast, did it matter? Here, the masses completed works of flabbergasting scale. There was no choice but to place faith in many hands making light work against the possibility of too many cooks spoiling the broth. For it was not the contribution of the individual that counted, but the total output of the social organism.

We continued walking, and as dusk fell a mist descended making it difficult to see the path ahead. Wind picked up, and angry limbs started shaking in the undergrowth. Eventually we arrived at a car park six kilometres below the summit. Day trippers were dropped off here during the day by buses that wound all the way up the gentle back bowls of the other side. It was now dark, the buses had long gone and only two people hung around on tarmac that glistened with night dew.

'You won't finish' the loiterers cooed. They were people carriers, waiting for us to break and provide them with their last catch of the day. So they followed us for the next two kilometres, calling and coaxing, and only giving up and climbing back down to shelter when the ground started to patter with rain.

It got wetter, and windier. A storm broke. Somewhere in this sideways weather, the forests fell away and out on the exposed roof of Emei, the hawkers had packed up and were huddling inside the battered mountaintop structures. A few hotel touts in raincoats braved the wind and downpour up here.

'Come inside!' they said.

We found refuge in an old guesthouse. It was damp, the wet floorboards were sagging. A terrible stench wafted up from open sewers. The sheets were soiled with dirt, the windows let in the draught. But at least with the smell of excrement, cold limbs and sweating torsos (management had generously donated an electric blanket the size of a tea towel), we were up long before dawn.

By this time the weather had calmed. Maybe there would be a mountain sunrise. Yet once outside, One Thousand and Ten Thousand Buddha summits lay screened off by fog. Pilgrims were already out there in the dark by the Golden Temple. They stood in long lines, bowing, chanting and waving giant incense sticks while the monks inside the temple banged gongs, and calmly led a packed congregation through the first worship of the day in a hall of gold coloured statues. The sun never did make it through the thick cloud at the top. But this was Sichuan, a province the sun did not know well. Thus the coming of the Buddha's Halo was a rare event indeed.

A small army of labourers was renovating the path we followed on the descent. Theirs was a different kind of ritual to that playing out on the summit. They were walking stones up here, up fifteen kilometres of incline, each man carrying one at a time. They were the masses working another of their amazing toils. The old trail ran alongside the one under construction. It snaked round the mountain gradient, cutting back and forth down the valley sides then down a long spiral section hewn vertically out of limestone on which more fairy-like gangs of elders danced. At its base, this path merged with other pathways that wriggled back and forth through the subtropical foliage and beside the river to a pavilion that could only be reached by bridge. Over the falls here the water crashed, spraying steam into the forest.

These valley thoroughfares were used by the bus loads of day-trippers who climbed no higher. And near the entrance to the mountain, the usual mess of trinket sellers had moved behind new stalls that still smelt sharply of coniferous wood. Other hawkers were selling ice cream, which the tourists were feeding to the monkeys. All of these mammals chattered mockingly and lazed around the pavilions and restaurants as the forest evaporated abruptly.

The river had been diverted from this area and its bed bulldozed flat. Workers were busy hacking down trees. From here the labourers started on their huge trek up the mountain, each with a stone, each replacing one tiny part of the decaying pathway. I asked one of the stall owners what was going on down here at the foot.

'We are building a car park, with a road and hotels' he said proudly.

This mountain had broadcast faith. Now the evangelising came from the State. Advancement and development were coming.

7. Progress

Chengdu was a city under a watery assault. The sewers had overflown and vehicles abandoned. Even the umbrella sellers retreated from the streets. Kristel and I turned up the TV volume and watched Charlie Chaplin reruns, while our neighbours next door alternated between bouts of blistering argument and noisy make up sex. The Chaplin silent miming I noticed, had been dubbed in *putonghua*. This idea, well-intentioned as it was, seemed thoroughly to have missed the point. In any case, after three days and three nights the torrents suddenly ceased. Kids ran outside to splash in the drainage overflow. The sun peeked out and hawkers and commuters returned to the streets to find their vehicles blessed with a natural hose-down. We ventured into the city back streets. Here, hooked meat hung from the rafters of wooden shacks and rubber gloved women shelled live crayfish - tails in a bucket, heads winking in a molehill left on the pavement. The shellers were as fascinated by me as I was by their work, and when I turned to leave the plumpest one called out

'You try *waiguoren*. Great taste from the river!' It wasn't much of a recommendation.

'The rivers are dirty' I said. Even top officials agreed most of them were full of industrial slag. She shrugged generously.

'True' she agreed 'so are the fields. But we eat the vegetables'. I could not argue with this.

Scattered around the city of Chengdu we found teahouses of smoking elders and wicker chairs; opera performances where men sang like cats on heat; tea served from pots with metre long spouts. I found a sign on a shop front that declared '*Smoke Wine*', and in the city's central square, a gigantic marble statue of Mao. It was of the type which on the East coast had long ago been torn from the public places and shunted off into retirement.

Former president Deng Xiaoping was especially revered in these parts. It had taken a Sichuanese like him to unleash the new economic pragmatism on China, when against the prevailing wisdom Deng had proclaimed

'It doesn't matter whether a cat is black or white as long as it catches mice'. With this emphasis on results over ideology, Chinese mercantile life had begun to reclaim itself from the state. Deng was a true son of Sichuan, with his plain-speaking and practical policy-making, the product of phlegm and mud. In this town Deng Xiaoping made a far more popular candidate for being cast into bronze than Mao. So I gathered the only reason Mao still stood here was simply because the local authorities had been too lazy and disconnected to take it down back when other cities were doing so.

Inside the Green Ram Daoist temple I caught a monk's eye. Sorrowful pools of wisdom they were, which widened as he leant towards my ear. I felt ready to receive any profound insight he might offer. But then this monk opened his mouth and whispered

'You are lucky if you buy a prayer'

Daoism, with its non action and belief in the balance of the forces, seemed the most practical and Chinese religion of them all, with its endless array of deities from whom you could buy *guanxi*, and the monks who made little pretence that they were anything more than tax collectors for them.

We paid a visit to the *Da Xiong Mao* - pandas (literally in Chinese, *big cat like bears*) - who woke to eat early every day, torrential rain or not. On the first morning after the rains, we visited them, watching them sit like giant sloths, grinding bamboo inside the cells and bleating like deep-throated sheep. There were thirty of them here at the Panda Research Centre just north of Chengdu - more than anywhere else on earth - all cute cuddly teddies.

During the Great Leap Forward of the '50s, peasants had hewn down much of the forest around here to fuel the useless 'backyard furnaces' that were supposed to create the steel in the quantities needed to overtake first Great Britain, then the United States. Bands of pandas had dwindled, left with a small series of disconnected forests to make the best of. Now they were too few to find each other, too anti-social to search too hard. Like army ants in the rainforest or Europeans of the colonial age, the Han had been multiplying and spilling abroad. Their movements, it soon turned out, had not been confined to the lowlands.

For we were to leave Chengdu, this laid back capital of 11 million, the major urban centre for the 90 million toilers of Sichuan - a province with a population greater than Germany, Turkey, or two Spains;

and a cuisine hotter than any of them. I liked the place, this centre of the most populous province of the most populous nation. Yet in many ways Chengdu was a typical Chinese city, home to stifling multitudes - just one more hotbed of noise and dust, of construction and billboards, of cars and people and bicycles all clogging roads, temples, malls and clumsy pavements.

Back at the hotel, the passionate neighbours left, screeching at each other and banging suitcases against the wall. I listened to them clatter down the stairs, the woman cursing her man, he firing back. It was such un-Chinese behaviour. Did they care nothing for face? In the lobby I arranged travel to Tibet through a tour company. It was the only way. To get up to the plateau by road was difficult. Foreigners were banned from the Eastern roads, which were precipitous mountain tracks used mainly by military supply trucks. Occasionally though hitchhikers slipped through locked behind a few crates of supplies, or hidden under a tarpaulin. Back at the University of Educated People, Professor Darling one evening had cracked open a beer and said

'My nephew sneaked across the Sichuan border on his bicycle'
'How did that work?'

'He and his friend oiled their wheels and chains so thoroughly they didn't make a sound...then they whipped across while the guards slept'. Darling chuckled at the audacity of it.

But Kristel and I would be taking an easier entrance to Tibet. We were not going to cycle across the border by night. We would simply fly into Lhasa as part of a domestic tour package once our permits had come through. Our tour group would be run by Chinese, for Chinese. Our comrades would be Han lowlanders. We were to explore with them their borderlands, the dim fringes, which in the old imperial order, were thought peopled only by savages.

On Tour

Our plane juddered nervously above plains which soon disappeared under Sichuan's defining cloud ceiling. It was a fearsome relic of the old China, a dirty fume-spluttering monster. It flew at West Sichuan's foothills in a bizarre game of bluff, edging above the ridges and spires as if to taunt them. This was how we passed into the bleak spaces of the Tibetan world. Some called this place the land of snow; others, the land of tears. It was the roof of the world and for the Chinese government, '*Xizang*', the Western Storehouse, just one of 34 administrative districts.

These mountain chains - the *Hengduan Shan*, and their eastern adjunct, the Himalaya - were some of the most formidable land barriers known to man. Yet air travel allowed the illusion of victory. A few horizons passed, and green valleys began to appear, etched from the dandruff, the evidence of man. It seemed a nourished neck, the Lhasa valley, as it loomed out of these grass tributaries - green farmland and smattered dwellings hemmed in by mountainside. We landed sloppily at an airport that was a clutter of military boxes and camouflaged hangars, colonised by teenaged Han soldiers who slouched deceptively in all this fresh air, like resting termites. They looked bored.

Our guide waited out there too.

'Call me Donald' he said, wincing and pulling sunglasses over his eyes, a man persecuted by the sun. He was a stout fellow of stained skin and he was to lead nine of us in a battered bus around the tracks of Tibet. We climbed in: it was full.

Mr. Chang, a spritely Chinese elder whose walking stick seemed to be an ironic statement, grinned mischievously and said

'Young people are always so busy'. He wore shades too, and sun cream and a winter jacket that made him look something like a skier on the slopes above a European resort. Eight year old Hong Jia jumped on his seat and shouted

'I don't want to eat the food!' His mother feigned an artistic pose in her fishing hat, pretending apparently, that Jia was not in fact her son.

A skinny student sat at the back trying to keep the row to himself. His name was Yu (Fish) and he owned the kind of pasty skin that lent a man an air of frailty. Perhaps the boy had been sent up here by rich parents - to be cleansed in the wilderness. Grudgingly Yu shifted himself into the corner for a chap called Xing. This new arrival was a rotund kind who fidgeted compulsively and eyed the foreigners nervously.

And unfortunately, there were a few of us *laowai* on the bus, which somewhat destroyed the wilderness fantasy. After all, you couldn't very well have your own native adventure with the other big noses tagging along. The bus motored off along winding paths of fresh asphalt and mountains reared on three sides. The plains were populated by tiny plots of rapeseed and grass sprinkled liberally with the odd hut. And the skies? Navy blue, cloud free! The road soon found itself tracking reeds and a river, the Yarlung, a great greyness reflecting in splinters the sun and the hillside. We soon stopped for a break. Hong Jia ran towards the river, threatening to splash his mother when she came to pull him back. Mr. Chang strode off behind tall rushes.

'Don't come with me' he called. Yu huddled by the van, inside a military overcoat a few sizes too big. And as I watched Mr. Chang disappear off to the call of nature, one of the foreigners approached my side, and spoke.

'Been a while since I've seen the sun' he reckoned 'You?' The questioner was tall and American accented. He smiled like he couldn't help it. The man's name was Jim, and he had been teaching peasant kids in Sichuan.

The other *waiguoren* was Amy, from Melbourne. She was taking a break from the orphanage in which she worked, deep in the province of *Shaanxi*.

'It is mainly unwanted girls we care for' she said softly 'they get abandoned on us. Left on the doorstep'. As she spoke she ran her fingers through her hair delicately, as though afraid it would all fall out. Amy's stroll too, I noticed, was a gentle glide, one that seemed to avoid intrusion on life - she seemed to have borrowed the walk of a most respectable Chinese girl.

We four foreigners threw stones at the water. It was a rather aimless thing to do, and the Han looked on, curious. Xing scowled - watching us play as though he were some kind of big cat tracking a safari group. We re-boarded. The bus grumbled off through golden flats and crossed a bridge over the Yarlung where a couple of teenagers with Kalashnikovs stood guard. It couldn't have been a bad posting during the summer after the glaciers had thawed a little. The work however was real. There were separatists, agitators, and hooligans to quash. There was China's old Asian rival to check. Over the freezing passes south of here China and India had once fought a border war. India had expected to teach the little effeminate upstarts to the north a lesson. Instead it found its fearless Pathan troops bombarded, outmanoeuvred, scattered and slaughtered by the People's Liberation Army and its hardened veterans.

Everyone wanted a piece of this high ground, said Chinese government strategists. Tibet had always been part of China they said, Tibet was yoked to the motherland via the unbreakable placenta of history. And in any case hadn't the poverty stricken Tibetans always been destined for domination at the hands of a larger power? If it wasn't China, then it would be the Indians or the yanks they said. It would be reckless for China to allow this to happen.

This was of course also a theory of self-justification - one that carried that strange reek of China, and its ancient paternalistic obsession with hierarchy and control.

All afternoon we moved back and forth across the river, which flowed behind us. It moved from here into eastern Tibet, where it curled southwards and plunged through the mountains. In Bangladesh it collided with the sea and was known as Brahmaputra. It was known there in its swollen fertility, as a son of the giver of life, as well as the bringer of death. In Tibet too, this river was a sacred one. Even its fish were holy. It had hewn here for itself a corridor insulated by hillsides. And on these hills were scatterings of prayer flags - cloud whites, sky blues, earth yellows, watery greens and fiery reds - a representation of the elements, weathered and rotting, and glowing radioactively in the late afternoon sun. For the Tibetan culture was an ancient one - and these figments of native *Bon* animism had only more recently been recycled into a Buddhism come up from Han China.

The bus dribbled to a halt at a lonely Han restaurant, its breezeblock and gold characters garish against the rock and dust.

'*Aiah!*' exclaimed Mr. Chang 'I am so hungry' and he turned to peer jovially at little Hong 'I could eat a whole young boy' he said. Hong dropped his mouth open and was promptly safely scooped up by Ms. Jia.

'Don't listen. No one will eat you' she said 'but you can eat. You must be hungry. Here we will eat. It is safe'. Indeed it was safe - safe Han food, made by Han and consumed by Han. It was the regular drill, the plastic table covers and disposable chopsticks. But the vegetable was a little sparse and the meat indistinguishable. Most of the ingredients had been driven some time ago from the lowlands, up the long winding tracks of West Sichuan and I wondered whether standards slipped for the Han of the plateau. Our comrades gobbled noisily.

'Not bad ah?' said Mr. Chang with his mouth full. He picked up his stick and prodded Yu, who looked a little less ghoulish now he had a bit of food inside him.

Kristel was talking with Amy.

'What's your work like?' she asked. Amy clicked her teeth and said

'Hardening'. The waiters cleared the plates. 'Many of the babies get dumped with us because they have deformities. Many don't survive because of their injuries - often they have been neglected. Someone left a baby girl on the doorstep just two weeks ago. She was dressed in a dirty shawl and had a cleft lip. This baby had some kind of infection and my friend who is a nurse said she didn't have long to live. She never cried, so the Chinese nurses called her *Xing Yun*. 'Lucky''

Noticing the food rapidly dwindling Amy paused to steal a few morsels. 'This girl died five days ago' she added 'while I was singing to her'.

After that story there didn't seem to be much worth saying, and it was all I could do just to listen to Hong Jia struggling with his mother.

'Finish your rice!' she was saying

'Don't want to!' said the little emperor, shoving the bowl into the middle of the table.

By the time we got back on the bus, the rocks of the roadside had been sprayed orange. Xing hadn't joined us at the table, but when I left the restaurant, I saw him standing by the river, still smoking.

The mountains slowly flexed and rose to eclipse the light, and the bus groaned into the outskirts of Lhasa. Shops and faceless new-builds strung out along the arterial routes like scattered trash. Here was a valley adorned with smoked glass and concrete, bright signboards adorned with gold characters, concrete, construction, more dust...On first appearances Lhasa was a typical Chinese city. It had the same flat roofed apartment blocks, row after dreary row, with no noticeable design change between them apart from the occasional faux-terracotta roof. Only the number of people wandering or out on their bicycles suggested that this was not just a lowland transplant, for the streets were almost empty.

A series of pillars followed the road, reddened by the last of the sun. They were carrying track for the new Lhasa to Golmud express railway. That advancement was about to carry more Han settlers and tourists right here into the cultural heart of Tibet. They would come on pressurised carriages containing oxygen bars. In an emergency they would be able to recuperate at one of 60 medical stations to be thrown up beside the rails. It was a railway that had been built against the odds - much of the tracks lay across permafrost and even the Swiss engineers invited to assess its viability said 'It can't be done!'

But in the new China nothing was impossible - no project too large, no construction over the odds. Man could, and would, conquer his environment because that was what the Chinese had been attempting since the dawn of their civilisation when the first dykes had been built to control the floodwaters of the yellow river. This track taking shape beside a pitiful road and a sprawling river was to be the world's highest railway line, a display of ambition and will.

The bus made its final stop at nightfall. We had arrived. This hotel was a Han one of plastic and arbitrary colour. But we hardly noticed. Breathing in this altitude had been exhausting enough for one day. We negotiated our room key and crashed.

In the small hours of the morning the phone rang. I picked it up.

'Want a friend?' asked a woman.

'No' I said 'Do not want'.

In Lhasa even the drill for hawking prostitutes was the same.

Backward and Feudal

The skies were clear. The sun was out. There was no pollution in sight. Then we discovered the old town, the Tibetan heart of the city where the mess of the Han petered out against daubed white stone and beamed doors. Divided windows were framed in heavy blackened wood so that they looked like portals to alien worlds. No building was taller than three stories. Covered stalls lined the roads, and the authorities had helpfully rigged up street lighting in the central area with chandeliers so elegant they might have been stolen from the Moscow subway. And the crowds were back. They were not the Han masses, but Tibetan townspeople wearing ankle-long *Shuba* robes, flogging tat or yak butter. Goods were being unloaded from man-powered carts. The pilgrims were here too: Dropka nomads, and wild Kampha people with their hair in plaits, and many of the farming folk of the valleys.

Tibetans had mechanised prayer. Not only did the wind blow

prayers off to the heavens from flags all over the hillsides, but pilgrims and elders shook their own prayer wheels - little ones on sticks inscribed with sutras. At the temples they pushed man-sized ones clockwise. These were adorned with holy verse, which through the act of spinning were reeled off to the heavens. And the Barkhor, the great market-stall surrounding Tibet's holiest temple was also a circuit spinning clockwise. The nomads and peasants and traders and monks all ambled this same direction around it, chanting and swaying amongst barrels of flaming incense and the flapping hawkers. There were policemen loitering on the corners and lurking under stall tarpaulins - they usually wore shades and although the sun had varnished them all. Mostly they appeared to be Han.

As we walked amongst the colourful crowds, I found a hand on my shoulder. An old Tibetan woman draped in heavy sheets stood there spinning a wheel in one hand, and tapping me with the other. With the face of an old walnut, she smiled toothlessly and thumbed at her friend, who looked even more browbeaten by the weather than she was. They wanted water. So I let them drink from my bottle. One of the Han officers stood with his back to us. After handing back my bottle both of these women took it in turns to stick their fingers up behind the copper's back. They tittered like children because he did not see their disrespect. It was an odd way to express gratitude.

As we continued the crowds jostled into a bottleneck which then spilled into the Barkhor Square. Thousands had perished in this place in the failed uprising of '59. In 1999 in this same square, eleven Tibetans had been gunned down. It was an incident that had made it into the Western press mainly because a Dutch tourist present had also gotten himself shot in the arm. Now on these flagstones on which blood had spilt came the rest of our tour group, freshly bussed round from the hotel. Then two Tibetan giants began a play fight in front of the stalls and the incense. They were Khampa tribesmen in colourful rags and plaited hair. And Ms Hong grasped Jia tightly by the hand to make sure the cheeky nomads could not spirit him away. Mr. Chang smiled and tried to engage them in banter. They stopped their fooling to stare at him. He turned away with a frown and said

'They don't speak the common language'

Yu was there at the back, with Xing - both of them just standing, anxiously surveying the place.

Across the square billowed smoke from stone street urns. It smelt sweet and pungent - like marijuana (it wasn't). Here on the edge of the square was Tibet's holiest place, the Johkang Temple. Our group marched towards it, waving away smoke, picking past the lines of pilgrims, who whooped and howled at the paying tourists jumping the queues. Surrounding the entrance cluttered the truly devoted, who lay on their faces and mumbled, and then we were moving through the black frames and white stone, where eaves of mauve and gold heralded the circuit of the inner courtyard. Here the faithful spun their prayer wheels and pushed at the large static ones that they passed: we seemed to have found the largest prayer factory in the land.

In the inner sanctum under the rancid stink of burning yak butter, the pilgrims wailed to the Gods. Effigies of demon slayers hid as beacons of light in sooty alcoves, each with their own small following. It was a heady, mediaeval place - gothic and dirty with its own micro climate - a dark, slippery humidity, in which eyes took time to adjust. Candles flicked more plumes of smoke at the devout, prayer wheels rattled, a bees drone - *Om mani padme hum* - slid from cowled figures on the floor, and Han tourists darted insecurely from one deity to another like lizards caught out in the sun. I did not stay long inside before I had to head back out to the light. I found Xing standing by the entrance, facing off the hollering pilgrims, and smoking. He turned and fixed me with a stare.

'It was dark in there' I said.

Xing shook his head and walked off, flicking his cigarette butt on the flagstones: the temple was barbarian. So were most of its visitors.

I started off on my own while I waited for the others to extract themselves. Down a side street I bought a roundel of bread. A streaky-faced boy asked me for money. I was about to break him off some bread when instead a swarm of children ran out from another alley. They leapt at the loaf, grabbing it, attacking and clawing it to pieces which fell to the floor. Someone shouted and the kids scattered - a Han policeman had been watching. The beggar child bent down and began to pick at what was left. I had not previously noticed the gaggle of prayer wheel spinning elders camped in the corner, but now they were chuckling.

I set off back to meet Kristel and join the tour bus back on the square, strangely disturbed. There were soon to be stronger reasons to feel this way. For tonight Donald was organising 'Tibetan Cultural Evening'. There would be exotic Tibetan dancing, chanting and bells, grilled yak. There was going to be a brief performance of the Tibetan epic 'King Gesar', a 1000 year old tale of world creation and the work of the messiah. It would have to stay brief, for the original epic - at one million verses - was thought the longest literary creation in existence. Our Han friends had already signed up. They were going to join the other Han at the hotel in watching the minorities perform their delightful dances and eating the barbarian food, but safe from the savages who would still be out there, roaming in the dark. When we set out to find an alternative dinner, we were accosted only by the occasional 'Hullo!'

Mr. Chang looked groggy next morning.

'Interesting' he sniffed 'the dancing was interesting'.

'And the wine?'

'Also interesting'. Today we were headed to the Potala Palace, the symbol of Tibet, home to the Dalai Lamas, UNESCO World Heritage Site and wonder of the modern world according to the American Society of Engineers. The outer quarters were a castle of white cliffs, the inner chambers were vermilion battlements crowned in tiny golden hats. The Palace had been vacated by the fourteenth Dalai Lama since his escape over the mountains in '59. But even without him the palace dominated the central valley. It had managed to escape some of the more extreme communist policies while an estimated 6000 monasteries hadn't. Since then the authorities in Beijing had labelled it a 'national cultural treasure' and stamped its image on 50 yuan bills. In hierarchy conscious China, that made it only second to the Great Hall of the People on the 100 yuan as an architectural symbol of the nation.

'Interesting Building' said Mr. Chang with a detached frown. Potala glinted, its whiteness coming from a plastering of Yak yoghurt. Hong Jia put his face to the window and waved at a soldier slouching in the car park.

We climbed out and moved in, following the army's footsteps. The PLA had found a use for this relic of feudal engineering and taken up residence amongst the Potala's 1000 rooms and 10,000 shrines. Soldiers loitered inside, sat in gloomy pockets underneath ancient scrolls. They haunted the dank corridors and sunny atria, and added splashes of olive to the place's fabric. The prescribed route passed through a corridor lit by the candles of yak butter. The passage turned onto a hall, inside of which were eight metal coffins, rounded cones each containing a previous dalai lama. They had been stacked behind one another like awful beehives.

The 14th Dalai Lama's chambers were several stories above this place, an eyrie at the roof of this palace. His bedroom was cluttered with warm embroidery and furniture which had been touched by tourists for almost half a century. A People's Liberation Army guard sitting near the bed stretched his arms.

Mr. Chang strolled to the window.

'It's very busy outside!' he shouted.

Yu was standing at the door looking blank. Mr. Chang hurried over to him and dragged him towards the window.

'Look!' he cried 'Most interesting Mr. Fish. Look! You can see all Lhasa' And Yu looked, his eyes bulging, taking in the scene: the clutter of modern Lhasa far below us, the shops and the houses, the streets, the flagstones, the people...all had become Lego contraptions - specks under the mountains.

'But no tall buildings?' continued Mr. Chang, scratching his chin. 'Lhasa maybe needs some tall buildings'.

Up here Heinrich Harrer had witnessed the Dalai Lama at play. The Austrian had escaped from British India during the war only to wind up here as an advisor to the Tibetans. Harrer had watched the young 14th Dalai Lama look out from this nest through a telescope surveying the valley and his people. Down there, the people had gone about their business on the Lhasa streets oblivious to the eye of their god-king. Now he was over the mountains, a recipient of the Nobel peace prize, and an exile in an alien state. Meanwhile the Han were with us here to nose about in his bedroom, gazing at the city he had known and lamenting how little the old street patterns had changed.

At the foot of the palace a square had been laid. It was of the windswept variety that could only be the work of the old socialism. Photographs from the 1950s showed this area in smatterings of old tumbledown dwellings huddling against the Potala, built in the old style of whitewash and timber. Since then the authorities had demolished these and replaced them with flagstones. With its context removed the Potala seemed an austere museum piece. It was just another Chinese monument which the government had patiently restored, even whilst still managing to modernise the city. Instead the square had become the city's centrepiece, created under the then-governor - now president - of all China: Hu Jintao. He had been called a technocrat, a reformer. He had cut his teeth here in Xizang province, rolling out the economic advance. But Hu suffered greatly from altitude sickness at that time. He had not spent a lot of time up here witnessing the itinerants bludgeon out this man-made plain.

But the concrete seemed familiar territory for our lowland friends. There were bus loads of them reeling off photos of the palace, the flag and each other. The hawkers were up here too with their camera films and ice cream and fake Tibetan tribal dress for the posers. But the square was so vast it swallowed the snapping tourists and their hawker entourage.

Ms. Hong dressed up in Khampa clothing, pranced and preened. And little Hong grasped her hand, and jumped up and down.

'I want to wear the clothes!' he screamed. Yet his mother did not seem to hear, and carried on prancing. Mr. Chang turned to Yu who had been gawping at Ms Hong, and said

'You try too. They are more colourful than you are!'

And poor Yu was needled until he too succumbed to the wearing of quaint tribal clothes, standing forlorn in a colourful oversized gown - in the middle of this empty place. But Xing was not larking. He stood by the flagpole, watching silently, smoking in his brooding way.

Donald rounded us up. He had us all herded into a restaurant. In this place Mr. Chang was soon wolfing down hunks of Sichuan beef. Hong Jia slurped at cabbage. Even Yu managed to join in, splashing soy braised pork over the table. This particular moment echoed Lin Yutang:

> 'What shame is there in enjoying one's food, what shame
> in having a normal, healthy appetite? ...[We Chinese]
> have bad table manners, but great enjoyment of a feast.'

Usually I agreed wholeheartedly with this Chinese spiritedness. Enjoyment of eating was more important than manners. But for some reason I was suddenly embarrassed by such poor etiquette. *Tsampa*, or barley porridge was the Tibetan staple. It felt some kind of crime to enjoy one's food when it was this dreary foodstuff that was usually trotted out as the centrepiece of a meal.

Donald did not eat but watched the Han intently

'Not eating?' I asked in English.

'Later'

'You don't want Chinese food?'

'We are all Chinese' said Donald, blinking 'all our food is Chinese!'

'Why are there soldiers standing outside?' asked Jim

'To keep you safe' said Donald.

'Safe from what?'

'Safe from crowds' he answered threateningly. Then he flinched, and cast a regretful glance towards Xing. 'Don't need them often' he added.

'What about Han and Tibetans. How do they get on?'

This seemed to cross the line: it was too much. Donald tapped his glasses and hissed

'That's enough!' All the spilling and slurping covered what might otherwise have been a moment of some awkwardness.

A few minutes later Mr. Chang fastidiously wiped chilli oil from his mouth, preparing perhaps, to make a speech. Soon enough indeed, he was delivering it.

'In Tibet we have been building roads and electricity and shops' he crowed

'The Chinese have been developing Tibet very quickly!'

'Are Tibetans Chinese too?' I asked.

'Yes' he said without much thought. But then he pointed at Donald with his chopsticks and exclaimed 'These are our China's Little Brothers!'

Donald looked as though he had pulled a facial muscle.

'Do you like Tibetans Mr. Chang?' I asked

'All Chinese like Tibetans' he claimed 'They are a very colourful people. And they need us'

'They do?'

'Tibet is backward. And *fengjiande*' he explained. Backward and Feudal. 'Before, the people did not even wash'. Mr. Chang's thought process was clear. The barbarians needed civilising. They had always needed civilising. They had needed civilising in fact ever since the 7th century, when the armies of the Great warrior Songtsan Gampo had marched out of these mountain fastnesses and utterly wrecked the Ming dynasty armies of lowland China. And what back then, had China given in exchange for such destruction? The legendary Princess Wenchang, whom Songtsan Gampo had wed. It was the beautiful Wenchang who had first brought Tibet the humanising power of Buddhism…apparently.

Kristel and I left the others to the bus, for our comrades were heading back to nap. Away from the Chinese concrete, narrow back streets split from the boulevards and soon we were lost once more amongst decaying whitewash and begging grannies. These wrinkled sprites had collected piles of *fen* - a mythical currency denomination, a tiny subdivision of the yuan. It was a denomination so small I had never actually seen it in use on the Chinese East coast. But in the land of tears they were valid currency, swapped in the market and scattered on altars, collected by the many beggars who had always been tolerated here, encouraged even. For life was bitter on the plateau. Giving to panhandlers seemed only a simple acknowledgement that life for all depended on the whim of nature, and her mercy was often scant.

Back on the Barkhor circuit the crowd had thickened. But it turned out that these were no longer chanting pilgrims with their heads bowed to the floor, but baying locals flicking their limbs to the heavens, their faces contorted like those of the more frightening deities. A Tibetan man's nose had been bloodied. Out in front stumbled a shaven-headed Han man stripped naked to the waist – was he the perpetrator? The Tibetan pedestrians melted before him as though he were a leper. Someone at the back of the crowd threw a rock. It landed threateningly close to the Han man. He appealed noisily to nearby police. These armed men shuffled uneasily and fingered their weapons. They were heavily outnumbered.

As the crowds wheeled into the main square the Han man turned and fled. There on the edge of the Barkhor square, he was bundled into a waiting police van. Official reinforcements turned up in a new fleet of bread cars and the mob quickly disbanded itself, dispersing into the regiments of the pious prostrating themselves before the Johkang. I did not truly understand what the Han man had done to offend these people. But I did know this was the sort of crowd behaviour that scared the authorities. Then they knew what they had always known, that the savages of their borderlands were wild and feral and would answer best to a rod of iron.

Friends with Foreigners

The next day we were back in the Barkhor square. Stark in the middle of it slouched a sullen leather jacket-wearing guy who was probably younger than the late twenty-something he looked. He carried with him a book. It was titled '*How to make friends with foreigners*'. But he did not appear to be having much success. His cheeks were dirty and his mouth mournful, attributes that seemed unlikely to help his quest. But neither was his approach any good, and I watched for a while as he hovered on the outskirts of another group of *laowai* then dove into them like a female duck scaring an intruder away from its young. He tried this unfortunate method a couple of times before finally steering towards us. Amy saw him coming and turned her back. The friend maker seemed to take this quite hard, hanging his head and retreating. I decided to make it easier for him and walked over.

'Having any luck?'

'Luck?' he said, repeating me. 'No luck' he said 'lots of waiting'. He said these words very deliberately, as though he were determined not to spoil the moment by speaking too quickly. Then he pulled a photo from a wrinkled wallet - in it a Tibetan stood at Beijing's Tiananmen Gate.

'My brother' he stated proudly, and then 'China makes him fat!' He sniffed and dropped his voice suddenly self-aware 'Duck, steam buns. Pig...' he said rather randomly 'I want to join him. I want to study there'. The boy's name we discovered, was Tsering, and he was studying English at a school near the Barkhor.

Flush with achievement at this first interaction, Tsering followed Kristel, Jim, and I away from the Han. We followed clockwise the pilgrims, with the strange whir of their prayer wheels spinning in the breeze. Tsering was still with us when we halted at a cafe. It was another place of yoghurt covered stone where a herder in a felt poncho manned the entrance.

Bob Marley and his wailers hollered from a cassette in the

stereo.

'*Freedom!*' cried Bob. The Cannabis stench of burning incense had by now spread over the low roofs to dirty a large slice of sky. Here we overlooked the city centre and the prayer flags which rose from all the dirty whitewash. Below in the Barkhor moved still the people, all swirling colour. A rugged Tibetan woman with a dimpled smile and the pigtails of a girl took our order. While she was doing so an overweight Dutchman accompanied by two similarly large women shouted

'Take this back' and the woman left to sort out the command 'it's not real orange juice...' I heard the Dutchman complain.

'My father is a teacher' said Tsering 'an English teacher. He said go to the Barkhor where the foreigners go. At first all I could say is hello. For seven years I came here to speak with foreign friends. Now I want to say more difficult words' He thumbed through his book but then shrugged as though he had not found what he was looking for. 'I must practice' he said dolefully.

And behind me the Dutchman continued

'...what kind of customer service is this?'

'If I can practice I can get to Beijing'

'This is squash. On your menu it says orange juice. I'm not paying for it'

'But in Beijing maybe I will get fat?' he grimaced.

'Everything is terrible in this land. What is wrong with you?'

Kristel leapt up from the table, and stormed over to the Dutchman. She leant into his face and said

'You want fresh orange juice? Travel to Spain or Florida. They grow oranges there'

'It is not your business'

'It is. You're a representative of our civilisation and you came here for customer service? Perhaps you should have stayed at home'

The Dutchman did not reply, but got up to leave, mumbling under his breath and dragging his suffering women with him. Tsering's mouth flickered. I almost thought he might smile. Instead he leaned in secretively and said

'Come to the hills'

We finished our drinks then jumped on a local bus out through all those gaudy suburbs. Eventually we reached the edge of town, where a crew of itinerant Han were slopping concrete into muddy foundations

'Bringing harmony to the land!' shouted a construction billboard. There did not seem to be a whole lot of harmony here, just the wilderness being tamed like it had already been long ago in the lowlands. Behind the building work we climbed a flinty hillside where strings of prayer flags fluttered in grass.

Tsering sat down.

'The Chinese are making ugliness' he said

'They say they are developing Tibet'

'Tibetans did not ask for many Chinese. More are coming all the time'. The wind whipped straggling prayer flags off the ground. And he fiddled with a blade of grass.

'Sometimes they fish from the holy river' he said as though even the last taboo had been broken. Then a few minutes later Tsering suddenly observed

'Tibetans love the Dalai Lama'.

'But the Dalai Lama has left Tibet' I said.

'He will come back' said Tsering with a confidence so strong it was probably be false. The Chinese were insistent that the Dalai Lama recognise Chinese sovereignty before talks could begin. The Tibetan Government in Exile insisted this would only undermine their negotiating position. The barriers between these parties seemed as insurmountable as the ranges laid before us. The 14th Dalai Lama was in all likelihood going to die abroad. The communists would choose his successor.

'One day I will go over mountains' reckoned Tsering, and he stared at the peaks on the other side of the valley as though he were planning the route. His people were routinely shot for putting these sorts of sentiment into practice.

Kristel had bought some prayer money at the market - paper prayers to the Gods to be burned or thrown to the wind. She shoved wads of it into our hands. Jim stood already at the summit with arms outstretched. Then all of us were at the top, hurling the colourful notes of prayer to the wind where they eddied and scattered across the valley. Tsering's eyes were no longer narrowed, but curiously lit.

Donald and the tour bus were headed to some geothermal springs the next day. It seemed likely there were better things to do than hang around with Chinese men in Speedos, so Kristel and I decided to give it a miss. Instead we agreed to go with Tsering to the Ganden monastery, original home of the Yellow Hat Sect and its founder, the very first Dalai Lama, Tsong Kapa. We began by joining the bus very early next morning. It was packed and restless and outside two Tibetans were arguing. One of them pushed the other. In return the victim plucked a watermelon from a nearby stall and smashed it over his attacker's head. The watermelon had been a lowland one, shipped up from China's Southern tropics. On the bus, these pilgrims hooted with laughter at the sight. As light erupted across the golden roofs of Lhasa the driver jumpstarted the vehicle. We were off, through the outskirts, past the miserable new houses bathing marginally less miserable in the soft dawn, the shops and bordellos were left behind, the valleys narrowed. We passed two young boy soldiers on a bridge who waved.

As the asphalt of Tibet's first city fell away, the bus bounced over rough rutted track. Its movement was rockingly rhythmical and I fell asleep. I awoke to find the bus stumbling around some final primitive hairpins. The monastery occupied a summit. It was a scrabble of whitewash and gold perched above the valley, which lay in a quilt of emerald below. It had been built as a fortress protecting the sect and its leader, the Dalai Lama, in an age of tribal incursions. Last time Mongols had been the invaders. The Tibetans had sent them away as Buddhist converts. The Dalai Lama claimed descent from this heritage, for he was an incarnation of Drogon Chogyal Phagpa, the monk who had single-handedly evangelised to the Great Khan, Kublai.

The pilgrims disgorged from the bus excitedly, racing past straw and animal faeces, and into the darkness of the temple. Here they prayed under the sutras inscribed in Sanskrit, the heavily coloured *Mandalas* symbolising the sum total of existence. They lit incense under swaying fabrics and the gaze of brass demon slayers whose enraged faces belied their underlying compassion - for they were the last defenders of *dharma*, the path of virtue. Around the temple's forlorn little collection of buildings, beggars spun prayer wheels, and monks cleaned the stonework with brooms. In an outhouse we found an artisan painstakingly crafting wooden print blocks for use in painting. He seemed to be pretending not to notice the irritable braying of the animals outside. We climbed the peak behind Ganden, where the dope-incense could be smelled burning off from the monastery behind. The altitude was high and it took all of us some time to catch our breath.

Two athletic young monks were kicking a wall below. They attacked then span off from it in some martial routine. A soldier leaned against his military post and watched these monks playing. He wielded a pot belly - the result perhaps of too many noodle soups from the monastery canteen. Monasteries such as Ganden had been used to warfare. In the old days it had been the monks who kept the peace in these valleys, levying armies and defending the realm. They had rushed from the strong points and wiped their enemies off the mountain. Marauding bandits, Nepalis, Mongolians, Han Chinese, all had been given a taste of this odd Buddhist ferocity. More recently, the feisty monks of this particular mountain had rebelled after the commies had banned display of the image of the Dalai Lama. They had stubbornly dug in and clung on as their forefathers had done for centuries before them. This time though, Ganden had been sacked. Later, Red guards had blown holes in the great monastery and set fire to the remains of the revered Tsong Kapa.

The People's Liberation Army still maintained a small outpost up here to prevent a repeat episode. This whole land was wild: not only the mountains, deserts, or pack animals which were barely domesticated, but also the people, the nomads and traders – and especially the holy men.

In the afternoon Tsering took us to his home. He lived in the heart of the Han mess in one of the sprawling blocks of Maoist communalism. His family home hosted a couch and cupboards, the toilet though was simply a hole in the recently laminated floor.

'My father also works at the factory. He teaches, then he goes to the factory' said Tsering 'But when my sister got a job in the same factory, he did not like it. He said 'Stay at home. Find a husband' But she does not listen. She says having a husband is slavery'. Sister was home early today too. She sat there on the couch, slim, attractive, and scornful. Mother and aunt were also home, both spherical women in heavy cotton dresses who fussed after us with butter tea and *Tsampa*.

Jim had found an image of the Dalai Lama sketched in his guidebook. Once invited, the older women scrambled to gaze upon it. The bronzed sister however only crossed her arms, daring us to accuse her of interest. Finally though the temptation proved too much even for her and she jumped up from the couch to catch a glimpse. She then pulled a metal locket from under her blouse and opened its secret catch. Inside smiled another image of the Dalai Lama. All such images were banned in the new China.

Jim asked to borrow a knife. Mother ran out to the kitchen and sought one for him with which he cut the image from the guidebook.

'Remember us' he said, handing the Dalai Lama to Tsering. All of them giggled, including sister, whose haughty exterior had been broken. This was an admission of complicity - the rules had been broken. And it felt edifying. Almost beaming, Tsering put a finger to his lips. It was a futile gesture because the laughter continued.

'The Dalai Lama is the very best' he said, his eyes starting to water.

We finished the *tsampa*, and downed more of the tea. Then we left. Tsering led us back out to the road. Slowly the smile faded and his whipped expression began to return. He stared sadly at the potholed ground. We said Goodbye.

No Problems

The next day, we left Lhasa. We left Amy. She had taken very badly to the altitude and so had booked herself onto the next flight back to Sichuan. The remaining *laowai* and Han crammed into our little bread van, and we chugged out towards Tibet's second city, Shigatse. It was dark when we set out and the streets were quiet. It was officially 10am. Because across the vastness of China there was only one time zone. There was unity and stability to preserve and so the authorities were having a go at controlling time itself, run to suit Beijing's sunlight hours far to the country's east.

I asked Mr. Chang about the trip to the hot springs that the Han and Amy had taken yesterday.

'Interesting' he said 'very interesting' and he pulled out his digital camera and showed me his snaps. He had indeed been wearing speedos - rather heroically I thought for a man of his age. So had little Jia. Yu, however, had not. He had sat it out in a heavy overcoat while the others splashed around in a gigantic metal tub. Mr. Chang seemed to have gotten quite enthusiastic about the female company, and a high proportion of his photos featured either Amy or Ms Hong in their one piece swimsuits. Xing was nowhere to be seen. I imagined he had probably been sulking somewhere outside wondering what the hell was up with the yaks.

We had a new driver. His name was Mr. Hu. Like Donald he wore sunglasses, but unlike our guide, he was tall and ungainly and walked like an amateur on stilts. Still, he was all the more likeable for being an optimist. Mudslides had written out a more direct route to Shigatse.

'We'll be in Shigatse by the afternoon' said Mr. Hu 'It will be no problem'. After a couple of hours we passed the very thermal springs the others had visited the previous day. I was glad we had not come up here. The bathhouse looked like a misshapen pressure cooker, a relic of Soviet-type planning. And in this pristine valley of grass and wildflower, it appeared a particularly incongruous piece of litter.

It was soon lunchtime: it would surely have been illegal to miss it. So we parked up and ate boiled eggs and salted vegetable out on the grass. There were colourful nomads here grazing a few goats. They approached, gesturing aggressively for cash. Ms Hong moved her boy towards the *laowai*, because we were now certainly the lesser of two evils. Mr. Chang threw money at them and started snapping. And the nomads ceased begging and posed with their horses, with their vibrant cloaks, lank hair and dirty faces. A gang of children arrived having spotted the party up the valley, and they made for Hong Jia with their hands outstretched. But he darted back onto the bus and hid. The life of these people seemed a strange existence, with the wandering of the land, only the occasional stop to cadge from the suckers on buses who almost certainly couldn't ride a horse or raise a tent. But they also seemed to be masters of frugality and making the most of it. For as Donald hustled us onto the bus and Mr. Hu primed the engines, I saw that our nomads were already raking through the card boxes and plastic bags and other leftovers we had not picked up.

The track soon thinned, and then gave out. Now it was just the vehicle against the grassland, the wide open spaces. But Mr. Hu increased his speed. Yu started to look even whiter than he usually did. And as the bus cranked up the next pass, he threw up. Down valley, across valley, up valley - and again down, across, up, we travelled, with Yu retching all the way. On the last of three passes we reached the height of 5400 metres where ancient prayer flags blazed against the snow. And Mr. Hu stopped the engine so we could all enjoy the view, the horizon obscured by the young ranks of mountain.

But Ms Hong complained.

'My head hurts' she said.

'Continue' ordered Mr. Chang 'It is too high for us'. Yu lay spread-eagled across the backseat like a limp eel, taking shallow breaths from the oxygen bag. That Xing was affected too I only guessed because he had not gotten off the bus for a cigarette.

Back down in the valleys a large patch of water was coming our way. Mr. Hu grinned, gunned the engines, and aimed for it. The bus hit the water and slid. But this was a muddy swamp, and after a few metres, we were stuck. Mr. Hu revved the engines, spraying slurry up the windows. Yu in the back flapped a hand and groaned weakly. Mr. Hu tried his futile trick a little longer. The vehicle only sank deeper. Mr. Hu jumped out to inspect the back wheels, which had almost disappeared. He scratched his head as though this had all been most unexpected. Donald, Jim and I got out to join him, and Xing followed to light a cigarette.

'*Mei wenti*' (no problem) proclaimed Mr. Hu, and he hauled a number of spades from the boot. He threw them out, and together, we had a go at digging out the bus. This team effort seemed to work, and soon afterwards we were racing back up the mountainside with Mr. Hu hunched right over the wheel, like a fanatical bird watcher. Later on the endless hairpins I noticed that the bus wheels were beginning to float out over the track edge, especially on corners. Mr. Hu now began overtaking the slower traffic, the construction trucks, army vehicles, even land cruisers brimming with rich tourists, while huge boulders stared up from the valley floor like pieces from a model railway. Mr. Hu must have been blessed by the Gods. It seemed prudent at least, to assume that this was the case.

Then a pillow sized rock spoiled all the fun and we bounced into the mountain. Apart from the casualty holed up at the back, we all clambered out to survey the damage. It seemed that an axel had been damaged and a wheel had bent.

'*Mei wenti*' said Mr. Hu cheerfully. 'Fix in Shigatse'. Such puny irritations were not going to slow us down, and we raged up the next hairpins of the pass, where large chains of local Tibetans were also shovelling mud from the tracks. The task was monstrous. With every rain, these routes became smothered in debris, and hundreds of miles of tracks needed clearance using only the raw effort of man. This effort was a gift from the Chinese, an export of their greatest strength: their capacity for mobilising the masses. Because Tibet had become another front for the state in its attempt to tame nature: the Chinese would conquer the mountains just as they had long ago the lowland floodplains.

Down in the next valley - a rubble wilderness - a grating began to emanate from the rear of the bus. We stopped again. Now the exhaust pipe had snapped off and was dragging along behind the gravel. *Mei wenti.* Of course, we could get it fixed in Shigatse. In any case Mr. Hu had brought along a spare clothes hanger. It turned out to be especially for occasions like these, for with this item Mr. Hu tied the exhaust back on. It was with some relief that our decrepit junk box later rolled into Shigatse.

Dusk had fallen. Ragged children lined the streets. They waved to the arriving tourists and chased the bus through the dusty streets, past the white daubed buildings with their timber frames, the more recent carbuncles, a couple of donkeys. The place looked less Han-influenced. It was harder to reach after all - and further from Beijing: there was no rail connection planned for this town.

It began to rain. While Donald went to sort out a hotel, Mr. Hu deposited us at the Tashilumpo temple. The place was another spectacular agglomeration of gold topped stone hiding below the mountains, a maze of shrines and crimson outhouses. Red robed children ran between the buildings clutching paper sheets and pencil boxes. Tashilumpo was a renowned school for young monks - not only in spiritual matters, but in temporal ones too. The children were taught how to parry and thrust with words, how to debate and reason. Two centuries back however, the monastery had been sacked by Nepalese Gurkhas and the proud Tibetans had been forced to appeal to the Qing for help. The Chinese had been gracious enough to help kick out the invaders. Afterwards they had set up a military garrison, and invited themselves to stay. Their near continuous involvement up here since that time was a central plank in the communist claim to legitimate rule.

But first and foremost, Tashilumpo was home to the Panchen Lama, second in the Tibetan pantheon. The Dalai Lama's chosen Panchen Lama however, was not at home. His predecessor had died quite mysteriously. The then Governor, Hu Jintao, was rumoured to have been involved. The present Panchen lama, the 11th reincarnation of lama, the *Amitabha*, the Buddha of infinite light, had been 'discovered' by touring holy men back in 1995. But then the boy had vanished just a few days after his inauguration - along with his entire family. The communists had since chosen their own Panchen Lama. This one was faithfully studying in Beijing, that renowned seat of Tibetan Buddhist spirituality.

'I don't want to see more temples' said Ms Hong. Mr. Chang pointedly shut his camera case. There was no Yu. He had been whisked off by Donald direct to the safety of the hotel. Kristel and I entered the shrines. A few boyish monks hovered - in Tibet parents often donated a child to the care of the monasteries where they would be clothed, fed and schooled. A lone monk sculpted yak butter under a brass effigy of Tsong Kapa, the original Dalai Lama. There were no beggars, and no prayer wheels.

Outside we rejoined the others. The rain still fell, running in rivulets through the alleyways of the temple grounds.

'I'm hungry!' whined little Hong, and his mother frowned and stared at the rapidly forming puddles. In the dark Mr. Hu announced his return with a flash of his headlights. It turned out he had gone to get the axel and the exhaust fixed.

The hotel was a pretty typical place. The hostesses even wore the kind of red *cheongsams* that gave them all the appearance of provincial hookers. Indeed it later turned out that this was exactly what they were. Inside in a private dining room, the local police threw a banquet for local officers from the People's Liberation Army - uproarious toasts were going on in there. The others split up to sulk in their separate rooms. Mr. Hu meanwhile found himself a few bottles of beer and squatted down in the entrance lobby. Kristel and I headed out to dine on one of Shigatse's back streets.

When we returned later Mr. Hu was still in the lobby. His bottles were empty and he had removed himself to the reception desk, where he was badgering a clerk about something. As we passed, he turned round.

'Seen Mr. Xing?' he asked
'Not seen' I said.
'No one has seen Mr. Xing' he said.

'I saw him at the temple' I said. That was the last we had seen of him, the floodlit silhouette of a smoker sheltering from rain under the temple eaves. Perhaps the monks had decided to take him hostage. Mr. Hu shrugged.

'*Mei Wenti*' he slurred. And then: 'I fixed the bus'.

Fortunately, we had other plans.

Raping the Sacred Mountain

Next morning we were up and out before our colleagues woke. They would be heading back to Lhasa today with Donald and Mr. Hu and his unique brand of recklessness.

We had been promised a land cruiser. But it turned out there was not one available. Instead we had been allocated a bread van - one of the modest delivery vehicles of Chinese city life. The new driver looked like a retired boxer. His name was Mr. Cha.

Kristel and I climbed in.

'Speak *putonghua*?' I asked

'I do not speak English' he said

'But I speak a little *putong...*' I protested

Mr. Cha interrupted.

'I do not speak English' he said.

Mr. Cha was not paid to communicate with foreigners. That job was reserved for our new guide, a merry looking Tibetan lad who looked as though he was playing truant from middle school - definitely he looked of the line of Tibetans who held that their race had been birthed from a union of rock ogress and monkey. Mr. Cha tutted and started the engine, and we crawled back out onto the streets. The kid called himself Duke. He grinned when Mr. Cha barked orders at him, and nodded facetiously in response to the brute's questions, which came thick and fast amongst relentless acceleration and smoking.

Outside Shigatse we ran on a stretch of metalled road. There were villages along the route, linked by sparkling electricity pylons and phones lines - the promised development of Tibet. But a few miles out the asphalt abruptly turned to rutted track, and then a few miles after that, even the track was gone. Rain had been here in the night and this valley was now another swamp. But Mr. Cha it seemed, was the practical sort. He swerved the vehicle expertly through freshly formed lakes and pools of mud, and stopped for nothing. Duke sat stapled into his seat, grinning that grimace.

By lunchtime we had left the greenery and swamp of the valley. The grass had given up and we were in the desert, a moonscape of mountains and rubble. This place had not seen rain for some time. The hamlets here, which were few and far between, looked to be sickly shelters of stone and daub. They were mounted by struggling prayer flags, and often surrounded by patches of barley.

Between these sparse habitations rolled the army trucks of the liberators. The soldiers sitting in their backs looked like bored youths. But I noticed these ones had evolved. It seemed the longer the Han stayed in this land, the more they resembled their hosts: their faces took on a deeper tan; their skin weathered; their eyes narrowed from long periods of squinting in the sun and the wind.

In the next valley a band of nomads chased yaks up the mountainside. And on the pass above it we met once more the great Tibetan road gangs who were digging out the roadsides and repairing landslide damage, picking their fight with a threadbare landscape. At 6200m, we were soon travelling over the tallest pass in the world. Out there was Everest, one amongst many giants in the Himalayan front range. From here, the track wound back down the unfathomable depths, through arches in the mountainside, past the gnarly geological formations which occasionally jutted into the road. No-one uttered a word.

The plateau was endless. It made up most of the autonomous region, a vastness twice the size of France. The Tibetan world included vast tracts of Qinghai and Sichuan provinces, corners of Yunnan, Xinjiang, and Gansu. At the height of its glory it had encompassed much of lowland China, Central Asia, even Burma...since then it had been boxed back into its highland core by nomadic tribes, internal strife, the Chinese and their administrative divisions. We passed all afternoon sun-drenched valleys, passes of rubble, and beds of cracked mud. I dreamed of it too, mud and stone intermingled, and when I awoke I could not remember which features had been real and which had not been. I also awoke to a dispute. Kristel informed me that Duke and Mr. Cha were arguing about correct documentation. It was an argument that was soon over, for Duke had been forced to give in. He sank back into his chair wearing the smile of defeat.

A fleck in the distance turned out to be a checkpoint. Since it was manned by Han soldiers, Mr. Cha took care of the formalities. Amongst his countrymen he backslapped and teased. He swapped some immensely funny anecdote with one of the guards, then climbed back in, stuck on the grumpy face he seemed to reserve for barbarians, and started the vehicle once more.

Rubble, hillside, valley; more rubble and hills, another valley…the scenery had been looped. And just to confirm this, another post now loomed in the distance. Duke leant over and murmured something to Mr. Cha. Whatever it was, it caused Mr. Cha to chop the air with his hands. They bickered strongly again, and once more Duke ended up having to resign himself to loss. We slowed as the checkpoint arrived, this time manned by the police, who hid inside a sturdy administration house made of stone. Yet instead of passing under the checkpoint here, Mr. Cha threw his weight on the accelerator, leaned right over the steering wheel, and swerved off on a track skirting around this block. It seemed Mr. Cha and the boy were intent on avoiding the payment of a park entrance fee.

We made off at speed, spinning on the scree. Yet several hundred metres down the line, just when we seemed to have made it home and dry, a gigantic ditch appeared between us and the main route, which we were attempting to rejoin. Mr. Cha slammed on the brakes and we came to a halt right at its edge. We all climbed out and considered fishing around for rocks with which we could dam up this fissure. But the ditch was as deep as it was wide, and it stretched between the mountain on one side and between us and the main track all the way back to the checkpoint on the other - surely by deliberate design.

Behind, lights were already flashing down the track. A dirty little police motorcycle was coming. It seemed so incongruous to find such a thing out here - this symbol of urban control whining around in the wilderness. The motorcycle arrived carrying a bloated copper. He was wearing shades.

'Where are you going?' he asked. None of us replied. And since none of us replied, there was going to be some explaining to do back at the guardpost. After all, there was not a whole lot to do out here apart from monitor traffic and I imagined catching out such miscreants as ourselves might be the week's highlight for a policeman. In any case Kristel and I and Duke and Mr. Cha all clambered back on board. Mr. Cha crunched into reverse and we backed up the half-mile to the checkpoint where Mr. Cha parked up. Fat cop removed his glasses and puffed out his cheeks, which glowed under all of this effort. He entered the building, followed meekly by Duke and Mr. Cha. Kristel and I sat in the van watching dust attack the windows. The driver and the guide were inside the building for half an hour. Then they emerged: Mr. Cha first, Duke tiptoeing behind. With disgust Mr. Cha lit up a Red Pagoda Hill cigarette. Duke was still smiling. The fat cop followed and he too was smiling. For in his podgy hands, he carried a few notes - several hundred *yuan*.

'*Guiding shi guiding*' called the copper cheerily. *Rules are rules.* He was obviously not the type to count bribery as rule breaking.

The rubble beds continued. Then after an hour or two we reached the end of the line. Our lodgings were here in a valley which formed a monumental wind tunnel. It was again rubble strewn, and populated by just couple of yaks, an incomprehensibly lone beggar, a few scruffs of lichen. There was also here a whole century's worth of waste, clods of human and yak shit, desiccated and untouched in this place where even bacteria survived with difficulty. To the side squatted Rongphu monastery. It was another whitewash affair dominated by the stupa sitting in its forecourt. Rongphu pressed itself against the mountainside, hiding from the gale. By adding relative scale, this positioning though emphasised the hugeness of the valley and its walls.

At the valley's end towered Everest, flickering in and out of cloud wreaths. Great Earth Goddess - *Chomoloungma* - was Everest's Tibetan name. And following the lead of this happy minority, the Chinese had also adopted it. The British had known the giant as 'Peak B', then 'Peak XV'. It had finally been labelled Everest in 1865, by British India's Surveyor General. This did not please the authorities of the new China whose media had just recently written that the British were '*raping the sacred mountain of Tibetans by giving it a false name*'. In his office on the campus of the University of Educated People, Lou Da had shown me this headline and crowed

'The British continue to oppress the Chinese nation!' The headline had seemed a simple testament of the Chinese Communist Party's utterly underrated sense of humour. The original survey team had attempted to establish local names but ran into difficulties. Both Tibet and Nepal had lain closed to foreigners. Since the mountain straddled the Nepali border too (*Sagarmartha* they called it) surely neither the Tibetans nor the Chinese had any monopoly on names.

Kristel went to bed. Meanwhile I discovered a dingy hall of softwood walls. In it roared a hearth beside which smiling Tibetan girls in shell suits doled out roundels of Tibetan bread fresh from the kitchen. Here the Chinese and the Tibetans sat in separate groups, smoking and goofing and bolting bread. Mr. Cha and Duke had already found the place, and although they were not seated together, they were both drinking Chang, an alcoholic barley water. Mr. Cha played cards. Duke sat on the edge of a group of laughing Tibetans, grinning, and pretending not to notice the eye daggers Mr. Cha liberally threw his way.

I begged successfully for a flat bread seeing as Duke did not seem inclined to sort anyone else any dinner. Then I retired too. Several times during the night I awoke gasping. The blankets were as heavy as the air seemed light.

Duke was supposed to be hauling us out of bed and dragging us off to base camp the next morning. The sun had come out to bless the valley and it looked altogether less menacing than it had done before. Everest had mainly freed herself from the cloud: only the odd wisp remained hanging about her midriff. Mr. Cha was outside stroking his vehicle as though it were part of the family. But Duke was nowhere to be seen.

'Where is the boy?' I asked.

'Not seen' he said and he climbed underneath the van with an oil can. I wondered whether Mr. Cha had finally given in to his desires and done in the guide. We tried walking up the valley ourselves, but did not get far in the altitude. Plodding geriatrically uphill suddenly seemed to invite heart attack. So we gave up. At our closest point, Everest was still far away, the clouds still sweeping her bows. She was a lighthouse, an apparition, an iceberg.

This was certainly the end of the line. The end of the earth. Mischievous Monkey from the Chinese classic 'Journey to the West' had bet the magical powers of heaven that he could travel to such an end of the earth. He had travelled forever across the continents and eventually arrived at a mountain of five peaks. There he relieved himself at the base of the middle peak and left in triumph certain he could prove his win to heaven. But back in the court of the Jade Emperor, Lord Buddha had opened his hand. His middle finger stank of urine and Monkey suddenly realised that in his entire journey he had never even managed to leave the Lord Buddha's palm.

Neither would the world's tallest mountain escape the palm of the Han. An asphalt road was in planning, better to bus up the domestic hordes. There would be hawker stands selling ice cream and '*I climbed the Great Earth Goddess*' t-shirts. There would be tour caps and megaphones, and hotels and brothels. There would be karaoke and dumplings, and coaches and coach parks. The Chinese would probably lay flagstones all the way to Everest's summit and cover the crevasses in ropeways.

Poor Boy

Duke miraculously appeared back at base.

'Where have you been?' I asked. He shrugged.

'In the kitchen' he said 'with my friends'. Perhaps he had sold us out to chat up the bread baking girls. But we could not delay any longer if we were to make it to Gyantse today and then get back to Lhasa in time for tomorrow's plane. So we set off back up and down the freezing passes and more hours passed in the wilds. Eventually we hit a road junction, the first for many miles. The route to Yondrok lake was closed, the way barred by PLA trucks. We had been due to travel this way but heavy rains had washed the tracks right off the mountainside. We could not pass and would not see its milky waters, nor the pinch point at which the government planned to build a giant hydro-electric plant that environmentalists claimed would turn the lake into a cesspit. Instead we started out the way we came, trundling back through the vertiginous deserts and over the winding passes with the brutish driver and the imbecile of a boy. By sundown we once more arrived in the dusty streets of Shigatse, the frontier town, a shelter from wilderness.

We were off again the following morning, winding once more amongst the grasslands. Half way between Shigatse and Lhasa, Duke turned to Mr. Cha.

'Stop' he said

'Why?' asked Mr. Cha, stabbing a lit cigarette in the boy's direction

'This is my home' and he nodded out the window to the hamlet that was passing.

Mr. Cha guffawed

'Poor boy!' he shouted. But still he consented and we soon rolled off the track to a tumbledown cottage where the barley plots vied for attention with a few chickens and a stunted goat. There Mr. Cha pulled up haphazardly. Duke flung open the car door, ran to the front door, and then paused for just a second to prepare a cocky swagger. He pushed open the door, and called an assembly. His mother, a gaunt woman, brought round butter tea and bowls of Tsampa. Three bedraggled boys and a couple of girls ran leaping into a living room where we sat on wooden benches laid above packed earth.

Mr. Cha stood at the door looking gloomy while Duke threw notes to the bouncing kids and passed more to his grateful mother. He was clearly the man of this house.

I felt only a little mean, sitting there in their home, drinking their tea and eating their porridge, and wondering if the money that should have bought us lunch over the past three days had gone first to the policeman, and was now also disappearing here in the bills being passed to this woman and her ragged family.

Back in the Bread van, Mr. Cha put on his best face of thunder. Duke attempted to engage him. But he found himself fobbed off with an aggressive shrug, which made Duke press himself back into his seat and switch on the grin. On we paced, wheeling across the grass and avoiding the odd pond. The eeriness of the valleys was compounded by the conversations remaining unspoken within the vehicle. Finally the grasslands began again sprouting the evidence of civilisation, an electricity pylon here, a mobile phone mast there. At the sight of all this modern magic Mr. Cha was prompted to make a phone call. It was a tense one that involved a whole lot of staring in Duke's general direction. The boy meanwhile sank ever further in his seat. I couldn't see, but I felt sure he would still be smiling.

Homes and shops too emerged from this ground, and soon we were again within the Lhasa valley, rocking back through the suburbs where the asphalt and neon heralded relief. For here in the Han city nature no longer dominated fate. The modern world was back, breaking through the wilderness and promising the good fight. And when we pulled up at our hotel where Donald waited outside looking naked without his sunglasses, it felt for some reason like arriving home.

'So you ate flatbreads' said Donald, one brow raised 'Tibetan food? You should not have to eat Tibetan food' he threw a brutal look at Duke, whose grin had become a desperate parody of itself.

In the bus on the way to the airport the next morning things seemed to have returned to normal. Donald's shades were back on. Mr. Hu was driving once more, swerving and chuffing merrily with one hand on the steering wheel.

I looked at Donald, who bared his teeth.

'What happened to Mr. Cha?' I asked.

'The Chinese?' he nodded sharply 'Fine'

'And the Tibetan?'

'Lost his job' he said, and sticking a finger in his ear 'He was not used to carrying money'.

Safety in Numbers

We unloaded at the airport and boarded the plane that humped us over the peaks and dropped us back under the stuffy ceiling of Sichuan amongst the masses once more. Down there humans clogged the streets. They were storming the temples of Chengdu, along with its tea houses and department stores, and its station too.

We boarded there a train bound for Hangzhou for two more days of crowded carriage, games of cards, snacks, and frantic lowlander conversation. The train jogged back south across the plains of four rivers and squeezed out through its mountain walls. Somewhere at a tiny halt amongst the cornfields and steaming hills of Guizhou province, a hugely obese man clambered on and climbed into the sleeping bay above me - it was rare to find someone so large in the Middle Kingdom and I could not take my eyes off him whenever he ventured down. I watched him even when I could not see him, for the shape of the bed above me shifted in tune with his fidgeting. At night thoughts of being crushed in my sleep kept me awake. So I decided to cancel the early morning wake-up call scheduled for the next day, by turning off the main speaker switch.

When Kristel and I rose next morning at 9am instead of 6am, our comrades were not amused. They had not received the radio wake up. With all the pouts and hunched shoulders, these men and women already displayed the unmistakable symptoms of noise withdrawal. And to judge from the accusatory stares, a few of them already had their suspicions about who might be responsible. It was one of those foreigners, either the yawning girl or the boy. Neither were capable of appreciating the harmony of the Old Hundred Names awakening in the morning; the people rising together as one.

8. Glitter

There had been no change in Hangzhou. The city remained occupied by construction cranes and swarming labourers, sledgehammers, cement mixers, steel girders. The itinerants had gone nowhere, still building and begging and scouring the bins for bottles. The hawkers were hanging around and so were the touts and the slap-happy taxi-drivers. The multitudes of cap donned tourists still huffed from one attraction to the next. Chinese progress was a comforting constant. So too was the lake, which rippled gently, mocking all the strenuous energy underway on its edges.

The University of Educated People though, had taken on a monastic air. Lampshade wearers gently rolled out turf and watered the lawns. Teams of acrobats lounged in the shade of the 13 storey library they had almost finished building. Beside the security kiosk where a guard had fallen asleep with a newspaper over his face, Mr. Ji sat furiously mopping his brow.

'Been looking for you' he said

'For us? You must have been busy'

'Busy. Yes. Everybody is busy except the students' he said 'I am busy. But it is said he who toils with pain will eat with pleasure'

'I see'

'It's an old saying. The students don't care for such things. It is old thinking. They want money without toil. How can they know the best in life when they do not work hard?' he ran a hand through his greasy hair and wiped it on the pavement.

'Yesterday I called my student. He is watching television all summer. I said why don't you help your father. He told me his parents are very proud of him, he does not need to help. They threw a banquet and invited all the neighbours. He must rest, ready to study hard next term they said.' He pursed his lips and whistled 'I told him he doesn't study hard enough. I told him when I was a boy I helped dig up vegetables. I studied English after I dug up vegetables. I asked him how can he make his parents proud watching television? He says they don't care. He is their only son' Mr. Ji stared at the patch of pavement which he had just stained. It sounded like his pretty boy was having a rebellion of sorts. Mr. Ji tilted his head and carefully enunciated his words.

'I want him to learn your Queen's English' he said 'can I practise first with you?' He did not wait for an answer, but returned to form

'Say something. Anything' he said

'We have just returned from holiday' I protested

'Excellent!' he exclaimed, clapping his hands together 'Please, again'

But instead we walked to our flat and left Mr. Ji behind.

Lou Da, we caught on the stairs. He claimed to have been washing. Indeed the powder was in his right hand.

'Yes you have' I agreed.

'Mei-xie and me have moved into Dave's room for summer' he added. For British Dave had gone home.

'He said he was going to come back and open a tea house' said Da.

But British Dave had previously said something similar to me. He had nodded so heartily I suspected the audience he was most trying to convince was himself.

'Now he is getting an education. Masters at Oxford? His parents must be so proud. More studying, more success. Dave will make much money and meet many beautiful women if he returns.' This was how it used to work in China. It did not bring British Dave back. Perhaps it would work better for Professor Darling, who with his five degrees, had a continual collection of different female student shoes piled on his doorstep just as Emma had returned to the States to sit out the summer.

Chang Er came by the next day to tell us that the rabbit had died. The students had already buried her in a flowerbed behind the administrative block: two weeks ago apparently, while we were in Lhasa.

Lou Da phoned.

'I told you it would die' he claimed. It had only been a rabbit. More often they were eaten than loved… But this particular rabbit had greeted us when we returned from classes and spread the flat with its quirky rodent personality. Its death filled us with melancholy.

'Don't be sad' Da said 'China is always so full of sadness. If we reflect, the tragedy is sometimes too great. We Chinese cannot bear it' He clicked his teeth 'In history the Chinese people always just suffer loss. Chinese cannot feel sad for animals when life is so cruel to humans'.

Thieves and Brigands

As the central Government had weakened during the drawn out death of the Qing dynasty, China had erupted. The Yellow river flooded even more dramatically than usual - the peasants rose. These rebels called themselves the Nian, the '*hands take incense sticks to the Sky Lord*' followers, and plundered the east. In the west and southwest the Muslims rose too. But the movement which had inspired them all lay at the heart of Han China: the Heavenly Taiping, responsible for the greatest rebellion in recorded history.

I had read of it first in the flashbacks of Amy Tan's novel, '*One Hundred Secret Senses*'. The tale had been based at the end of the conflagration at a time when the rebel leader had died scouring the streets of Nanjing for food. He had been searching for the 'manna' God had promised to send him from heaven - but there had been nothing for him but poisonous weeds. This leader was Hong Xiuquan, a man who had earlier come to believe himself the younger brother of Christ and formed the sect of Heavenly God Worshippers - the *Taiping*. Nurtured deep in the hills, these God Worshippers had roused the footloose and the discontented, and bled China white.

I got my hands on historical accounts and autobiographies. The more I read about the rise and fall of the Taiping Heavenly Kingdom, the more the episode appeared one of history's most pivotal - and bizarre. The movement had begun as a small sect in the area of Thistle Mountain, deep in China's far south, where their theology began to coalesce around the ten commandments and a belief in one God. Tension between the God Worshippers and the Qing state soon spilled into outright hostility, and a deputy magistrate who had been sent to put the group down had been killed. Then as so often happened in times of dynastic weakness, what had been a localised revolt, snowballed. The years preceding the rebellion had been cursed by famine, drought, and displacement of Hong's people, the minority ethnic Hakka. These events made for an attractive recruiting sergeant and the Taiping's ranks swelled with uprooted Hakka, angry peasants, and a large number of laid off miners. The most devastating civil war in recorded history had begun.

Many of China's most splendid citadels - including Hangzhou - had been thoroughly razed. Such a serious conflict had been spurred by some of history's weirdest theology: all three of the highest ranking

Taiping leaders had spoken at some point for one or other of the Christian trinity. Hong had had his visions and decided upon theological matters; through the third in command, the 'West king', the Taiping had received visitations from Jesus; through the second in command, the 'South king', spoke the voice of God himself. In social matters, these rebels of the Heavenly Kingdom had implemented policies radical before the term had been coined. By 1850, foot binding and private property had been abolished in Taiping controlled areas, the sexes had been declared equal. Mao and the communist leadership had later declared the Taiping proto-communists, the Taiping take on Christianity may have been some distance from communist atheism - yet they were people of faith too. At its height, the Heavenly Kingdom had cobbled together much of Southern China. But between the rebellion's beginnings in Thistle Mountain and its end in the bloody recapture of Nanjing died an estimated thirty million - more than in any conflict until World War II.

We had planned for some time a trip through the Heavenly Kingdom. Now we brought it forward. Without the rabbit the flat had become more empty than ever - and still it seemed claustrophobic. So we caught another train working the deep arteries of China, a beast that spluttered and grumbled right into its dirty heart. And because this was a branch line the train that ran on it was an older model, one defined by wicker bed matting and sunflower seed husks cementing gaps in the plastic floor. Out came the cards, the beers, more seeds, the creeping smell of fresh sweat. A gambler crowed to his colleague: 'you're an old man, a fool!' and aging fans swatted the heat uselessly.

The rail journey was anaesthetising though with the heat and the rocking of the train; the activity of roadside China compacted and tinned. I never felt more content than on a long distance journey, when the monotony and routine of life is ditched, and sloth excused. The other end is still unknown and lies in possibilities that cease to exist even on arrival. This was especially true in China where arrival required effort and concentration and the confrontation once more of the commie blocks and grey skies, the lurid frontages of shops designed by Chinese Warhols.

From Zhejiang to Jiangxi we travelled. By the following morning we were huffing back through the wilder province of Hunan, where the food was famously hot and the attitude hotter. Outside flew the stereotypes of the south, the sweltering dwellings of whitewash and tile, hills of bush hugged limestone, and everywhere waterlogged paddies worked by dark peasants. They were bent double over their crops, parrying the sun with lamp shade hats. These field toilers had never been renowned for welcome. Jesuits who came here in the seventeenth century were slaughtered for sport. They had dressed in Chinese robes and had queued their hair in an attempt to fit in and sell the good book. Still they found their heads lopped off and mounted on stakes. Mao too had been raised in this province of *laowai* haters. In the '20s he had even joined in with the Hunanese suspicion of other Chinese with their call for an independent Hunan - *'Hunan for the Hunanese!'* It was the Chairman from Hunan who had drawn down the post-liberation bamboo curtain and kicked out the foreigners.

One evening over hot-pot, Chang Wen had fused his brow and said

'Be careful. The people of Zhang Zha Jie are thieves and brigands'. Zhang Zha Jie was the end of the line. It was not even in Anhui. It was lost there amongst rock pillars and fern carpets - in hills not long ago outside the writ of government. The town fell between the borders of provincial administrations and far from the central authorities. It had always been haunted by bandits and rebels, and when rebels found the reins of power, Zhang Zha Jie would simply shelter the next generation of rebels. The Taiping rebels had never controlled this place. Back when they were the rebels, the Communists had had a go at running the area. But the nationalists had smoked them out, and they had been forced to join the migration 12,000 kilometres west then north remembered as the Long March.

Now the province was open - and under some sort of control. We were arriving with a host of foreigners. These ones were domestic ones, from Shanghai and Zhejiang, from Guangdong and the Pearl Delta, from Jiangxi and Guangxi and Shaanxi. There were Northern foreigners down for the southern summer, and Western foreigners come out of the desert to walk the jungle. But out in the wilds of the city the other foreigners provided no shield. Kristel and I were soon accosted by an uneasy gang, the taxi drivers of this town. They were carnivores who circled the tourists, rubbing their fingers and cooing, as though this might hypnotise us into accepting one of their inflated offers. It turned out there were enough tourists for everyone however, and only one hardy tout stuck by us on our trek down the streets of smoked glass, past all the rubbish heaps. He was a moustachioed little hunchback.

'How are you getting out to the park?' he nagged 'getting out to the park by taxi?' and then 'in my taxi I can get you to the park'. It was a clever ruse, this continual changing of the same sentence. And in the end I turned to him.

'We are going by bus. Please leave us alone'

'Exactly. Going by bus. But the bus station is not so close. I'll drive you there for ten'. In Hunan's heat we gave in to persistence.

Off we chugged in a fit of wrecked exhaust, Kristel and I and the moustachioed hunchback. Through the crumbling concrete and new plastic of the town we raced, out to the fields, past the peasants and rice and the odd water buffalo, all immune to this blazing sun. Before long the taximeter displayed 140 RMB, and the first of the rock columns already leered from the horizon.

'You said it would be ten' I protested.

The little moustachioed man shrugged. 'I was going to drive you to the bus station for ten' he said 'but there was no bus'.

'How do you know there was no bus?'

'Buses don't go to Zhang Jia Jie' he said.

'If buses don't go to Zhang Zha Jie, why did you say you would take us to the bus station?'

He fiddled with his struggling fuzz and said with impeccably good logic

'Because you wanted to go to the bus station'

'But now we are not going to the bus station. We are going to Zhang Jia Jie'

'Yes. Because there is no bus'

'Then we are leaving' said Kristel 'no money for you'

Moustachio shrugged and stopped. The magic words had been uttered. *No money*. I hauled out our luggage, and Kristel and I set off in the direction of the rock. He crawled after us in the vehicle.

'No wait!' he shouted 'It's dangerous out there. It is hot. Too hot. And there are lots of thieves'. It did not seem to have occurred to him that it was the taxi drivers we feared. Perhaps he worried that should something happen to the foreign clowns, it would be he who was held accountable. For a halving of the displayed fare we agreed to continue.

We got back in and on we roared, past the first of the limestone pinnacles, winding through a valley of overhangs where hunks of rock had been sliced from the cliffs.

The driver pulled off into a car park.

'Here is the park' he said 'be careful of thieves' and raised his eyebrows paternalistically. We did have an inkling that this was not in fact the park, but it was exhausting fighting this indefatigable man and we wanted shot of him. Kristel paid. Moustachio span his banger in the gravel and tanked off. We found ourselves outside a decrepit concrete bunkhouse once painted white, one which proclaimed itself a hotel. We took a room with rotten headboards and the belligerent fatty who called himself the manager said

'You did not pay enough!' and refused to switch on the air conditioner. The heat and damp were committing battery, and we were hungry. It is a rule of nature that the poorest negotiations always occur at a travellers lowest ebb.

The real entrance to the park was a few kilometres down the road. It was an *'enlarged potted landscape and also a miniature fairyland'* according to local pamphlets. Government literature also promised rare animals. There would be giant salamander, Sumen antelope, South China tiger, leopard, macaque, even unicorn...

The following day we joined the rabble - another medley of hawkers and tourists - paid an entrance fee, and obligatory insurance. It turned out the insurance was to protect the park - from us, in case we decided to sue it. With our fingerprints we activated the electronic entrance gates, and then we were in amongst the hordes of amateur geologists examining the rock faces. They ran their hands over the bases of limestone towers and plagued the fern-lined paths with their sweaty exhaustion. We all slowly shunted past the sign: *'lets enjoy the green trees and flowers'*. For some reason the place was particularly full of Koreans, with their cameras and chinos and caps they were the ubiquitous East Asian travellers.

A pretty button-nosed hawker girl sidled up beside me.

'50 yuan for guide' she said

'No thanks'

'Over here you can see the top of Tanzi mountain' she said, hopping to keep up.

'I can't pay you' I said

'Over there is the river' she said, and waved off-handedly.

'We don't want a guide. No need' said Kristel.

Smiling as though she could read our thoughts and only needed to cut past this polite charade of protest, the girl continued. She waggled at clefts in the cliffs and called out incomprehensible names for bits of rock. For an hour she tagged behind, mumbling brightly until we tried to escape, running around corners and hiding behind trees. She was utterly unflappable, and kept up.

Down by the river where yew trees drooped towards the fast flowing waters she overtook us and I walked into her outstretched arm. She screwed up her face and said 'Now you pay me'

'I can't pay you' I said 'We said no need for a guide'

'50 yuan'

'We can give you 50 yuan' offered Kristel. The girl broke into smile and tapped her palm.

'But you have been practicing your English with us' Kristel continued 'And we are English teachers. We get paid 100 yuan for one hour. There are two of us so that is 200 yuan. If we give you 50 yuan then you need pay only 150'. Kristel tapped her palm.

The girl pouted.

'I have no money. You have money'

'Foreigners are not all rich' I said.

She frowned.

'Yes' she said 'all rich'. Kristel picked up the pace and turned the corner.

'That's not true' I said hopelessly, but the girl just sneered. We merged with the crowds and became stuck together on the path for some time, both of us ignoring each other like a long married couple.

People clogged the riverbank, pushing and shoving, stretching and contracting in a frenetic semi-standstill - like a paralysed millipede. But I finally caught Kristel up and left the aspiring guide scurrying instead after a dazzling Korean. Kristel had found an escape route. It led away from the river up steps to where the masses had fanned themselves out along the tops of viewpoints. From the valley rose the rock columns, which were straight from Conan Doyle's Lost World. The valley looked like dough squeezed through a sieve. Pillars emerged through it to grow mouldy and sport foliage. Behind the valley hills began to roll. In that direction, the clouds had broken. In poured a fretful screen of sunlight behind which lay a wild Hunan of hills and fields ripe with weeds, and a single ruined house. In two hundred years this region had burned in no less than five brutal wars - including the Taiping rebellion. Over the same period close to a hundred severe floods had burst from the basin of the Dongting lake. In the face of nature's little jokes, the locals had clung on with a Chinese tenacity.

Then an old man tried to wrestle off my backpack

'I'll carry, you pay!' he shouted. And like that the spell was broken. I was back amongst jabber and snapping, amongst the torrents of peasants from the surrounding area who had decamped here to try their hands at hawking. With guidebooks and watermelon, walking sticks and bird whistles they came, a summer vocation of the new China - and they claimed banditry had declined in these parts.

We waded through these waves of rabid merchants and hid in our hotel until nightfall. The manager laughed at us as we walked in dishevelled.

'Buy anything?' he called.

'No' I said

'The farmers have not yet eaten you?!'

'Not yet'.

Later in bed I tossed and turned and sweated and moaned. Kristel was not happy. Then the phone rang.

'Hello. Want a friend?'

I hung up - and ripped the phone from its socket for good measure.

Escaping

The train to Guilin, one province south, was to leave in the early evening. We had bought the first available tickets - overnight hard seats. It was time to get out of this hell hole. But we still had a day to spare. So we gave in and paid the manager for air-conditioning and locked ourselves inside the hotel room, fearful of the heat and the tourists, but especially the hawkers. In the dusk we crept out to find and board our transport. Squashed against a window we were jammed in with four Korean girls and a local Hunanese peasant woman. But when her baby screamed at the sight of all these foreigners, the peasant sensibly moved back a seat. The Koreans seemed to have chosen one another for balance, for two were sprout thin. It was the other two who seemed to control the groups' food rations. They were not the only other companions here either, for this carriage was rammed with vegetable sacks and clammy bodies.

Truly this was the local service, but it was already making good progress through the darkness with the windows flung wide and the chat merry. Once again the carriage had turned into some model of rural China. Peasants spat and grinned and feasted on sunflower seeds. For hours we rocked through the darkness. Fans swatted aimlessly once more while naked bulbs faded and brightened. The seats truly were hard, and when Kristel drifted off to sleep she did not slump forward, but remained bolt upright, jammed between me and her Korean neighbour.

Then the train wheezed and halted in the middle of nowhere, which was a surprise, for the middle of nowhere was a precious commodity in lowland China. It turned out we had broken down. It was 3am and still sweltering. The fans switched off. So did those unreliable lights. A topsoil of sunflower seed husks and cigarette butts began to form across the carriage and bitter smoke wafted through its entrails. Fidgeting, scratching, teeth grinding, seed flicking, grimacing. The passengers were not happy. I lost the patience to continue reading. Kristel sighed. I checked out the neighbours and wondered who would snap first and lose face.

'We hate Brigitte Bardot' said one of the Korean girls without provocation. It was one of the plumper ones, who, it seemed, had little interest in disproving stereotypes. 'She came to Seoul and told Koreans they shouldn't eat dog' she complained.

The heat, the lingering smoke and the building detritus, seemed to be making everyone a little delirious.

'Delicious!' shouted the Korean, flailing her arms. Perhaps she was still talking about dog.

Passengers clambered out of the open windows as the doors remained locked. Two bored attendants had nothing to say about the breakdown as they had not heard from the driver. They lit up and blew smoke down the carriage. A man held his little boy so he could pee through a crack in the train's belly. The thin Koreans slumped against one another, propped like two flimsy cards, and the other plump Korean said of her hosts, the Chinese

'We say they act like pigs and eat like pigs' she said. I got up, clambered over the mess and tried the doors at the other end of the carriage. All locked: how very suffocating. But the windows were still open, and outside hung the sweet whiff of corn. Neither Kristel nor I joined the escapees relaxing outside.

It turned out to have been a wise decision, for a couple of hours later they were still out there, falsely confident of our joint predicament, when a sudden jolt announced our departure. Only one escapee dared race for the window. He was rewarded and hauled back through by the helping hands of the Old Hundred Names. Sadistically, the attendants whooped for joy. The rest of the escapees could only watch as their ride picked up speed and left them stranded in the dark. I stuck my head out of the open window and watched the ends of their cigarettes narrow to infinity.

Dawn the following day revealed that the earth had broken out in boils - beautiful boils. These were the karsts of the south, huge limestone formations carved by glaciers at the end of the last ice age, they were the 'Jade Hairpins' described by the Han poet Han Yu, a bizarre chain of mossy mounds. Peasants were already up and tending the paddies, pretending the land did not contain these obstacles. They had furrowed around them creating in the crops concentric ripples where the ploughs had been. But the carriage was still asleep, and the two fat Koreans snored together. Kristel slept too. It was just me and the oblivious peasants outside. In this timeless landscape I liked to think this train, a messenger of the modern world, was invisible.

It was only once urban China invaded in fits of corrugated iron and concrete that my companions were roused. They woke to see the outskirts of Guilin spilling around the formations. Myth claimed that these gigantic rocks had been carried by labourers on a journey to plug up the South China Sea. They had not made it, and their ridiculous cargoes had been marooned around the river valleys of these parts. The modern Chinese had managed to abstain from levelling these rocks in the usual bid to make a God of man. Instead the locals had strewn their mess around them so that the karst jutted out of the town in a series of green islands. We arrived and left the Koreans to pick a fight with the cabbies at the station. Instead we flew up a karst in the centre of town and nested in its top like squirrel monkeys. From there we looked out onto the other islands and whiled away the afternoon pretending not to notice the usual street life clatter below. Dressed in captured Qing uniforms, the Taiping had once come to siege this place, this town of rocks. But the ruse had failed and the town's great gates had been closed. A month long attack using cannon mounted siege towers fared no better in breaking the defenders and instead the Taiping moved north into Hunan, from where we had just come.

Rolling out of town on a jolly old bus, we quickly re-entered the paddies and rows of maize, all sprinkled with shacks and old junk - a rusty bicycle, plastic bags - and many more of the molehills and gigantic witches hats that had petrified to karst. All along the route families of peasants were bringing in the harvest, cutting and threshing rice and tying the stalks into bales. By the time we arrived, it was dusk. A deep dusk strewn with clouds of crumpled coal. The crimson lanterns of Yangshuo reflected in puddles, a town rife with pizza joints and burrito houses, whitewashed and flying-eaved, a dragon that danced past them all along narrow cobbled streets. Drummers followed on its heels, and hypnotised by drink, the *laowai* of the Red Star and Blue Lotus bars had stormed outside. The hawkers out there did not look like they were missing a trick - they were purring purveyors of fans and scrolls. They strung up t-shirts daubed with the Chinese characters for '*Be quiet, please!*', '*You are Evil!*' and my favourite, '*The Foreigner is coming*'. I bought this last one, just so the Chinese could tell.

In the morning we hired bicycles and rode out into the valleys where we and the other tourists sparred with construction trucks shipping in materials to help fuel Yangshuo's tourism boom. Families were out collecting the harvest. On one patch worked a girl and a young boy busy with a lathe while an older man lounged there watching from a skirting ditch, fanning himself. Beyond them glinted ribbon - the river?

'The Li?' I asked the boy with the lathe. He shook his head.

'Floods' reckoned the older man. And he got up and pulled the boy to him protectively 'the Li is flooded'.

We followed a track towards the ribbon and passed three men napping in a thatched roofed pavilion. The muffled yapping of a dog floated from a nearby home. A teenage boy sat on a stone wall above the water, fishing with cane and string, while below him passed plastic canisters and fallen branches. A water buffalo tethered at the bottom of the steps was having a hard time holding its footing. It snorted like a wounded hog, struggling to stay put. Downstream we discovered later, the Li had burst its banks spectacularly and forced thousands from their homes. The rice crop had been decimated and government aid trucks had been sent to four affected counties. It was difficult under the sunshine to imagine such trauma, for the floodwaters of this town only glittered lazily.

We stood down in the water and watched eddies form around the drowning palms. A topless elder floated by on a raft. The years before the rebellion had been a time of flooding and drought: signs from the Gods. The Taiping may not have pried open Guilin, but they did learn the value of the waterways here on the Li. They had seized all river-going vessels, practiced naval logistics, and sailed into the heart of China.

Later in Yangshuo's night market a wild haired woman shrieked

'Take a photo!' She brandished a dog jaw balanced on a fat butcher's knife. 'Take a photo!' There were here rows of fishmongers selling fish in various states of repair, and outside under bulbous clouds, ranks of busy chefs flicking woks fuming with ginger and chilli. I found a cheery girl manhandling meat in a pan.

'Have or not have rat?' I asked her. She shook her head and laughed prettily.

'Squirrel?'

'Not have'

'But you must have cat'

'Last year we had cat. We also had squirrel. We had rat. Now we have only fish. Want fish?'

'But in the South you eat everything' I protested. That's what they said in Hangzhou at least, which truly was saying something as the citizens of Hangzhou were not fussy. Southerners eat anything with four legs, they claimed - anything except chairs that was. They would eat anything that flew except aircraft, and anything from the sea except ships. The girl giggled and shook her head again.

'Not for tourists. You will get sick. Know SARS?'

Did I know SARS? In China it was impossible not to know

SARS. There were SARS scanners at the transport hubs, and quarantine rooms there for the victims.

'They say it started near here' I said.

'No. In Guangdong' she reckoned 'Foolish people, the Cantonese!' She flashed a wicked grin and flung mushroom into the pan. Guangdong folk I met later swore that Guangxi had been the originator. And besides, the province had relatively recent form, for the place had provided the central government with some of its most disturbing reports during the last great famine, when Mao had tried to kick-start economic growth with the 'Great Leap Forward'. Instead peasants across China had died in their millions. Many had been reduced to barbary - bark had been stripped from trees, chalk had been consumed. In parts of rural Guangxi the dead had been eaten, and in some hazy reportage, suggestions of babies too. In this region shaped by shortage it did not seem at all unlikely that some villager might have dined on Civet cat and transferred the SARS disease across the boundaries - and set off the international lockdown.

'Want or not want Fish?' repeated the wok girl.

'Want' I said. She grasped the most energetic one, a lively mandarin wriggling in a bucket. This one didn't like being thrown onto a bed of onion and garlic in the middle of a hot wok. Neither did it like having beer poured over its back. But it tasted delicious.

Next morning dawned, and soon the morning mist was left fighting a rearguard action, trapped against the karst. The morning sun began to spill under these strange shapes, bathing the town in a mellow citrus glow. The hawkers were just beginning to set up for the day, ready for the tourists to waken. We found a place of panelled teak and figurines collected from across Southeast Asia; of Chinese waitresses slouching good-naturedly while two young boys argued over a coffee grinder. One was boasting '*My* Daddy ate snake!' The manageress was drinking at the bar. She was a rather distracted-looking Frenchwoman.

'My son - he was brought up here' she said 'The other one is his cousin'. It turned out both boys had been brought up here. She had lived here with her husband for a decade and a half, and so had his brother and his wife.

'How come?' I asked.

'My husband and Jean were brought up in Indochina. It was

their home, but when the French lost the war, they had to go back'. Her brow tightened and she shouted at the boys, one of whom was now wrestling with one of the waitresses perilously close to a large bodhisattva. This had no effect. She got up to separate them all manually, the waitresses from the boys, and the boys from each other.

'It was their dream to go back' she said on her return 'but until very recently it was not possible. After we married, my husband left the army and moved us all over here instead'. These parts of China reminded them of Vietnam she reckoned. There were similarities: the karst mountains looked like islets from North Vietnam's Halong Bay; the burrito houses and bars and foreigners might have been airlifted from wartime Saigon. It seemed to me that even when this stunning region was not consumed by war or disaster, it was recalling it.

The Frenchwoman sluiced herself another coffee. 'It is funny...' she began 'how memories are better than the reality. We live thinking of what comes next and what has gone. And we paint the past only as we want it'. The Frenchwoman became distracted again by the boys, for one of them now stood on a chair, perilously close to knocking decorative plates from the top shelf.

'*Fais attention!*' she screamed. Her boy leapt off as though the furniture had bitten him, and she refocused.

'To return to his childhood home would probably only disappoint my husband she said'. She seemed to believe that he was better off here in the town of his idealised past.

Another China

We left in the evening for Shenzhen. It was a sleeper bus, and on the bunk next door a British boy was wrestling himself into an impossibly short bed. The driver of the bus meanwhile had been having his own wrestle – this one with reasonable standards of driving. Harvey was eighteen and had been teaching in a small village school deep in China's South-west, in the province of Yunnan. I asked him if he had any photos of the place.

'No man. I don't take photos. Rather have the real memories, not told how to remember from a photograph - know what I mean?'

'That works if you have a good memory'.

We held on tight as the bus was flung round mountain bends.

Then wide-eyed, Harvey claimed

'They've got the best dope down there. They sell it by the kilo. Everyone smokes it. The tribes people grow anything and the men are whacked out all the time' He said 'but I feel sorry for the women, doing all the work and all...You get any dope in the East?' He sat up stiffly.

'I don't think it's so easy' I said, recalling the drugs exhibition from Shaoxing, the jet planed dealers shot in the neck.

'Even the cops smoke it in Yunnan' Harvey reckoned 'sometimes they sit outside and play cards with traffickers. We reckoned they were up to the necks in it, taking bribes and turning a blind eye when they shipped it in from Burma. They've got tribes to keep happy too - the Miao, the Dong. They're all growing weed and the Burmese are growing opium'. He talked like this for some time, encouraged here and there by the odd nod from me. He discussed different types of high, how much opium could be smoked until one puked; how the tribes-people relieved the foreigner of his cash; how the police relieved the foreigner of his dignity; and how the local communist cadres relieved the foreigner of his ability to think freely.

Somewhere in the middle of these anecdotes, Kristel had fallen asleep. And eventually Harvey too, grew tired of his own voice. Instead he occupied the soundscape by snoring loudly - like a water buffalo in floodwater. The bus continued teetering into the night and I read alone under lights that flickered. I was coming to the end of the Lin Yutang book. It had been written in the 1930s, during the reign of the nationalists. Lin had clouded his final pages with his own once youthful emotions.

'I pictured the saviour of China' he wrote 'I would believe in a revolution, any revolution, and in any party, any party, that would replace the present government of Face, Fate, and Favour by a government of law. These three have made the rule of Justice and the weeding out of official corruption impossible'. But whenever the peasants rose in anger and overthrew the old system, face, fate, and favour still managed to worm their way back in. And despite the best efforts of the communists, the old China of the three Fs was still around...

Kristel prodded me in the belly. Flashes of sun were breaking through a forest, another one of steel and glass. And now instead of the suffocating darkness of the Guangxi countryside, we were racing down the bright boulevards of Shenzhen, the legendary boomtown of shopping malls and consumers that twenty-five years ago had been a bunch of villages.   Apparently this was the future, this grid of malls and skyscrapers and packed factories where the herds of beggars were periodically swept off the streets by police because they did not have residence permits.

Harvey was already up, and chewing gum for breakfast.

'Shenzhen' he said vacantly 'I hear it's wild'.

It was supposed to be an economic frontier town of hookers and fast-talkers, of villagers arriving full of hope to the city about which it was said *'You think you are rich until you arrive'*.

'Maybe I can find something here' Harvey said dreamily 'I'll find a girl. Have some fun'. The bus pulled into Shenzhen bus station. By the time I hauled my bag out of bed, Harvey had vanished.

Kristel and I caught a cab to the border. Shenzhen sprawled right up to the barbed wire. There it ceased. Over the other side the hills seemed green and verdant.   Straddling the fence was the concrete administrative station. We climbed to it washed along with floods of businessmen and day-trippers. Queues, passports stamps, lino floors, no mans land - cameras scanned for SARS. LEDs flashed: body temperature 36.5 degrees. Then there were different border guards and more stamps. We had arrived in Hong Kong Special Administrative Region of the People's Republic of China. Here we boarded an MTR train to Kowloon and watched as the dwellings of the New Territory sped past. They were the gaudy ones of Zhejiang's rich peasants, but decked with a car or two. There was not a vegetable plot to be seen.

Outside Kowloon station a paper stand carried recent copies of *The New York Times*, *Le Monde*, and *Corriere della Sera*. A bomb had gone off in Baghdad's Sadr city. Across the road stood subversives of the Falun Gong. They were middle aged middle class women in sun hats wearing the studied affectedness of art students. To a fence they had chained placards: enlarged photos of human suffering. I pointed at a picture of a dead man sporting some kind of trauma to the chest.

'What happened to him?' I asked

'Torture' volunteered the shortest.

'Where?'

One of the other women - a Sunday school teacher type in a flowery blouse - pointed back over the border

'In China'
'But this is China'
'The other China' she said.

Over the next three days we crossed the harbour on the Star Line Ferry and ran up the world's longest series of escalators in Central. We sat by the window in a dim sum restaurant in one of Hong Kong Island's many towers and ate urchin and yam dumpling. We took a sampan ride around Aberdeen and lay on the beach at Repulse Bay, from which the British had once evicted the pirates. We drank in a Bavarian tavern and shopped in *Mong Kok*. We visited the library and the Happy Valley and the tops of Hong Kong Island. It was a way of life that seemed familiar, but it was difficult keeping up with it on a mainland salary. And the places through which we travelled in this China had been infected with the seditious presence of the Falun Gong. By transport interchanges and on shopping streets they lurked, inflaming the people with their free speech and leaflets.

I remembered our first days in Hangzhou when all of those faces had looked monotone and indistinguishable. We had gotten used to it. Now it was this China's diversity that seemed discomforting. For there were not only Chinese wandering these streets, but Africans, Indians, and great numbers of Europeans, all diluting those delicate Chinese features.

If this was not confusing enough, in this China, the television was broadcasting BBC, and people opened department store doors for one another. But I was truly shocked in a lift as a Chinese mother leant over her humming boy and whispered

'Shhhh…!'

There were rallies in this China - held legally too. So Philippine maids outside City Hall picketed assembly members as they left in their Mercedes, and supporters of the pro-Beijing Democratic Alliance for the Betterment of Hong Kong demonstrated under a flyover. The latter waved yellow flags and yellow banners. They even wore yellow, the colour of the emperor. And two of their speakers with apparently extreme shouting disorders had - most unfortunately - been allowed access to megaphones. Kristel and I walked into the crowd to watch. The mop haired man beside us pulled a spectacular double take.

'What are you doing?' he asked fluently.

'I've come to see what you are all doing' I explained

'We are supporting solidarity...' Then one of the megaphone squealers put out a new broadcast. I could not understand any of it, but I suspected it was Cantonese.

'What is he saying?'

'One China' he said

'One China!' replied the crowd, and the most enthusiastic vigorously assaulted the air.

One last time we crossed the glittering harbour on the White Star Ferry. The Falun Gong naturally, were hanging around on the other side. There were dozens of them, a few students and housewives, malevolently placard waving. It was a well oiled machine, this Falun Gong, well organised and financed. But membership of the Falun Gong had been banned in the other China since a few thousand of them had converged on the communist leadership compound in Beijing to demand better treatment. Like Hong Xiuquan the Heavenly King, Li Hongzhi - head of the Falun Gong - had developed 'supernatural powers'. These were not those of communication with God, but a mastery over his breathing supposed to return man back to the path of morality.

The communists carried the burden of the dynasties. For who were the Falun Gong? They could only be the Taiping resurrected. The Falun Gong were the rebels who had risen so many times before to sweep out the old dynasty. They were the Yellow Turbans and the Five Pecks of Rice, the White Lotus and the Boxers (who burned charms and ate the ashes which they believed would protect them from weapons). They were a millenarian movement whose ideology competed with that of the state. For whether they came as a fanatical sword bearer or a Granny hanging out by a park bench, the state knew a rebel when it saw one.

On the Beach

Next morning the South China Morning Post ran a story on a pro-democracy activist who had just been arrested on a business trip to Guangdong. He had been caught by the police with his pants down in a brothel.

'I've been framed!' he claimed. Maybe he had, maybe he hadn't. In any case he had gotten unlucky - or tempted fate. It wasn't often that the cops clamped down on prostitution, which both the traditional and the modern China seemed to have turned a blind eye to. But what was not very well hidden in this story was an underlying fear: anxiety over the state of the motherland, the menace lurking from across the border. For all its attributes; its key position in the global economic architecture, the international connections, the plurality of its society, this city seemed a lonely one. Hong Kong was weak, tiny, and insecure. It was haunted.

We set off for Macau on hydrofoil. It had only recently returned to the bosom of the motherland and still hung with the ghosts of the Portuguese who had ruled it. It stank of the Mediterranean, of olive oil and dried meat. It was a town of scooters and cobbled alleys, jewellers and pawn shops. The people ambled with a laid-back assurance that was not from the mainland. In Macao the authorities were encouraging casinos to move in and build the city a gambling future. In the mainland, gambling was a decadent vice and the Communist Party had banned it. So Macao was becoming a kind of Chinese Atlantic City, looking not to the world, but to a vision of itself as a niche dependency - a place to which the mainland party people and addicts flocked to on organised coach tours.

In the no man's land between the China of Macao and that of border town Zhuhai, peasant ladies camped themselves in the parking lot.

'Umbrella?' they pestered. We did our best to ignore them, and filled out the health declaration cards that we had been handed, as foreigners.

'*Do you have any psychological illness?*' asked the card. And then

'*To your knowledge, have you been infected with SARS?*' But it seemed more prudent to be asking people venturing out, not in. Perhaps they should have quizzed them on their eating habits too.

A police officer in an outsize cap stamped our passports, and we were once more upon the Middle Kingdom. Out in the streets the itinerants were spitting, a crush of traffic had already ground to standstill, and the place was in the midst of a feverish construction boom. Zhuhai, just another boom city of the Pearl delta, had once been built here to siphon foreign wealth from Macao. But after all of the frantic progress, perhaps the balance was tipping.

From the motorway the Pearl Delta was a sweep of palm trees and prosperous housing. We bussed into the heart of the delta to the city of Canton, now Guangzhou, another skyline hijacked by towers and cranes, of which Wen claimed

'It's full of murderers'. Other Chinese had long been suspicious. These southerners were often the first exposed to foreign contagion. The Qing had once forced Europeans to trade solely in this town, and bottled their influence. Through it the Europeans had sold tea back to the Chinese, as well as Christianity, opium and venereal disease. It was in Canton that Hong Xiquan the Heavenly King had become inspired to begin his mission to save all of China. He had arrived in Canton to take the civil service examinations, a fiendish exercise which candidates had spent their whole lives preparing for - a test of their knowledge of the Confucian classics. Hong had failed like 99% of those who took these exams. Instead he had read of the Good News in pamphlets written by a Chinese missionary and begun his trip back to Guangxi. On the journey home he had suffered some sort of breakdown. His family had hidden him indoors fearful of his behaviour, for they would be held accountable for his actions. As he recovered Hong began to receive visions. The first involved an elderly man complaining about men worshiping demons rather than him. In the second, Hong saw Confucius repenting after being punished for his lack of faith. In the third, Hong imagined himself carried to heaven by angels whereupon he was met by a man wearing the robe of a black dragon. The man had endowed Hong with a sword and a magic seal, and instructed him to purify China of the demons.

We had a few hours to kill until our train left for Xiamen so we hunted for the chapel of the Southern Baptist, Issachar Roberts, who had once preached to Hong Xiuquan in Canton. We wandered the docile streets of Shamian Island, where the colonials had once been exiled to. Here Kristel and I discovered lethargic itinerants, Italian colonnades and a Catholic cathedral, but no chapel. Roberts' house of God it turned out, had in fact been based outside the colonial district. It had, in any case, vanished long ago disappeared - swept away by progress.

We paid a trip to the nearby market instead where aisles of star anise and dried orange peel mixed with coils of dried snake and deer penis. A butcher was busy walloping hunks of beef. I approached and asked

'You sell monkey?'

'Not have now' he said 'too many police!' So SARS had toned down this market too. The police were indeed busy. We watched them down by the cinnamon stalls, snapping counterfeit DVDs they had seized from an unlucky hawker.

We caught our train, a breezy sedate village that moseyed up the coast, past the beaches, through the hills, away from Hong Xiuquan's Heavenly Kingdom and into rugged Fujian province. Sleep oozed through the land and the train, and the hot carriages were soothed by midday snoring. Palm merged to fern, fern to paddy, and paddy back to palm. At the heart of this kind of Chinese California lay the migrant city of Xiamen, a city of sparkling glass and fresh towers, and another of the former special economic zones where the communists had experimented safely with enterprise and foreign investment before it had been unleashed upon all.

This was the hometown of Fong Shen, another friend who had studied with us in the UK. We needed to find an internet café, to let him know we had arrived. We searched the guide book, identified the address, and walked through its door. A child sat there on the floor, hitting the buttons on a computer control pad.

'Is this the internet café?' I asked.

'No...' he said, his eyes stuck on the screen 'this is my home'.

'Sorry'

'The internet cafe was here before' he explained patiently 'other foreigners have come here too'. The boy pressed pause and pointed through the wall 'there is a new one open on the next street' he said. Not even guidebooks could keep pace with this change with Chinese characteristics.

We later met Fong Shen on the waterfront. He was there stoutly fighting seagulls off his ice cream, flinging a digital camera at them. He saw us and smiled while a gull got a beak full. Fong Shen ferried us about in his mother's car and we soon discovered Xiamen was a city of light. It splashed off the roofs of Xiamen university, on the eaves of Nanputuo Buddhist temple, on the Krupp canons up on the fort bought from Germany with which the Qing had never managed to harm the enemy.

This was another of those coastal towns that had been only a village until recently. Xiamen was so new that most of its inhabitants had been born elsewhere, somewhere in the hinterlands. In the evening the town burst to life, and those who had hidden from the heat of the day emerged to wander. Great gangs of prostitutes were already out manning the street corners and the exits of nightclubs.

'*Yaotou*' (headshakers) whispered Fong Shen and he nodded towards a group of youths flirting there with the street women.

'We are all foreigners here' he reckoned 'everyone comes for the new life. I was not born here. My parents were not born here and nor were my grandparents. My family has a typical Xiamen story'. His grandmother had lost her first two husbands during the liberation struggle, and she had insisted her third husband stay out of it. For him she had birthed her twelfth child - Shen's father, Fong Dong. All but two of the children had died by the time the Cultural Revolution came round. Fong Dong was left to find himself hauled up before a revolutionary committee and condemned for being the son of a coward. He had been sent to the fields for re-education, and on his return he had enlisted in the army. After some years of loyal service Dong had been honourably discharged, and with the money he had saved, he had begun dealing cars - surreptitiously at first, since owning a business had been technically illegal.

Shen's mother Ying had been a fervent red guard at the same time Dong was being re-educated. She had harangued teachers and witnessed the beating of a monk. She had since landed a coveted place in medical school and became a distinguished doctor of medicine.

'My father has always tried to fit in' claimed Shen 'My mother, she rules the home'. It was symptomatic of their social influences he admitted. Fong Dong tried to appease the society that had once cut him out; but brought up feted by the state, Fong Ying's right to command was ingrained. In this new China of opportunity, it always felt odd to look around at the urbanites of the generation above - the leather clad taxi drivers, the chefs, the entrepreneurs - and know that many of them still wore deep scars from a chaotic youth.

Shen insisted we visit the old colonial isle of Gulang Yu the following day. We caught a crowded ferry across a narrow strait which had on board a sign. '*No Tossing*' it said. The island was cluttered with European villas which had spawned several famed concert pianists. This claim was now telegraphed to visitors through hidden roadside speakers. The sun died and drowned in the ocean. Sea gulls patrolled, and peacocks mewed from a park below.

Jinmen, the next island out, was a geopolitical quirk. For it belonged to the Republic of China, not the People's Republic of China. We could see its dark bulk just across the water. It had been held onto by the retreating nationalists at the end of the civil war. Somehow they had kept it through the Korean war - when it had been shelled heavily - and beyond. It was Taiwanese territory according to Taiwan, and Chinese territory according to the communists - for Taiwan remained one province amongst many: just a rebel island. In Beijing, it was still known as 'Chinese Taipei', and one way or another it needed to be liberated.

We headed back to the mainland to hang out on beaches strewn with abandoned pillboxes. They were thronged with comrades swimming under floodlight. No one seemed concerned that there were enemy soldiers over the water for no-one had fired shots in fifty years. The propaganda war had not tailed off as dramatically however. Even behind this beach sat a gigantic sign that during the day was supposed to be visible from Jinmen: *'One Country, Two Systems, One China'* it proclaimed. On Jinmen apparently the nationalists had matched this effort with their own: *'Reunify China under the Three Principles of the People'* (nationalism, democracy and 'people's livelihood')...But this just didn't have the same ring to it.

Fong Shen stood trying to make out the characters hulking on scaffolding twenty feet high.

'If Taiwan splits from China' he reckoned 'China's soul will also be split. It would be disrespect to our ancestors, those who made China one'

'It is worth a war?'

'Yes' he said without hesitation

'And what if China loses?'

He gave this some thought, suddenly finding his fingers a major source of entertainment.

'If there is war this town will be destroyed. The Taiwanese have missiles aimed at us. But if China loses...' he began 'it will probably be the end of the communist party. And perhaps the end of China. If Taiwan goes, then everywhere will go'. The precedent would be set he reckoned. A thousand interest groups would rise. China would unravel like bad knitting - Tibet and Xinjiang would leave. Then Guangdong, Yunnan, maybe Sichuan. That was the nightmare scenario. The state would splinter. There would be violence and famine. Unification, disintegration

- it was history's cyclical pattern. But whereabouts in it the new China found itself, remained anyone's guess.

9. Dust

We were home by the end of August. Lotus had already overrun the West Lake with pink egg-shaped heads which in another plane of time seemed to be strangling one another. Hangzhou's botanical gardens with its pine groves and thickets of bamboo, had been overtaken by tribes of domestic campers. They tramped the grass and the shrubs and arranged the necessary noise to create this home away from home. The set pieces of the gardens - the bridges and rockeries merging with the trees where man and artist sought harmony with nature - seemed resigned to defeat on their own territory. Tour buses still limped between the sights, and ferries belched across the lake. A respectable mushroom restaurant had vanished. We turned up at the address by cab one evening to find all that remained was a field of brown rubble. Amidst the chattering herds, the young man with the melted face still dabbed his frightful keyboard under Hefang Jie's Qing dynasty eaves; and the forlorn panda of Hangzhou zoo had died.

'No one knows why' Lou Da said 'we find this an unexplained phenomenon'. With this statement I could only guess that Lou Da had not visited the zoo for some time.

In the neighbourhood, much had changed. A new pavement had been laid all the way to the supermarket to replace ditched and shattered flagstones. Mrs. Ping was already making use of it with her key making machine, and because sunshine and new pavements precluded any gutter play, she sat and taught her boy on the machine and showered the road with sparks. More hairdressing salons had opened and a pizza joint on Zhoushan Road had closed and *re*opened. It had been sold on, gutted, renovated, refurbished. In one summer the place had been converted into a fine eatery by ex-students from Educated People. It was already renowned in the neighbourhood for the smelly perfection of its home cooked *Dofu*.

The pig-tailed fruit stall girl was sat back on the streets where she flicked mud at passers by. And the Xia's water store? It had been flattened. Crushed to an empty space, ready for the next tiny redevelopment.

'Xia went to Zhoushan' roared Mr. Zhou of the fast food buffet, whose custom had dried up during the school holidays. He stood there puffing a cigarette absentmindedly, as if attempting to compensate for his lost neighbour. 'Mr. Xia thinks he can fish!' he shouted. I hoped the Xias had landed on their feet out there on the island they had apparently left for: Mr. Xia smoking on the prow of the boat while his curious son hauled in the bountiful nets. Mrs. Xia of course, would be hunched over a desk somewhere, plotting how to sell fish to fishermen.

By the time purple Mangostine fruits began spilling across the road to be run over and crushed, I had the feeling that summer was wrapping up. Then Fong Shen arrived. He had flown up to Shanghai from Xiamen, but then run into trouble.

'I'm going to be late' he said on the phone 'Security won't let me on the train. Getting the bus'. We crossed town in rush hour on our own packed bus. It rumbled past the police department where kalashnikov wielding kids from the PLA stood guard next to a sign that said *'if you are stolen, call the police'*. It curb crawled city hall where a few former pedicab drivers had been protesting for a number of days. Their vehicles - which had been a ubiquitous part of the streetscape back when we first arrived - had been banned by town edict for being unsafe. These drivers had no place in the modern Hangzhou and their protests were being studiously ignored by officialdom. Fong Shen waited with his camera (which was almost as large as his head) swinging like a hyperactive pendulum. It turned out Shen had gone to some trouble to bring with him three cans of deodorant - a present for the caveman bought at a specialist store. Then at Shanghai railway station the guards had seen it from the x-ray machine, hiding in his backpack.

'They said it might be a bomb' he smiled 'I might be blowing up the train'. Shen shook his head 'We have problems. We have *Uighur* terrorists and angry workers'. It sounded more to me like China had problems with petty individuals making the most extensive use of their powers.

We stayed downtown by the bus station amongst Grannies and their wicker bags, for we had another guest. Soon I saw him coming from a long way down the street, this solid fellow lumbering through the bicycles and street sellers - it was Chang Wen.

'You are thinner' he greeted me. Then as if he had suddenly remembered his own dire warnings, he turned to Kristel and exclaimed 'and still alive!' But once we began to catch up, it sounded like it had been Wen who had had more to cope with.

'Cheng Hualing has a new plan. She talked about it all the summer' he frowned like a bull chewing on really average grass 'she wants us to move in with her parents'. But the home she wanted them all to move into was still conceptual. It was a pristine white tower set in gardens of luxuriant flowers. At least that was how it looked in the promotional material the developers had produced. The end product was still three years away from completion, but most of the flats had already gone. Indeed a desperate middle class mob had appeared outside the developer's offices on the first day of sale hoping to secure a flat for themselves or their offspring. It had taken a van load of police officers to restore order.

'Prices will be much higher by next year. They rise all the time. Soon they will be too much for a driver to afford' admitted Wen 'so better to buy now. We can move in too'. He pursed his lips 'I'm not so happy though. In the old days the wife came to live with her husband's parents. Cheng Hualing thinks we should reverse this. Can you imagine?' It sounded like some sort of Chinese male hell.

Cheng Hualing seemed to have Wen well-trained. Today for instance, they had been shopping, an interest over which they seemed to be bonding.

'I walk around. She spends my money' Wen said without humour. It was hard work, this courting business. But at least Hualing had released him early today. So Fong Shen, Chang Wen, Kristel and I made the most of this time, hiking up in the hills.

As dusk neared we arrived lakeside and wandered until we arrived at the Jingci temple. It was deserted apart from a tour group from Taiwan led by a monk in a tutti-frutti robe who kept his audience rapt by speaking with the spirits. Amidst the stink of incense wafting in curls through the last rays of light, we stood near the dining hall. But then a local monk sneered, said

'*Fuck Off*' - the most surprising response from a monk - and shooed us away. The temple's famous bell rang out to mark sundown, echoing across the courtyard. But as we walked out of the temple grounds the tolling of the bell became subdued by rush hour traffic.

'There is 60% chance he is not a real monk' said Wen 'Just

another greedy Chinese man. Spoiled by his parents. Too good to find a real job'.

'It's difficult to become a monk' said Fong Shen 'Just like it is difficult to become a teacher'. Chang Wen fell silent. Just like anywhere else the path of a young person was enabled by parents here (was it different anywhere else?). It was all about *guanxi* and finance. It had been no different for Chang Wen.

We occupied a lakeside table at a tea house, drank of best Dragon Well leaves, and watched boats gliding on the darkening waters. Over the other side of the lake the city lights fired up, and the girls on the table next door chattered excitedly about boyfriends. Seated here under the emerging stars, there seemed little doubt that Hangzhou was the most beautiful town in China.

Chang Wen had been watching this drifting off on my part. Now he chose to give this away. He smiled broadly

'I know what you're thinking' he reckoned

'You do?'

'Yes' he said 'You are thinking, it is time for dinner'.

It was close enough.

Cheng Hualing turned up a few minutes later. She looked pleased with herself - clearly not everything had changed over the summer.

'New top, new shoes. It's been a busy day' she said. Then she grabbed Wen by the arm and steered us off to a restaurant.

Shen leaned over as we walked

'Typical new Chinese girl. Definitely a Little Emperor'. But when Chinese made claims such as this it was telling of their own upbringing. As a '75 baby Shen had come before both reform and opening and the one child policy. That meant he had an older brother and could remember rationing.

At the restaurant we were ushered into a private room where we seated ourselves on red chairs bowed with gold. Cheng Hualing stole the top chair - the one facing the door.

'You're the guests, you order' she said with a flick of the wrist. But just as Kristel began speaking with the waitress Hualing changed her mind: she ordered snails and cow gut and pigeon soup.

'You'll enjoy trying it!' she shouted. But we had been there before.

Then Cheng Hualing fingered a vinyl folder. It was an album of model poses shot around the West Lake sights: of her spread-eagled on the steps below the stone pagoda; holding herself back by her own hair amongst the tea plantations; come hither eyes telegraphed blasphemously outside the gates of Lingyin temple. She had gotten them done by a professional.

'Look!' she said and pointed at herself in the one where she lay on the steps.

'Cost me' said Chang Wen.

'I'm the modern one!' screamed Cheng Hualing. And as if to further prove this she shouted

'Yoga!' and then 'Do you like yoga?' I did not know whether she acted this way in order to impress the Western guests or to amuse herself. But in any case she dropped to the restaurant floor, spilled the photos all over it, bent her arms backwards until she was stood arched in the air, with her belly angled to the ceiling. It was a bizarre scene - the amateur gymnastics and the mess of artsy photos against the old staid garishness of the bright chairs and the plain linen tablecloth.

'I'm 70% sure I will pass my driving test next month' said Chang Wen trying to ignore his future wife, who had collapsed in a giggling heap on the floor. On my other side Shen leant over again, grinning like a prankster.

'Wives in China are expensive these days' he said.

Cheng Hualing for example, was worth a car, a bread van, and an apartment - preferably in the same block as her parents' one.

Quality Teaching

The first sign that employment opportunities at the University of Educated People had expanded was a seven foot giant bending under the door of the main administrative block. His name was Johann, he hailed from a town on the Dutch border. He was a huge chain smoking German with feral eyes and whiskers of barbed wire.

'I am a missionary of language' he said 'I was in Taiwan just before. On sabbatical'. Then he mumbled something about a wife and daughter back home, and I remembered British Chris's theory of foreigners: perhaps Johann was taking a sabbatical from trouble.

Then we caught a white boy and Chinese girl on the stairs to British Chris's old room. His name was Richard, an American. Her name was Zha Li, and she was a child of the new China.

'She invited me to the fishing pond by nine streams - you know the place?' Down by the nine streams meandering through misty forest, he had gotten sick eating the fish he had caught from the pond. She had nursed him and once he had recovered, decided not to leave his room.

'I like to shop' stated Zha Li vacantly. It turned out to be her favourite hobby - one she indulged with vigorous assistance from her father, who had made his fortune building electronic components and seemed to consider the creation of *It* girls as some sort of progress.

We discovered a Japanese teacher had also joined the University of Educated People and moved into the flat below. Reiko was her name, a spritely type who had been convincingly staving off middle age. Reiko was from Hiroshima and she had one vice - the insomnia of the workaholic.

'I sleep at 10pm. I wake by 2am' she said 'but I will never disturb you. I am busy arranging flowers and preparing classes'. Within a week I had her pegged as the most industrious person alive.

'I am so lazy' she told us 'but we live only once'.

One morning I bumped into Vice President Yao storming around the campus in a bright yellow shirt, directing students and teachers with an unfathomable energy.

'Hello Mr. Yao' I shouted cheerfully.

He nodded.

'You are learning the common language. Good' he said 'Ready for classes? We need our foreign friends to help our China to get stronger. Wishing you many ideas and prosperous learning'. I had learned more respect for modest Mr. Yao when Lou Da told me he had once been manager of a collective farm.

'Many opportunities for making money' Da had said 'but instead he came to work for the public institution'.

And later heading up the stairs of the foreign teachers' block I discovered Mrs. Ho. When she saw us she leapt up from the stair she was sat on.

'Mi Jin and Han Jie. Long time no see!'

'Hello Mrs. Ho' I said 'Where have you been?'

'In the country' she said 'My mother is sick. So I looked after my father' This kind of counterintuitive statement made perfect sense for the older generation.

'Professor Darling is very happy' she said, changing the subject 'one of his students has looked after him very much'.

We knocked on the professor's door and stayed for Gin Martini. He was glad to hear a run down on our travels. He liked the sound of the holy mountains. He tired as we talked of Tibet, but livened up once more as we described the South.

'I hated Hong Kong' he said 'Too many materialist folks hooked on consumer goods. They have it too easy to think'

Professor Darling explained that he too had been busy over the summer, and not just with the girls.

'I helped the school choose street names for the campus pathways' he reckoned 'We tried to choose names that reflect Chinese culture. I translated' Already the pathways had been signposted with these new assignments. The path leading to the girls' dorms had become the *'Road of Virtue'*. The *'Road of Honesty'* began at the administrative block, while the *'Avenue of cherished leaders'* ran in front of the library.

'There will be more discipline this term' he said 'curfews are to be more strict. Especially for girls'

'Especially for girls?' Kristel asked dangerously.

'Of course. They need protecting - even if half of those I met in college were just after my money. Have you ever talked to a young Chinese male? They have no honour. And the girls are very naïve. Would you let Lou Da loose amongst them?'

'Perhaps not' she admitted.

'If I hear Lou Da comes near any of my girls' he paused for dramatic effect 'I will cut his throat myself'. Bizarrely, I badly wanted to laugh. Fortunately, I managed to control myself.

'These kids need boundaries' he said 'there is too much licence. They need to shape up'. The university's plan involved continuing campus radio's wake up calls.

'Kids need waking' he reckoned. I asked him whether he thought we did too.

'Sure' he said. Later as we left I noticed the shoe pile outside the professor's door had thinned. Now it was just a pair of loafers and a single pair of flat-bottomed girl's shoes.

A day later the phone rang. It was Betty.

'I have a message' she said 'all teachers have been instructed to focus on teaching quality'

'Sounds like a good idea' I said 'teaching quality is important'

'You will focus on quality teaching?'

'Sure'

'Please tell Kristel as well'

'I will'

'About the quality teaching?'

'Yes. I will tell Kristel about quality teaching'

With this, Betty seemed satisfied, and she hung up.

It turned out to be an evening of phone calls. For later I found Lou Da at the other end of the line.

'I arranged for you to get paid over the holiday' he said 'but it was not easy'. When he paused for my acknowledgement, I gave him none. So he decided to expand on his heroic exploits.

'I asked the Finance Department about it' he began 'But they said it was not their decision. They said 'ask Academic Affairs'. So I asked Academic Affairs. But Academic Affairs said 'that is not our decision, ask Foreign Affairs'. So I was going to ask Foreign Affairs. But then I realised - Foreign Affairs is me! As Foreign Affairs, I decided to give you the money'.

'Excellent work' I said. He did not push this line any further, because I asked him whether he had enjoyed his meal out with us last term.

Later he turned up at our flat for a French lesson. I left him in the kitchen with Kristel for an hour, and came back out only to see him off.

'Lou Da has not been a good man' said Kristel. It looked like Da was in trouble. He may even have realised it for his smile was there, but it was surprisingly sheepish. I stared at him.

'This summer, Mei-Xie's father begged me to marry her' he admitted. I asked him why.

'Because he knows that I have taken her virtue' he claimed, and the grin broadened into something else - it was pride. 'But I have other options'. He rolled his eyes and pursed his lips in mimic 'be like a father to her. No man will have her if there is no blood on the cloth' and he

185

choked in some bewildered sort of scoff. 'Her father does not understand the city life. Small man. Still thinks like a peasant'

'You won't marry her'

'Maybe not. She is not so honourable'

Later there was another rap at the door. This time it was not Lou Da. Instead I found a small portly man with a face so sad and narrow, he looked like a horse. This was Professor Jiang, a teacher of English here who I had not spoken to before.

He said 'I need help. Got a project for native speaker' then levered himself into a chair at my kitchen table. He took a good look around, his lips quivering as though he were onto a particularly tasty sugar cube. It was a translating job, he said. It involved checking the grammar in a book he had written himself.

Professor Jiang's spoken English was very clumsy and I had great difficulty understanding him. His book, he said though, was about the lessons he had learned from life. I found it hard to believe he had written an entire book in English.

'I want the students here to use it in English class. So they can learn from my mistakes'. It seemed a curious form of public self-criticism. But then, according to the reliable accounts of Lou Da, Jiang's reputation had been under a cloud since a series of past indiscretions with his students.

'I'll help' I said. He broke into a broad smile of retreating gums. The worn leather satchel he carried I only just noticed. It turned out that it held the first shipment of paper to check. He pulled it out with some effort and dumped it on the table as he left.

I opened on a random page and read

'...just one woman good for me. Young men do not realise the important fact. Takes knowledge of behaving with women and knowing many women even after the marrying...'

The day before the start of classes a meeting was called for the ten English teachers, both foreign and native. Professor Jiang was there. He winked at me as though we both shared a dirty secret. This was a pre-term departmental planning meeting. Because Mr. Gong was busy taking a nap in the office on his foldable bed, it was Ms Lu the Vice Dean who chaired. She did this in a room of framed certificates and the lingering smell of disinfectant. But she had not prepared an agenda. Instead she waited until we had all crowded in and then asked

'What ideas have you all got?'

It turned out that no one had any ideas.

'You!' she shouted, 'What ideas do *you* have?' She was pointing at me. I made a mental note not to smile encouragingly at her ever again. My big idea for this term was going to involve bullying those boys who read papers under the desk. It was not an idea I wanted to share.

'What sort of ideas do you want?' I asked. She shrugged, defeated.

'Just a chance for fresh thinking' she said. What the hell. Term would be governed by fate, and fate, as many Chinese well knew, took care of itself.

I went to the photocopy shop. I turned round and found that the little pig-tailed fruit stall girl had followed me in.

'What are you doing?' she asked, fascinated that the foreigner could be doing usual human type activities - copying, and even some kind of speaking.

'Preparing for class' I said. A few minutes later she followed me from the photocopier to the printer

'What are you doing now?'

'Still preparing for class' I said 'I have to make lots of these' and I held up the paper. She was satisfied with my answers. Being alien, anything I did was novel; and strangely therefore, almost anything I might do, had become completely acceptable.

'What is your name?' I asked

'Ai Li' she said.

'Ai Li is a good name' I said.

'What is your name?'

'Han Jie'

'A Chinese name?' she asked, puzzled.

'Yes' I said 'But I have another name too'

'What name?'

'Justin'

She mulled this over.

'That is not a real name!' she shouted decisively.

'It is a foreign name' I said.

'What does it mean?' she asked

'It means…' I got my dictionary out '…*justice*' I said. She flashed a look of suspicion beyond her years. Then she smiled and said

'My name is prettier'.

'It is' I agreed. It was indeed. Ai Li meant *Lovely*.

Later that day a small rally for teaching staff was held in one of the university halls. Vice President Yao gave it a passionate ending, shouting about how we were all to do well in the coming term. He shook his fists and railed to the sky and I forgot that I had once thought him uncharismatic. Mr. Yao did not mention quality teaching.

Model Citizens

Bicycles returned and Zhoushan road became clogged again with people and speeding taxis. The students were dribbling back for our second term. The giant German holed up inside, I saw him through the window deep in study, practicing writing his characters in sweeps and flourishes that seemed ludicrously delicate for a man of his size. It was easy to spot what had changed - what had gone, what had come. But much had stayed constant. Rubbish still piled up on the roadsides and outside the communal skips, and dogs, sea gulls and bottle collectors were back to trawl amongst them. There was still no pavement on Zhoushan road and the kids walked in the road. The Irises behind the barbed wire the school had planted instead of a pavement though, looked gorgeous.

Progress had returned to the front door of the foreign teacher's block. Sixty or more workers were digging a trench for an internet cable from the main gates to the front door of the foreign teachers' block. They worked all day and most of the night, with the sound of drilling continuing into the early hours and beginning once more at dawn. For once they had technological assistance - a mechanical digger stuck in the mud alongside them. I began to return home a much longer route via the back gates of campus, for whenever I passed the digger its operator stared at me while his equipment remained in motion, and I feared he might maim his comrades. Still, with all the noise, the crowds, the dirt and the sleeplessness that clawed at our door, I felt at home once more.

To drive home the point, University Radio began its frenzied broadcasts again. Figures in combat fatigues began to parade outside. They were out there now, stomping past the cable trench diggers and noodle sellers, past Mrs. Ping the key maker and Mr. Hong the rubbish tender. They marched to the field were they muddied their plimsolls and chanted patriotic songs. Air raid sirens went off - each time these troops scurried for cover. Later we found out that these were not from a crack PLA unit, but were just Educated People's new students undergoing their compulsory patriotic military training. It had been this way across China ever since the students had been cut down at Tiananmen.

Then I was in front of the forty two again with the chalk and the blackboard and a small mug of green tea. Lei Shen sat on his own again. But so too did Tian Fei. Chang Er, she explained later, was sick.

I ran the class on inspirational figures. I explained mine: Churchill, Mandela, the writer Bruce Chatwin.

'Who are your greatest role models?' I asked.

'Yao Ming' blurted Fei Lian, who apparently thought himself a master of subtlety as he read a newspaper under the desk.

'A basketball star?'

'He is a famous Chinese all around the world. He gives our China honour' he said. I asked him if honour was important and he stared at me to see if I were joking.

'The most important' he said. Around the class arose a murmur of agreement. Class monitor Chang Xu stood up. She had come back refreshed after a summer housing street kids in Hebei province.

'Our sportsmen show us discipline. How to keep moving forward and not to accept second place'.

Tian Fei chose this point to stand up 'Do not forget China's true heroes' she said 'What about our chairman. What about Zhou Enlai, and Deng Xiaoping?' The mention of such names seemed to hush everyone else into submission. 'Zhou Enlai especially' she said 'his thought was always with the people, never with himself'.

'It is true' said Chang Xu, standing up to join in, unwilling to let Tian Fei take all the credit. 'Zhou Enlai is a hero to the Chinese people. He was loyal, he was patriotic and he was never selfish'.

'Anybody else?' I asked. There were no takers. To disagree with the choice of Zhou seemed to be heresy. I never could understand this choice. I understood the appeal of Mao whose strength had united the country and freed the masses from the tyranny of foreigners, warlords, and landlords. I understood Deng's value too. He was after all, the man who had brought reform and opening and lifted millions out of poverty. But Zhou Enlai? Conventional wisdom allocated him love for his steady hand, for his moderation of the Helmsman's excesses. In the Cultural Revolution he had pushed the students back to university after they had spent months on the road rectifying their teachers. He had intervened to save historical artefacts targeted by red guards. The giant sandalwood bodhisattva in Lingyin temple's main hall had been rescued by a simple phone call.

Yet to me Zhou embodied the politician. He had swung between factions as necessary. He had avoided the chop whilst more forthright men had been punished. Zhou had always been careful to sing the chairman's tune. While Chang Xu called this quality 'loyalty', it sounded more like cowardice. Then I wondered if the elevation of Zhou had been a conscious decision by China's rulers. Zhou the loyal had been a consensus seeker, one who submitted to authority even as authority failed. He seemed to be a model of citizenship in the new China, where to challenge the consensus was to invite anarchy.

At the end of class both Chang Xu, the class monitor, and Tian Fei came to the podium. Lei Shen grinned and watched from a distance.

'What do you think of our Zhou Enlai?' Xu asked expectantly. Tian Fei looked suddenly unsure, perhaps recognising that I may have been put on the spot. I thought about it for a few seconds.

'He was a great man' I said, avoiding possible political trouble. Xu raised her eyebrows, then smiled.

'See you next time' she said, and she walked out of the room, where her comrades waited for her.

'Is that what you really think?' asked Tian Fei.

'No' I admitted 'But what could I tell Chang Xu?'

She sighed.

'You are thinking like a Chinese' she said. She did not mean this as a compliment. I was far behind the Chinese rebel when it came to imposing my values on the world.

Next week I ran a class on injustice. I had a vague idea the themes would be familiar - the plight of the peasants or official corruption perhaps. I should have known China better.

'Injustice is oppression!' called Fei Lian. This sounded like a stock phrase he had been taught in political class.

'So what kind of injustice do you want to fix?' I asked. He pondered this, surprised at being asked to justify his previous statement.

'Hatred of black people' he said obsequiously 'In America there is a lot of this. Michael Jackson had an operation to become white but the American government would still not give him the rights of white people' he added, looking most serious. I explained that in my opinion, while racism might be a feature of our West life, I did not think it was directly connected to Michael Jackson and his identity issues.

'Not true!' shouted Fei Lian 'We know that people of Westlife countries are often racist'.

'Perhaps there is racism in all countries' I suggested 'including China'. That shook things up, and suddenly they were all talking

'China?' asked Dong Jie.

'Not true!' repeated Fei Lian. And he stood up. 'Why do you say such things?' His classmates fell silent.

'Sit down' I said. Lian still stood there with his arms crossed like a wilful child. I repeated myself. He did not budge but said something in Chinese that was not designed for me to understand. So I walked to the door as deliberately as I could, and opened it.

'Get out' I said. We stared at each other. The words of the University Radio had never seemed so crystal clear. But then he did get up and out. And I closed the door after him. I walked back to the podium and tried hard to follow the lesson schedule.

Next day I found a note slipped under the door. It said in a meandering scrawl:

> *Dear Justin,*
> *I am too naughty and too childish. I really realised my mistake and defect. I am disorganised and have no discipline. By this moral I will rectify my attitude and change myself into a good boy.*
> *Your Student,*
> *Fei Lian*

Later he knocked on my door too.

'I'm sorry' he said 'I was too emotional. I lost a lot of face with my classmates'.

Kristel and I settled back into the routines of teaching. They had become very familiar. They involved the same radio wake ups, the same mess, chalk, and interruption. I built myself a new nest of chalk stubs. The podium became a shambles of paper and dust. It was truly mine, all mine. We ran classes on business terms, common slang, and concepts of politeness. We organised roleplay and forced improvisations from them. Then I ran a class on memorable memories.

As was often the case, it was Tian Fei who stood up first.

'I remember when my father died' she began 'my mother looked after me alone. She wrote calligraphy all day and sold her writings to earn money. One day when I came home she held me in her arms. She told me we did not choose to be women. That life is not easy for women. She told me to remember 'Women hold up half of heaven''.

Tiny Bai Nien stood up like an anxious meerkat. She seemed determined to overcome her shyness through sheer force of will.

'I doctored my exam scores once' she said 'so my parents wouldn't punish me for bad grades. But my father was too smart and found out. He threw water over me and beat me with a stick'.

In this open spirit most of the class told a realistic sounding tale. Many of them were about lessons at school. Some were about deaths in the family. There were stories of regret and nostalgia, youthful joy and minor struggles. Wang De stood up, big as an ox - not so long ago the men of his house were harnessing themselves to the plough.

'A smart man came to the village when I was little. I was looking for frogs and I saw him talking to the elders. He looked Chinese. But he did not speak Chinese. He was looking for a place to build a factory' he said 'I asked my mother why he did not speak Chinese. She said because he is a *xiangjiao ren* - a banana person. Later I found out that he was from Hong Kong, which...' he could not resist adding 'is China too'

'A banana person?' I questioned. Some of the students began to snigger.

'Because on the surface their skin is yellow' he said 'but underneath, they are white'.

I could not help myself. I laughed. The students laughed

harder. I tried to control myself by focusing on rubbing down the board. Dust flew. I sneezed repeatedly.

'Someone is missing you!' shouted a voice from the back of the room. We laughed some more but had nothing to say by the time the bell trilled.

Pilgrimages

The white flower of the Osmanthus trees bloomed in parks close to the lake. Back on campus digging and demolition was decreasing to a vaguer background hum. The cable trench had been finished and with their feeble sledgehammering, the acrobats appeared to be under a half-hearted spell. A 'French café' opened on Zhoushan road, its speciality was pure fusion and not entirely edible: Belgian waffle coated in pork floss.

We, the foreign teachers of Educated People had discovered early on that there was something that united us more profoundly than our common 'Westlife' heritage, and that was the University Radio broadcasts. Johann, the giant German dampened it by placing a bucket over the speaker closest to his window. This ruse, however, was uncovered and the bucket confiscated. Soon instead somebody disabled the speaker by disconnecting its wires. Despite protestations we all had our own warm suspicions about who might have been responsible. Still disconnection turned out to have been only a temporary solution.

Recently Professor Darling had pulled a policy U-turn and turned against the radio. We were glad to have him join our camp. Indeed he was soon leading it. Eventually he formed Johann, Kristel and me into a delegation and led us to on a visit to the school authorities.

'Radio instils discipline' protested Da, after we had marched into his busy office and caught him with his feet on the desk. But we insisted on seeing Mr. Yao all the same. Half an hour later he came down looking a little worn, and apparently wary of us.

'Please turn down the radio Mr. Vice President' pleaded Darling 'Our quality teaching is suffering. We need to sleep'. Vice President Yao looked visibly relieved. This was just a simple complaint.

'I can't do it' he said 'it is not my responsibility'. He seemed to be adhering to the lessons of Sun Tzu. (*Lesson 18: therefore, when capable, feign incapacity*).

'We do not have this power. But you do Mr. Vice President.

This is why we have come to you' said Darling. (*Lesson 23: pretend inferiority and encourage his arrogance*). Mr. Yao stroked his chin.

'Maybe we can switch off some of them near the Foreign teachers block' he said.

'The one outside the window?' asked Johann, hopefully.

'We need them all either off or turned down!' insisted Meny.

'I don't know if this can be done. Maybe just one' said Yao.

(*Lesson 25: when [they are] united, divide [them]*).

'There is very strong reason to help' said Kristel 'you pay for foreign teachers. But if they cannot sleep they cannot perform quality teaching. The radio stops quality teaching'. Vice President Yao visibly sagged. We kept up this line of attack, taking it in turns to dish it out (*Lesson 24: keep him under a strain and wear him down*).

'Yes' he said finally 'We need sleep. We need strong teachers. The radio must stop'.

For a blissful week, the radio volume was cut in half. But after that it slowly crept back up again. It was a classic Chinese feint (*Lesson 17: all warfare is based on deception*).

As I ran these days, I noticed the usual neighbourhood references such as Mrs. Ping the key maker and Mr. Hong the rubbish tender, had been joined. For by day Johann lumbered around while the students gasped at the sight of him. By night he parked himself at a street stall at the end of Zhoushan Road and drank draught lager poured from a plastic barrel run up from downtown. The place was Mr. Xo's. He did brisk business in plates of peanut or preserved vegetable, and fried fish if his wife cared to whip it up on the outdoor wok.

'This is the heart of the neighbourhood!' he claimed. Certainly Johann seemed to think so. But since the itinerants, teachers, students were all here for the food and the never-ending beer tap, Mr. Xo's was no idle boast. He was an ex-labourer. He had migrated from the countryside, slaved for years on the construction sites of the new China, and bought a lively hovel behind the stall: he knew what the people wanted.

I often found Johann being challenged there by the locals. Unfailingly they were despatched a little later, drunken and defeated. Johann drank into the night. He drank amongst grease and steam. He drank when it rained, stood inside the kitchen while the floor turned to swamp. He drank *baijiu* with the itinerants and beer with the students -

making them late for curfew. Sometimes I joined him.

The street did not tire early. Extended flat bed trucks rolled by carrying gigantic concrete tubes filled with smoking tubing.

'New plumbing' said Mr. Xo.

A stocky woman arrived with a tricycle and a game which involved bursting balloons with a wildly tuned electronic pistol.

'Doesn't work' said Mr. Xo.

Male students roamed in packs. Mr. Xo commented on everything.

'Noisy students' said Mr. Xo 'big trouble'. Johann often swapped cigarettes with him: Double Happiness for Dutch rolling tobacco. He would listen politely to Xo's aimless chatter and occasionally expound on his drunken exploits.

'I made a pilgrimage when I was a teenager' said Johann, licking his whiskers. 'I cycled around the distilleries of Scotland. I still have the scars' he said, guffawing and raising his trousers to display evidence of some nasty fall.

The raucous laugh was his defining personality trait - he found mirth in much. Just one time did he become so serious that I forgot this. On this occasion he had leaned over the plastic table and said 'Modern Chinese Characters. It is what I hate most about this new China'. He had swilled his drink and studied me for a reaction.

'When the communists came in they conducted a few studies on how to modernise the written language' he said 'it was too hard to teach you know, the old system. The one they still use in Taiwan and Hong Kong. So the communists were going to do away with the whole set of characters. The whole lot. Thousands of years worth.'

'But they didn't'

'No. They were going to go for the Latin alphabet. But there was an outcry. Scholars were jailed'. He knocked back the beer and called for another. Xo broke free from his banter with the customers and poured a couple more plastic cups from the barrel.

'In the end they decided to just amputate these old characters. Tear the limbs off them. Cripple them.' He pulled an insane face. 'That is a problem with people' he said 'They use the future as an excuse to destroy. They do not understand what they have until is gone'.

The Anniversary

One clear morning Mr. Jiang came by to discuss the translation.

'Can you work faster?' he neighed. But I was going plenty fast already. He had come round to nag twice already this week, and twice last week - all beyond a reasonable hour. I would chaperone him downstairs by the arm and take him out of the gate and onto the street. I was not going to change pace, I explained. Secretly I thought I might resort to burning parts of his book if he did not cease from pester.

It was at these times that I noticed the new Gatekeeper. This one did not nap inside the guard post. Instead he stood to attention for every vehicle passing through the gates. His name was Dehuai. He was a youngster with a round face of such merriment that it reduced his smart uniform to fancy dress. I began stopping to chat as I passed, and learned that he had never spoken with a foreigner before, had grown up in Anhui and had not completed secondary school.

One cold evening, Kristel left him a small bag of biscuits to help keep him warm in his little guard post. He tried to decline them. She insisted that we expected nothing from him; that this was purely a friendly gesture. He relented awkwardly. But once inside the light of his box - through which we could see in better than he could see out - we watched him smile gleefully and ravage the lot.

The temperature plummeted. Fallen leaves brittled with frost. On my way to class I could almost hear them crunch against the taxi horns and itinerant shouts. It was under these conditions that Dehuai called to me one morning.

'It is the 20th Anniversary in one week' he whispered in some kind of subterfuge 'the radio will play from an early hour'. I lowered my voice too.

'Anything else?' I asked, suddenly finding myself so caught up his delivery that I seemed to be playing agent handler. He scratched his nose and gave the question some thought.

'There will be a party for all students and staff this Saturday' he said 'everybody has to go'.

'Everybody?'

'Not me' he laughed 'I am not important. I am staying here. But Foreign teachers...they have to go'

I thanked him for this intelligence and later disseminated it to all occupants of the foreign teacher's block.

'I am going to be woken up every day by radio and then again on my weekend?' spluttered Johann at his door 'No way'. The German insisted he would not getting out of bed - 20th anniversary or not. But I suspected this was a battle he would not win. Kristel and I chose a different tactic and agreed to join in. Saturday rolled around. Today was twenty years to the day when Elder Wang had formally opened the University of Educated People. The radio fired up. We got out of bed, picked up tea and *mantou* (steamed bread roll) at the cafeteria, and joined the ranks of students already lined up outside in jogging gear outside the library.

We were organised into teams. Each team was given a red flag imprinted with yellow characters. I studied it with the help of my dictionary. It said *'20 years educating people intellectually and morally'*. The teams jogged out of the school grounds, past Dehuai the gate guard, out onto Zhoushan road, and towards the supermarket, the same one I ran to every other day. Mrs. Ping the keymaker continued her work but her son stopped playing and watched as the fifty of us passed, chanting slogans. Each team leader held aloft a flag, we were a parade of flapping red, catching the attention of the street people.

I ran at the head with my team's leader. He turned to me.

'I am so happy!' he gushed between breaths 'this is the first time I have talked with a foreigner'. He became so out of breath at telling me this that I had to take the flag off him. He was grateful for this excuse to fall back. I now led the team, waving the red flag proudly and fruitlessly trying to join in with the chants. On the other side of the road, I watched Kristel do the same. It was strangely exhilarating, pounding these streets in the crisp air, part of something.

When we finally made it back, the rest of the school's students were gathering in the grounds. I noticed the gardeners had been busy laying out the flowers again, this time combining them with clutches of red balloons. At the back seated in a camp chair, Professor Darling sunned himself. Reiko and Richard had staked their places too. But there was no Johann. To dampen the radio he had placed a bucket over the nearest speaker and was attempting an unsanctioned lie in. We stood there in the autumn sun as the students gathered, and the dignitaries took their places on a raised table far away to the front, seated before the library as though it were some kind of altar. They took it in turns to step up the microphone. From afar I could make out Vice-President Yao flailing his arms around. But I couldn't hear him. With a few thousand students lolling around and chattering good-naturedly it was impossible to hear even as the dignitaries had their words broadcast over Lou Da's prized speaker system. We all gave up straining, and instead joined in the chatter and played with the balloons.

By the end of the morning it was all over. The crowds were dispersing and the dignitaries were off to a banquet - we would be joining them in the evening. At the entrance to the Foreign teacher's block stood a red-eyed Johann.

'Couldn't sleep' he growled '...*twenty years of educating people intellectually and morally*' he mimicked. It appeared the buckets had stopped nothing. From the speakers hidden in the flowerbed under Johann's bedroom window, he had heard everything. He was too angry to attend the banquet that evening. Mr. Gong was not. Neither was Party Secretary Teacher Xu, who challenged him to a drinking duel and made sure the both of them were red faced and steaming before we had even arrived. Ms Lu the Vice Dean was there, and so was Professor Jiang, who was pretending to join in occasionally. I noticed he was not swallowing his shots, merely swilling the stuff against his lips. Lou Da was there too. He tapped me on the shoulder.

'I have heard of your work for Jiang' he said loudly 'He is getting a very good deal. Remember everyone is trying to make money. People will have no regard for you. They just want to get ahead' he looked blatantly at Jiang, who was too immersed in his drinking pretence to notice.

'His book is a business enterprise' he said 'in fact he has recently asked me to do him a favour too. He said to me 'pay the publisher some money and I'll pay you too'. He wanted me to pass this money for him. He said 'Da I have a reputation to maintain. But you are young and unknown. It will not matter to you''. Da snorted derisively.

'Jiang was too worried about losing face to do it himself'.

'So did you do this for him?' I asked. Da grinned.

'Of course' he said.

The more I thought about this the more annoyed I became. Finally I walked over to Professor Jiang, still laughing at the ongoing duel between Teacher Xu and Mr. Gong. He saw me approaching.

'Ah' he said 'my translator'

'Translator?' I asked 'That depends. You should pay for my work'

He feigned seriousness.

'I am making nothing for myself' he said 'so how can I give money to you?' But I did not believe this. I took the bottle of *baijiu* from Mr. Gong, who had been caressing it only half-heartedly. I poured two shots and shoved one rather rudely under Jiang's nose.

'*Ganbei*' I said. Jiang slowly picked up the glass.

'*Ganbei*' he said, and forced it down.

I refilled them.

'To your health!' I said. We downed them.

'For your wife' I said. He pretended to down his.

'You have something left' I pointed out most ungraciously. He knocked it back in earnest.

'We southerners' he began 'we don't...' but the audience was too large for him to contemplate finishing this poor excuse

'To the students!' I said mercilessly. And the glasses were drained.

Mr. Jiang's cheeks were beetroot. Mr. Ji popped round to prod the drunken teachers. He pushed Mr. Gong, and tapped Teacher Xu on the shoulder. She flicked him off. Then he found Professor Jiang in his state.

'*Aaii* Professor Jiang' he said in the most eloquent accent he could muster 'I am most surprised!'

Mr. Gong lifted his head at this cue, and using Ms Lu as a crutch, roused himself to his feet to slur loudly

'We shan't want to do this again!'

The next day Lou Da called.

'Professor Jiang has given me something for you' he said. Kristel and I headed up to see him in his office. He gave me an envelope: it was full of cash.

Fire

By November, lotus stems on the lake had crumpled to flaccid ribbons. Mr. Jiang came by and I told him the translation was almost complete. It was nearing bonfire night.

At the direction of Lou Da, I decided to visit the security department to see the Security Manager. He was a stocky little man with piggy eyes.

''Night of the fire' is coming' I told him 'and the foreigners would like to build a fire'. He almost fell out of his chair.

'Fire!' he shouted. 'Why?' he added, struggling to recompose himself. Why did the foreigners want to burn things? On hearing such surprise, Teacher Xu came from her office next door to see what the fuss was about. I explained to them both that this 'Night of Fire' was an important cultural event for the British. Yes we built fires and burned effigies. I smiled with as much charm as I could muster, and suggested it would be a useful education for our students. They would learn a bit about the foreigners' culture. With all the fire and burning, we'd certainly show them barbarian.

Teacher Xu stroked her considerable drinking chin, and nodded to the Security Manager.

'You can have your fire' she said. There were only two caveats: it had to be out of sight of the main school grounds, and at least fifteen metres from any building. This sounded fair to me.

I started growing excited. I told my students and Chang Er asked

'Will there be games?' Yes I said. There would be games as well as fire.

'What about dancing?' asked Lei Shen. Not really, I said.

'And fireworks!' shouted Fei Lian. We would not have fireworks. Scarcely a month went by in China without a report of some fireworks factory - illegal and often staffed by school kids - blowing up. None of the foreign teachers were willing to trust their health to Chinese gunpowder, even if the ancestors of these people had invented it.

Kristel and I scoured the area for a place to build a fire and found a secluded spot within the campus grounds. It was an overgrown area of weeds and building debris which had so far been overlooked for development. It was a place in which we could practice our rituals far from prying neighbours. Lei Shen and I searched the neighbourhood for firewood. The boiler houses held ample stores but were far from willing to part with it. Wood was a precious commodity, and an essential one: the forests were far away. I bartered at silly prices and even stooped to begging, but none of these boiler house managers was willing to budge.

The brothel lanterns began to fire up and it was getting dark. I was about to give up and turn back when Lei Shen ran up to me breathlessly.

'Got a deal!' he shouted triumphantly. He had been offered a tricycle trailer load of wood in return for the weekly wages of a peasant. It was too good an offer to pass up.

Next day the boiler house manager, a slight man with a struggling beard faithfully tricycled through the campus gates. The trailer was only half full of wood, but it was better than nothing. I directed him to our spot and we unloaded the trailer. Two lampshade gardeners had been trowelling up flowerbeds close by. The shorter one ran over.

'What are you doing?' she asked

'Making a fire' I said. She looked the boiler house manager up and down.

'You don't need' she said to me 'first ask me. There is wood here. Much wood' She grabbed me by the arm and marched me behind the nearest concrete teaching block. Then she thrust me forward past a unique row of trees.

'There' she said, with her hands outstretched. I looked. There was a whole field of debris: kindling, uprooted scrub, even huge beams from a demolished house. I wondered if long ago it had belonged to the family of Mrs. Ho. The boiler house manager, who had followed me over, ran back to empty the rest of his trailer like a child on sugar, and set about refilling.

As the boiler house manager peddled away with a brand new burden, Kristel and I lit a large fire fifteen metres away from Administrative Block A. The students began to arrive as night fell. Tian Fei was one of them.

'Fire drives away bad luck' she said gleefully.

'You believe in luck?' I asked.

'Of course I believe in luck' she said 'it is different to fate. That I do not believe in'. I headed back to the flat to collect a bucket of water and apples to bob. Then I headed back. I passed a grinning Dehuai.

'Having fun?' he asked. Something seemed to have gone wrong back there. The campus had been lit an eerie orange. I ran to the back of the block where I found fields of flame - at least thirty fires now burned out there. Educated People never burned fires. But tonight they were making an exception.

It took me some time to find our fire amongst the competition. It was the one which Fei Lian leapt over while his classmates watched him in amazement. It was the one with the guy beside it, the guy with the papier-mache face and felt cowboy hat that was not such a terrible likeness to US President George W Bush. The military fan, Li Xun was poking it gingerly as though it might leap up and bite him. Even Mr. Ji had turned up. Mesmerised by the fire tonight, he had no questions for me.

Professor Darling, who had been laughing at the back with Johann, lurched forward. He picked up the guy and with it under his arm, marched on the flames.

'Good riddance!' He shouted, and toppled the thing in. It went up in a flare of smoke, the hat melted to caramel. The foreign teachers whooped and chugged gulps from beer cans. I looked around. Even Chang Xu the class monitor was having a strange sort of fun, watching the effigy burn while her classmates' heads and bodies got wetted in the bobbing bucket. Some of the more impulsive boys joined Fei Lian as he once more began to leap across the flames, hollering like a Sioux warrior. Lei Shen slurped his beer and stared at the embers of the guy. He leant over with his hand cupped

'Behaving like this in China' he said 'is not polite'.

Party

We still pretended it was summer. So not far from the Broken bridge we held a barbeque. Sycamore leaves fluttered to the lake surface - its waters were becoming clogged with rot. From the hills floated the chirping of caged birds. Lei Shen chewed chicken wings whole - nothing was to be wasted, not even bone. It was what he had been taught since he had been a child.

'I have a job' he said 'I can work with my father selling cigarette lighters to foreign countries' It sounded good and I congratulated him. Many of his classmates were struggling to find work.

'I want to join' he added.

'Join what?' I asked.

'The party' he said. Lei Shen gave up on the final mouthful and spat a wad of gristle into reeds. 'The interviews are soon' he said 'It's good for business, increasing *guanxi*' He shot me a confirmatory look, to see whether I found this as impressive as he did.

I turned to Tian Fei.

'You too?'

She nodded.

'Of course' she said 'If Chang Xu does not try stop me'.

I knew already that she was sold, but I could not help myself.

'Why do you want to join?' I asked.

'I want to help change China' she shrugged 'We are so huge. There are so many people struggling. There is so much to do'. I wondered how long she would hold onto this idealism.

'We are still trying to achieve socialism' she added.

'*Really?*' I asked, incredulous - irritated even. Tian Fei was so stubborn. So idealistic. No, *ideological* and rigid.

'Then what about all this - those towers, the shops over there, all the foreign brand cars on the streets. Is your China really trying to achieve communism?'

She looked at me pitifully.

'Marx said the proletariat would rise against the exploiters' she said. 'But we did not even have a proletariat. We just had farmers. Now we have a proletariat. They work in the factories so hard. China is unequal. It has to stay socialist'.

'Do you hear this?' I prodded Shen. He shrugged

'This is what our leaders say'

Tian Fei began toying with a chicken wing. A couple of ducks dipped out of the water.

'How else can there be justice?' she asked 'The rich are so rich. The poor are breaking their backs. If there is no justice then I cannot bear it'

'Millions of farmers lives have improved' I said. But it seemed an odd position, defending the communist party. Tian Fei shook her head.

'We do not share. Even in the old China there was sharing. But not now. Everybody must look after themselves. It is a tragedy'. Her vision sounded like something from the hydraulic past, when the masses had been mobilised to communal dyke building to save the group where the individual might otherwise perish. She wanted to do something. She wanted to *act* just as Marx and the rest of the communist pantheon had urged. But had not the sage Lao Tzu said 'practice inaction and the people will look after themselves'?

'*Lai*' said Shen 'we are just people'. Because in any case, the chicken was getting cold.

Over the next weeks I found that almost all of my favourite students were set on joining the party. It made absolute sense. It was the way to get ahead. All those managers, those wannabe businesspeople, they wanted to join the party. The best and brightest left college, joined the party and became mired in its interests. Communist Party rule seemed self-sustaining. It would go on forever...or at least until the peasants decided they had not been sweetened enough and once more rose in anger.

I saw Chang Er and her boyfriend strolling through the campus one morning. Her mouth dropped when she saw me.

'Hello' she said, catching herself 'This is Bo'. Bo did not look at me but studiously stared at the administrative block. Why it merited a glance from anyone but a demolition crew was anyone's guess. He did not even look me in the eye as we shook hands. Most Chinese shook hands like a dead sardine. Chinese culture discouraged body contact between strangers. But this was the first time in China I found myself holding it against someone. I knew I was being unreasonable but I could not help myself. It had been a while since I had seen Er. She had not even been coming to classes. I could guess why and I decided not to make things awkward by asking her whether she really had been ill. Instead I asked

'Are you joining the party?'

She nodded. And becoming suddenly animated

'It will take a lot of effort!' she said 'I have been so busy' she glanced nervously at Bo, who was now making a rather intensive study of the weather too. 'We have to go' she said anxiously, and they left.

I dropped some paperwork off at Lou Da's office. He was in there examining his nails. I mentioned the upcoming applications the students were making to the Communist Party. This seemed to annoy him for he waved his hand irritably and got up to make a flask of tea.

'At university I was not invited' he said 'I fell out with my main teacher. He wanted money to support my application. But why should I give him money? Mostly his job was drinking tea. He got paid enough'. Had I not known Da better I may have thought such timing to have been an act of calculated irony.

I called Chang Wen later that afternoon. I knew he was not a party member, but I wanted to hear how things had worked when he had been a student.

'I was invited to join the party' he said 'But I didn't want to. I was thinking of joining one of the five other parties that are allowed by the Communist Party. But then I realised they just do what the Communist Party asks them. They are not real alternatives. There was no choice. Secretly I supported China Democratic Party - I told you this' Indeed he had. 'I did not want to say *No* to the party' he continued 'because perhaps in the future they would make my life hard. Call me counter-revolutionary, or 'running dog' maybe. Instead I told them 'I don't know yet. I worry I am not good enough for the party'. Every time they asked me, this is what I said. Eventually, they stopped asking me to join'.

We resumed Chinese class. Teacher Nan still cycled in. She had a modern villa up in the hills near the tea plantations of Dragon Well. Teacher Nan had gone on a group tour to Yunnan province this summer. She proudly showed us photographs from it: mountains, jungle, her tour cap toting daughter and a rounded man outside the whitewashed terraces of old Lijiang. Then she showed us pictures of home: one of her daughter - teary this time - on her first day at private school, another of her bureaucrat husband posing beside his Mercedes. Then I asked her whether she too was a member of the Chinese Communist Party.

'Of course' she smiled 'I come from a good family'. Surely this was the ultimate proof that party membership was no longer the preserve only of those who believed in Marx and his dictums: *from each according to his abilities, to each according to his needs.*

A week later I heard a knock at the door. I opened it to find Lei Shen stood there wide-eyed, and carrying in a wallet two slices of paper.

'My CV in English' he said 'to help my party application. Please can you check it'. I poured us tea and sat down to read. Under the title 'Lei Shen', he had penned a strap line: *I believe I can fly,* it said.

Then the document listed his education and work experience (his father's factory). It was the 'interests' section that truly caught my eye.

Alongside basketball, football, and seeing friends, he had added *discussing with foreign friends,* and *making fires.*

'They want to hear about fires?'

Lei Shen smiled confidently.

'Yes' he said.

Nurses

In the midst of term I came down with something. For a few days liquids drained from both ends and then I woke up to find I was too weak to get out of bed. Kristel finished her first class of the day, then cancelled the rest. She came back, dragged me to my feet, hitched my arm around her shoulders and walked me outside to the street. There she hailed a cab and took me to hospital. I was brought to an examination room and laid out on a stretcher. The doctor had a rare Chinese bald head and the kind of hawkish eyes that spelled no nonsense. He asked me to pull off my shirt and then began to poke about my belly. But he had left the door open to a waiting area outside, and now a couple of curious onlookers poked their heads in.

'What is the problem with the foreigner?' asked the first stranger, a middle-aged man in a tracksuit.

'Stomach problem' the doctor told them. This conclusion attracted more spectators. The nurse stuck me on a drip. Kristel went out and called the University. Lou Da was with us within the hour. He pushed past the small crowd that had gathered at the door and began to discuss charges with the doctor. I did not understand everything, but I did hear Da suggest they charged less for the medicine.

'He is a rich foreigner' said the doctor.

'Not that rich' said Da

'How rich?'

'4000 yuan a month' The audience cooed and the part about 4000 yuan seemed to echo.

'How much?' asked the tracksuited man, who was still gawping.

'4000' repeated Da.

'Not much for a foreigner' said the track suited man.

'Not much' agreed the doctor. He reduced the price with the consent of the audience. This was indeed lucky for the university, because under the terms of our contracts, it was Educated People who would be paying.

The next day I was able to walk to the University Medical Centre while Kristel was in class. It was a concrete cuboid with an interior borrowed from a Soviet gymnasium. Here they were going to stick saline solution into my arm through a drip. I taught in between drips. On my first evening in the Medical Centre there was another young man in there. He had floppy hair and a leather jacket that leant him some of the air of a Chinese Fonz, and he was there for no standard medical problem.

'…You're cute' I heard him say 'kiss me!' He had thrown this at the nurse, a handsome woman with - rare in China - an hourglass figure which she had hidden poorly in her nurse's dress. I watched her put the drip in my left hand. All the while she treated this boy like an amusing sort of pest, covertly flirting by ignoring him until he said something worthy of shooting down.

She fluttered out of the room. He looked around and noticed me for the first time. He frowned and then strolled over and slumped into a seat beside me.

'Hi' he said. His name was Ni Hai Hua. He worked for customs. He wasn't very happy because, he reckoned, all of the officers took money.

'I work on a computer' he said 'So I cannot'. The nurse breezed back in and Ni Hai Hua's attention waned. He leant backwards without taking his eyes from her.

'She is very pretty' he whispered. Next time she went out he leapt up and chased after her. He did not come back.

But I was not left on my own for long for Lou Da came to keep me company.

He sat teetering on the edge of a chair, and I guessed he was itching to ask me something.

'Go on' I said

'How do homosexual men meet in the UK?' he asked.

'I guess like anyone meets' I reckoned 'at bars or clubs, through friends maybe…or perhaps through dating sites or on a blind date.' For some time he sat there pondering my answers. Then he said

'Yes I know these things. But in China we think this problem is a mental illness'. Yet the Chinese psychological association had removed homosexuality from its list of mental illnesses a couple of years ago.

I began to notice rather uncomfortably the itch where the needle entered my skin.

'I have a joke' he said, brightening considerably. 'A Japanese man met a Chinese man. 'Ha!' he says 'The condoms we Japanese sell to you Chinese, are made out of used chewing gum!'' Da lifted his sage finger 'The Chinese man replied 'Maybe. But did you know that the chewing gum we Chinese sell to you Japanese, is made out of used condoms?'' He smiled expectantly. I managed a chuckle.

'I am going to write a book about China' I admitted at last. His eyes lit up.

'Will I be in it?' he asked.

'No' I said.

At lunchtime I headed back to the medical centre, and this time had the drip implanted in my right hand. Lei Shen turned up with Tian Fei in tow. I asked them how the preparation was going. Party interviews were looming. They looked at each other.

'Not good!' cried Tian Fei suddenly 'Chang Xu has been lying! She has told the Communist Party Secretary I am disloyal, that I do not have good character'.

'The study is boring' said Lei Shen, apparently unwilling to hear Fei continue. I guessed he had been hearing a lot about this recently. 'We have to learn the thought of all of our leaders' he said 'Now I read about Jiang Zemin. I read about Hu Jintao. I read about people who died a long time ago' he blew a raspberry 'We read that it is weakness to go to the temple. At least I agree with this'.

'Weakness?'

He nodded.

'Religions weaken people'

'Where did you get this idea?' I asked.

He dropped his chin and poked his tongue out ever so slightly, which I guessed meant he was thinking.

'I have experience' he said

'What experience?'

'My grandmother' he began 'She went to church often and finally became a Christian.'

'What is wrong with that?'

'She told my grandfather that he was going to the hell and she needed to save his soul. He cried that he cannot change. Now it is difficult for them to live together. My grandmother has become a little crazy. We cannot reason with her.' he repeated the raspberry thing 'her ideas are too foolish'. It seemed churlish to point out that they were no more foolish than Marxism. In any case, I imagined that Lei Shen already felt the same way.

The two of them stayed with me for some time while the saline solution dripped away. Tian Fei seemed to have forgotten about her rivalry with Chang Xu.

'Er says she is sorry she cannot come' she said 'she said wishing you a speedy recovery'. Then they left. The nurse was out getting some dinner and all of the lights in the room were out. Through the window I imagined the impossible: that stars were breaking the Hangzhou cloud-cover.

Ni Hai Hua was already there by the time I arrived the following evening. He was sunk in a plastic chair staring at the floor as though he was expecting something to burst through it. I sat down beside him.

The pretty nurse walked in. She seemed more businesslike today - picking up my hand, sticking in the drip, placing my hand back on my knee. She did not acknowledge Ni Hai Hua, and he remained oblivious. She left the room. He said

'Chinese girls are too difficult' not so much addressing me as talking to himself. 'I try-try. But nothing. They just want too much!' He turned to me for the first time 'Don't try Chinese women, foreigner. They just take your money. Not interested in love'. He sighed.

'Really?' I asked.

'This week a girl at work said also no' he said 'I gave her chocolates. But she said she wouldn't date me because we don't have the same interests' He threw his hands to the air 'I don't like to shop!' He laughed wildly and then hung his head like a beaten dog. He sat there for a further ten minutes.

'Where do you live?' he asked, suddenly mellowing. He had forgotten the girls.

Foolishly I told him. He nodded, then stood up and made to leave.

'See you soon' he said. It sounded like a threat.

I was left with shadows from outside that flit across the floor, and was relieved when Da arrived.

'I am a good friend' he said, looking pleased with himself 'I've come both times...More than Kristel even'

'Kristel is in class' I said. He waved this away.

'In China everyone wants to get rich' he said 'like your friend Chang Wen; like the students; like the doctor the other day' he clapped his hands on his knees and folded his legs like some delicate sage 'but there are more important things than money' he said 'Can I tell you a story about a landlord?'

I had no chance to reply though, for he had already begun.

'This man hoarded food during a famine and the peasants had to eat bark and roots' he said 'The peasants plotted to undo this landlord. They found a scrawny horse and told the landlord it shit gold and silver. So he bought it for 30 bushels of grain. He took it inside where he could keep it safe, then it shit all over him and his expensive carpet'. He chuckled. 'Modern Chinese are greedy. But they should learn!' However it also seemed that it was only privilege that kept Lou Da's hands free from the muck of business, for his parents were wealthy and they had bankrolled him on the path he had chosen. Da looked away.

'Everyone struggles so hard against everyone else' he said 'But why work so hard? I believe in nothing. We are all just waiting to die'.

But to me it seemed that Lou Da was only partly right. The Chinese could be greedy. They were also spiteful and rude. They were clown-like and childishly naïve, yet somehow so world-weary too. The Chinese were plumbing the depths and scaling the heights - and sometimes both at once. They battled remorselessly. Occasionally their compassion knew no bounds, yet it had been said that the Chinese did not know the meaning of pity. I remembered then why I felt such great affection for these people, for they seemed the most human of us all.

10. Butterflies

There came a knock on the door one morning some time before University Radio set itself loose. It was obviously not the work of Mrs. Ho - she would have cared little for niceties. I pulled myself into the nearest trousers and opened the door. Tian Fei stood there shivering dutifully, her arm outstretched. An object wrapped in clear plastic sat in her hand.

'Moon cake' she explained 'for the mid autumn festival'. On her back she carried a rucksack.

'New bag?' I asked. She shook her head.

'I need it to carry cake'.

A lot of cake by the look of it.

'Here' she said impatiently. Tian Fei thrust the cake into my hand before marching off to the first class of the day. I closed the door and put the cake on the kitchen sideboard.

Fei was not the only visitor today. Later Chang Xu brought cake and then Betty did too; Bei Nian brought cake and so did Lou Da. In dribs and drabs several students dropped by to dish out cake. Over the next few days the sideboard became full. There was violet cake and lotus cake, red bean cake and almond and egg yolk cake. There were bite-sized cake and pan-sized cakes that might almost have satisfied a sumo wrestler at breakfast. Kristel and I ate cake for breakfast, lunch, and dinner. And sometimes we snacked on cake in between.

Moon cake clogged Johann's doorstep. And Kentucky Richard's. And Reiko's. Anything could be put in a moon cake it seemed - from tarot plant to gooseberry, from dried scallop to abalone: the more expensive the ingredients the more auspicious. The rich apparently, were taking this to new heights with their cakes of shark fin or bird's nest (swallow spit).

The Mid-Autumn Festival celebrated myth, one of the legendary archer, Hou Yi. It went something like this: in the time of the Xia, before the Shang and their records, earth had been threatened by the might of ten powerful suns. Yet Hou Yi had saved everything by shooting nine of them down. Afterwards Yi had fallen in love with the beautiful maiden, Chang'e. Here the versions of the story differ. In one Chang'e mourned Hou Yi's death through drinking an Elixir that lifts her to the moon; in another Chang'e drank an elixir to save the people from Yi's tyrannical rule - and again floated to the moon; Another had Hou Yi giving Chang'e the elixir so she would become immortal. Unfortunately in this tale Chang'e drank too much elixir and floated off again - to the moon. My favourite though again placed Hou Yi as a tyrant, this time bent on discovering an elixir of immortality. His advisers discovered, it seems, a method of creating such a product by grinding 100 adolescent boys into a single pill. But Chang'e could not bear to see committed such a terrible crime. She stole the pill - and then flew with it to the moon.

However you looked at it there was a whole lot of moon-flying. It had translated into a whole lot of cake-giving. For the mid-Autumn festival had become a pleasant form of institutionalised corruption. It was a time when the Chinese hauled themselves around the social circuits to give gifts of cake to friends, customers, and business partners. Chang Wen showed up on our doorstep a day before the pinnacle of the festival. A man of protocol such as himself had not forgotten to bring cake. Indeed his came in a beautifully ribboned basket laden with pomelo fruit.

'This is one of many deliveries' he admitted 'I have brought cake to all of my professors and fellow teachers. It is getting very expensive. But if I don't get them good cake they will feel insulted'

'Would that matter?'

'My career would become quite short' he said.

By the weekend of the main celebrations Kristel and I were becoming heartily sick of cake. The masses were rolling into Hangzhou and congregating beside the lake. Everywhere they laid out sheets of old newspaper to protect their behinds from the frost. Then they bunkered down to drink tea and pick at sunflower seeds. They did this all day in the shadow of soldiers dressed in riot gear who appeared to be waiting for some kind of storm to materialise. But it was a long good natured afternoon. At dusk VIPs were herded into prime viewing locations inside the pavilions. They were shielded from any kind of crowd madness by a large wall of police.

Then rockets began to fly. They shot from boats moored in the centre of the lake and exploded in bright showers above the oiled waters. Soon the clouds blazed as they had done when we first arrived - with butterflies and imploding stars, smiley faces, stars. Some of the fireworks burst to reveal offspring which floated down on parachutes before erupting once more like the suns of Hou Yi. No-one was going to forget that gunpowder had first been used here in China to entertain and mystify like this. It had been discovered in error by men searching for the same elixir of immortality as the archer. The earliest of descriptions comes from a Taoist manual written in the 800s. It was, unsurprisingly, a record of surprise:

> *'Some have heated together sulfur, realgar and saltpetre with honey; smoke and flames result, so that their hands and faces have been burnt, and even the whole house where they were working burned down'*

It had not taken long for men to find a true vocation for such an elixir. Tang officials had wasted little time in commissioning flamethrowers and rockets, bombs and mines. They are credited with inventing the first firearms.

When the last sparks fizzled in the lake there awoke amongst the willow shadows a frightful cacophony. This display of sound and colour had been so engrossing I had managed that rare feat in China – to forget that the neighbours existed. But now they were on the move, shuffling amongst the newspaper, jabbering, and slowly churning towards the exits. The crowd moved with a life of its own - no one chose to participate, but all played their inevitable role in building this flood. For from a bird's perspective we must have looked a single fluid, swirling and dancing along the parkways. This stream spilled into town. Like the parks before them, the highways, the malls, and the towers too soon became thoroughly bathed in people.

Separation

Dog hot pot reappeared in the caldrons of side streets while the itinerants continued their bludgeoning of metal. The constant flow of trucks arriving to dump bricks was dwindling in the cold, for Educated People's great building projects were drawing to a close. Those floating workers who built this place were about to scatter in search of work. I disturbed one of Lou Da's French lessons to find him stood by our window. Kristel remained seated at the table regarding him like the strange insect that he was. Da stared outside. My moving in to refill the tea flask seemed to break this trance

'We will have to pull down their huts' he reckoned 'they spoil the view from the library'.

Not far beyond a sign that stated *'Abide by the Social Morality'*, outside the peacock runs beside the lake one afternoon an elderly man in a buttoned down Mao suit shuffled across the path. There he stopped and raised his head.

'What does GMT mean?' he asked in English.

The stragglers who passed were astonished to hear this Chinese elder speaking a foreign tongue. I was more astonished by the absurdity of the question. *What does GMT mean?*

'GMT means *Greenwich Mean Time*' I began 'It is a measuring point for time starting at the Royal Observatory in Greenwich, which is in London...'

'I don't even understand your explanation' scoffed Kristel 'how is our friend going to manage?'

'Because he looks cleverer than you'.

The elder carefully mulled the explanation. Then he gave a thoughtful nod and allowed himself a long exhale. It occurred to me that he may have wrestled with this question for years. Then someone in the crowd that had been steadily gathering shouted

'What did the *waiguoren* say?'

The old man shrugged

'I don't know' he said, reverting to his native tongue 'I didn't understand'. He didn't seem to care for clarification - and neither did anyone else. *Laowai* could hardly be expected to make coherent sense. It was not going to get better when Mao-suit changed tactic. Suddenly pointing at Chang Wen who had joined us, he asked in Chinese

'Where is he from?'

'Hanguorren' I claimed (Korean person). This came as no surprise to anyone. Apart from to Chang Wen. And to Kristel, who leant over

'Chang Wen is not Korean' she whispered

'I see' I admitted

'I'm not Korean' added Wen, just in case there was any lingering doubt.

'No I suppose not'

I turned back to the crowd.

'My friend is not *Hanguoren*' I corrected myself 'he is *Hangzhouren*' (Hangzhou person). After all, for the Chinese, the Korean people lived in the country of Han. Meanwhile the Han people lived in the country of China.

'Where did you learn English?' I asked the old man. But I never received an answer for we were interrupted and moved on by the police, two fatties with a loudspeaker and a golf cart who seemed concerned by the congestion. For over the course of these episodes we had become encircled. At the back the most desperate voyeurs had been clinging to willow and hanging over the water hoping to glimpse the free show - this elder and those foreigners, attempting to communicate...whatever next? But it was such an obvious rule. Nothing attracted a crowd as rapidly as a crowd attracted a crowd in China.

A few days later the Japanese national football team came to play a match against China. Their players were subjected to a good coin pelting. Then China played Hong Kong. Leaving Kristel at the foot masseuse I hid in the latest opened café and watched. One of these Chinas played in red, the other in white. I was a little confused so I called to a weasel-faced man drinking at the next table.

'Which is China?' I asked.

'They are both China' he said keeping his eyes on the screen.

'Sure' I said 'but which is the white team?'

'Both China' he repeated obstinately 'white and red - both China'. His skinny friend smirked and swigged from the bottle. Since this was a somewhat less than helpful answer I decided to search for a slightly better quality of conversation. So I left and tried Mr. Zhou's instead, where I found the German.

'Do you know which team is red and which is white?' I asked. Johann shrugged.

'Who cares?' he said, with beer foam caught in his beard. The government had for some time been accused from outside of stoking xenophobia, of nurturing a peculiar Chinese style of nationalism - an inferiority complex that needed righting, a just settlement to be sought for the injured feelings of a century of shame. The international sport of football - which had been invented in China according to Chinese fans and Chinese history books - was all it took to bring such feelings to the surface.

215

Then Mr. Xo tried to sell my jacket. I had left it at his stall one evening and returned for it the next day. Xo was already smoking outside, incongruously kitted out in shades and a military greatcoat. When I told him about my jacket problem Xo picked his nose absent-mindedly and asked

'What does it look like?'

'Black' I said

'I know!' he exclaimed, as though he was *the* neighbourhood fixer. When Xo strode across the road I followed at a safe distance. He barged into a shop. It was a clothes shop, one run by an ex-student from Educated People. Xo remonstrated with an assistant. An item was pulled from the rack and handed over. Xo turned marched back through the door, where he ran into me.

'This jacket?' he asked innocently. It was mine.

'Yes' I said, snatching it back.

'In there it was safe' he said. I forgave him quickly. In this China trying to sell off your customers' clothes seemed more indicative of entrepreneurial cunning, than theft.

Then came a bowl of snails. And not just any old snails either, but stewed giant land snails that smelled of nursing homes. These snails came in an enamel bowl slapped down in front of Kristel and I as we read outside Xo's. Really it was a little too cold to be outdoors but since everybody else also seemed to think so too today, there was a measure of peace to be found on the street. In any case, with the arrival of snails I looked up and found hovering there a Chiffon-scarf wrapped woman.

'What are you doing?' asked Kristel.

'I bought them for you' she explained proudly, prodding them into position under my nose.

'Why?' I asked

'Because I want to speak English' she said 'please teach me'.

It was an innocuous enough request. But it felt like the height of insult. For a year we had been outsiders. We were not Chinese. We were *waiguorren*. As foreigners we were always in some way cut off from the hive. Even a misplaced 'Hullo!' then might serve only to reinforce this separateness, to remind the foreigner of just how different he was. A request from a stranger for a free English class had a similar effect. Furthermore, it seemed this English class requestee not only considered she had an innate right to take our time, but assumed she could secure it by making a gift, thereby placing us under obligation? Suddenly I felt I'd had enough. Enough of grasping and relentless optimism. In fact, enough of this China in which we were *Gui*: Ghosts.

Kristel and I packed up and left. The scarf wearer sat behind with her snails. Foreigners must have seemed to her, thoroughly unreasonable.

It did not take too long to realise things could be worse. A couple of weeks later, Wen, Kristel and I we were walking out into the lake on a concrete walkway when we saw coming three broad black men. I was almost shocked to see them for these were the first black men I had seen in the mainland outside of Shanghai. I stared at the men walking steadily towards us, and so did Kristel. Only when I noticed Wen's open mouth did I realise quite how rude was this behaviour, and I managed to catch my manners before any harm was done. It seemed natural for any long term foreign residents to fall to conversation. Indeed the *laowai* tourist often seemed to give himself away simply by *not* acknowledging the other. It was a sign that until very recently, they had felt at home somewhere, that here they were merely passing through on one adventure or another. They had not yet developed that hunger for the company of other *laowai* borne from a period spent at the margins of an alternate reality.

These men were studying Chinese at the University of Zhejiang they said, and were all from Nigeria. One of the Chinese 'Little Brothers' scholarship programmes had brought them here, a relic from the days of the non-aligned movement which still played good politics in an age when the powers scrambled for resources around the dark continent. There was something that truly bemused them, said the first, who was also the tallest. He looked pretty bookish in his glasses and knitted sweater. But his eyes were wide and seemed to be assessing everything around us.

'Everywhere I've been' he said 'people stare'. He gestured with his hands at the expanses around us, the water and the people.

'Even now for example, the people are watching' he said. He was right. Several yellow men were watching this black man talking with a white man.

'And…' he continued 'often they point. Often they laugh. The kids, they just shout *Laowai, laowai, laowai*…Sometimes worse things in the countryside. We were in Henan. They wanted to show us an education initiative bringing city graduates to the villages. But the locals? They called us devils'.

'How did you feel?'

He chuckled merrily and the glasses slipped some way down his nose.

'I thought they needed an education' he said. I felt then that my recent irritations had been somewhat indulgent, that there were worse positions to be in. And surely too frustrations were worthy experiences. If they were received with humour, then lessons and anecdotes were there for the taking. And for free!

After the Nigerian and I bade each other farewell Chang Wen leaned over.

'I saw a black man spit one time' he said.

'You did?'

'I did' he paused thoughtfully, then added 'spitting is not so hygienic'

'People spit all the time in China'

'Yes. Because Chinese believe it cleans the body of toxins' he said 'but I don't know why a black man would do this'.

We passed a group of itinerants *(From Anhui?)* sweeping leaves off the pathway. And Wen blurted

'The Chinese are not racist'. Kristel chose the next moment to notice the willow that had been there all year.

'Look' she cried 'the leaves have gone'. Wen was left scratching his cheek. Then a few minutes later he finally let it out.

'We think these men look like Gorillas' he said.

Acceptance

Our students were wrapped up again, cursed by *ganmao*. The humidity that gave Hangzhou summers the grace of a steam room now began to gnaw the insides of limbs. One morning I was just spreading chalk shrapnel around the floor in a pointless effort to make things look better, when Mr. Gong popped his head around the corner.

'Where is Kristel?' he asked

'She is out shopping'

'Ah' he said dropping his head in apparent disappointment. But it seemed I would do, for he beckoned for me to come with and leave this important cleaning behind. He led me to his spacious office and foisted on me a mug of tea.

'How are you enjoying China?' he asked in French.

'I have enjoyed it a great deal' I said.

Mr. Gong nodded encouragingly. 'But recently I have enjoyed it less'. Mr. Gong nodded again and took a great slurp of tea.

'I remember this feeling, of being homesick' he said 'is that it?'

'Maybe' I said 'it is not belonging'

'Yes' he agreed 'the feeling that one never quite fits in? When I lived in France I enjoyed many things. The food and the art for instance. But I felt different, and this caused me terrible loneliness. All I wanted was to be back in China'

'Did you get over this loneliness?'

'I was surprised!' he admitted 'when I came back to China it was still there'

'You couldn't get rid of it?'

Mr. Gong cocked his head.

'I had moved outside this world and it looked so small from there. But in China especially we spend our time so closely together that we feel alienated when we are apart.'

'How did you feel when you returned?'

'Like a foreigner!' he laughed 'when I came back at the end of the Cultural Revolution, China was mad. Everybody was stuck in their own battle. The people against the government, pupils against teachers, communists against communists. But I could not take it seriously. I was not even there, just an observer, watching from a distance'. He shuffled his hands around the mug and then looked up, suddenly self aware.

'Lou Da is studying abroad next year' he said, bending the topic somewhat 'and Betty is thinking about it too'.

'Lou Da says he knows what to expect'

Mr. Gong laughed again.

'Nobody will be more lost than Lou Da' he said. It did not seem true that living amongst others broadened everyone. For some it seemed being peripheral blinded them to the new culture. Instead they found only an affirmation of their own lifestyles and identities.

Mr. Gong and I talked about more routine topics and after a while I excused myself. I went to collect some post from Lou Da's office.

He was seated at the computer.

'Professor Jiang is away' he mentioned casually 'taken a student away with him. Did he write in his book about how much he liked to help students?'

'No'

'Anyway. Have a look at this' he said, casually.

Da was showing me how people were conversing on the university's English language forum when Mrs. Ho popped by to exchange her old broom for one with less bristles missing. When she saw us both there looking at the screen she could not contain her curiosity.

'In your country' she said to me 'do you have computers?'

'Yes' I said 'we do'. She pondered this for a few seconds. Then she asked

'And televisions?'

'Yes'

'Telephones?'

'Yes'

She frowned.

'Is your country like our China?'

'No, it is very different. We speak a different language and our food is not so delicious'. Mrs. Ho nodded impatiently, not really seeming to listen after 'No'.

'My son wants a computer' she said 'a computer is too much money. When I was a student we shouted at our teachers and made them do homework. They did not ask about computers!' Mrs. Ho threw her eyes to the ceiling as though the earth had been asked for.

In the middle of that week, Ni Hai Hua, the man I had met in the University medical centre, turned up at the door. His breath smelled of alcohol and thus I was not desperate to invite him in. Instead we just stood there for a few moments, facing each other off. Meanwhile the stairwell was robbing the flat of its heat. So I gave in.

'Come in' I said 'sit down'. He did as I instructed and we sat there, our smiling face-off moved to the table. Then because Ni Hai Hua didn't seem to have much to say, I got up to fetch us both some tea. Suddenly Ni Hai Hua jumped up and protested vigorously. I pretended not to hear. So he lit a double happiness and moved to the window, where he smoked and studied my tea making. He did not stick around, but finished the cigarette with frantic little drags before heading back out into the night. What was it that he wanted?

The following day the cops launched a crackdown on the hawkers of Zhoushan East Road. They dismantled a cart selling homemade sweets and ordered a medley of noodle fryers never to return. But already by the following evening the hawkers were back. And so was Ni Hai Hua. He was sober this time, but still as strangely silent - a different man to the carefree talker I had met when I had been ill. This time when I let Ni Hai Hua come in, he accepted a tea which he gulped down quickly. Then once more he got up, smoked a cigarette, and left.

Ni Hai Hua began to knock door every other evening. I would get up, let him in, and sit back down again. Sometimes he just came in for a quick smoke. Sometimes if he knocked while we were eating then Kristel or I would find a spare plate and share it with him. Sometimes he would join us in watching a counterfeit movie, sitting meekly in one of my leather armchairs.

Ni Hai Hua's visits had not gone unnoticed.

'Your new friend' observed Darling one day 'Is truly the product of an agricultural society. That's how the peasants live. Whenever they fancy they turn up unannounced around each others' places. It is as if time does not exist for them'.

If Ni Hai Hua was not at work, we would often catch him just drifting around the neighbourhood. Whether I was walking to the supermarket or dining at a noodle stall; out on a run, or heading to Mr. Zhang's internet café - whenever Ni Hai Hua saw me, he broke out in smile and invited himself to join in. Whatever it was that made Ni Hai Hua a peripheral character in his own world seemed to create in him an affinity for *laowai*.

Darling's Descent

I continued to join Johann for beer at Mr. Xo's. It was the kind of event that Ni Ha Hua too would join. He would notice me in the middle of a wandering, then stomp over to the table, order beers all round and try to poach a cigarette from Xo. After that he usually just sat there, picked at peanuts, and struggled to understand the foreign tongue.

Xo had recently been focusing on becoming more entrepreneurial - and not just by attempting to sell his customers' lost property. No, Xo had anticipated the gap in the market left since the departure of the Xias and was now selling train and bus journeys as well as snacks and beer. We were unlikely to use his services any time soon however. For he had bragged after a few beers that he was charging twice as much as the Xias had.

'Sometimes I forget to go and collect the tickets too!' he laughed. Yet it was not a decent boast, leaving one's customers stranded, and I hoped Xo's was merely a Chinese laugh of embarrassment.

Darling began joining us at Mr. Xo's too. He had recently been spending a lot of time at the Administrative block putting his head together with that of Teacher Xu, the Party Secretary, discussing again names for the campus thoroughfares.

'I think she likes me more as my Chinese improves' he claimed. Then one frosty night he stepped up to the table in a foul temper.

'I despair' he said 'China is never going to get ahead. These people have a total inability to innovate. Copying is all they can do' Darling shouted for a beer.

'Take my students' essays. None of them are imaginative. All they can do is repeat to me what I tell them in class'. Johann grunted. Darling stared blankly at the stained table and drank until he fell from his chair and had to be carried home.

Recently Darling had been becoming close to a student who went by the English name of Angela. Whenever I dropped by Darling had received some gift or another from her parents: a carafe of Shaoxing yellow wine, a pot of crabs sent from the coast. Darling took Angela for lakeside walks and bought her little gifts of cake and ice cream. But soon this happiness too turned to disillusion.

'The Chinese find it so easy to lie' started Darling down at Mr. Xo's one night. Johann usually managed silence during these rants. But the rest of us were not so wise.

'Why do you say that?' Richard asked. Darling shrugged theatrically and pretended he was not interested in explaining himself. But Richard persisted.

'You cant make a statement like that without any evidence' he said.

'Angela was ill' began Darling 'I offered to pay her medical bills. She inflated how much they cost. How could she try to rob me?' he took a great gulp from his beer mug and proceeded to deduct a lesson from this situation. 'I fear the Chinese have destroyed their value system' he said 'there is nothing left here but making money.' Down there amongst the oxidised oil, amongst students, hawkers, and rats Darling began to preach. He railed about evangelicals and big oil, Nixon, Reagan, Bush. He prophesied the end of ambulance chasing, the state of Texas, the need for lawyers of any hue. A number of times he almost choked on his own words:

'The West has tried to export its cancer here…'

'And to think, in the States they call me a socialist…!'

But one evening in a more reflective mood he tapped his nose and said

'I discovered the true story of the German who was sent home. Basically Matthias was a great scholar but a terrible teacher'

'Did Lou Da tell you this?' Johann interrupted.

'I've heard the same story from different sources' he said indignantly. 'Matthias decided to ditch the language teaching and give lectures on German history. By lesson four, when the class reached Martin Luther and the Reformation, the pupils complained that their German language skills were not improving. So the school got on his back. They told him to liven up his lessons'. Darling swept his eyes from side to side as though phantom spies were checking in 'and that's exactly what he did. He walked right in there next class and asked 'does anybody know the German for *penis*?' He wrote *breasts* and *vagina* up on the board in German!'

'I've heard the story' said Johann 'But my students from Matthias' class say he didn't teach history. But he did discuss politics. He talked about the Chinese kidnapping the Panchen Lama, and of a plot to kill the Dalai Lama. He said the Chinese should not be up there in Tibet'

'That is just untrue' interrupted Darling 'it was all about sex!'

'It was not about sex…'

'Lou Da, the party secretary, and even the Vice President - they say exactly the same thing! Matthias was a sex pest'

'They all say the same thing? Come on…' he swigged and raised a violent eyebrow.

'Is this a question of national pride for you?' asked Darling.

'It is not about me. It is your motives that are interesting' said

Johann 'you seem to swallow anything these people will tell you.'

'It is clearly no use arguing with you' said Darling disgustedly. This episode brought the evening to a rapid end.

It may just have been my perception, but as I saw Darling over the next few days something seemed to have snapped. He was unshaven and his clothes were no longer ironed. He stopped me in the corridor and rambled incoherently about a party official moonlighting as a Daoist monk. One morning he leaned out of his flat door to claim the Swiss man who had been supposed to live in the apartment had actually been an intelligence operative - mainly on the basis that he had brought too much luggage with him to China.

Then a week later he issued a public decree.

'I'm going to divorce Emma' he said 'I've taken the ring off. My finger feels lighter already'. He wanted a child, he wanted a younger wife. Darling, it appeared, was sliding into mid-life crisis. But there was perhaps nowhere better to have it than here where the ties and responsibilities of the old world had been severed, where the values of the new world valued his unique wisdom.

Next week Lou Da finally discovered us all at Xo's. He sat himself down, turned to Johann and with typically diplomacy, said

'Smoking is a disgusting habit. Even more disgusting at table'.

Johann whinnied and blew smoke in Da's general direction.

Da turned to Kristel.

'Your boyfriend will meet someone he likes more than you one day, and at that time he will have to resist someone else's advances' he said 'that is the problem for women'

Kristel shot back

'Are you not worried Zhou Mei-xie is not resisting somebody else at this moment?'

Lou Da turned to Richard

'I read that poor Americans eat car tyres because they cannot afford chewing gum?'

'I don't know where to start with that one' Richard admitted.

Da then addressed the entire group

'Mr. Gong sniffs too much. Everyone knows that is why he will not be promoted above head of department'.

And finally

'Betty is having an affair with the head of the university restaurant. Everyone knows that. Apart from maybe you foreigners…You don't know much at all'

Darling leaned towards me threateningly and repeated threat he had uttered before: 'I'll slit Lou Da's throat if the bastard ever lays a hand on one of my girls' he said. He slurped a beer and suddenly became nostalgic and teary eyed. A couple of prostitutes peered through the steamy glass opposite, and Darling, fired by beer, peered back.

'We used to head down to El Paso and cross the border to see the whores in Cuidad Juarez' he said, squinting wistfully. 'Man you can do anything in a Mexican town'. Emma was not coming back from the States. Socialism didn't seem to be holding his faith anymore than marriage did. All of those truths which Darling claimed to have held self evident appeared to be slipping through his hands. Suddenly he appeared as lost as anyone.

Lovers

I noticed now the changes that the new season had been bringing - the sun weakened to a dull pink, the mist that once again veiled the southern hills. In restaurants across town waitresses conducted warm up exercises before opening for the evening dinner rush. Taxi drivers, we noticed, had even begun to wear their seatbelts properly - a local edict issued in the summer was finally being enforced. A new constant had been invading my life. For Ai Li the fruit store girl suddenly seemed to be everywhere, popping up like an apparition all over the place. She waved at me from the curb as I walked to class and laughed at me as I began my run to the supermarket. At other times she simply followed me around. She followed me from the fruit store to the flower shop. She followed me from the water store to the photocopiers. She stopped if I stopped. She walked when I walked. At the stall one afternoon I picked up an apple. Ai Li picked up an apple. I pulled a bottle of beer off the shelf. Ai Li lifted a bottle of coke from a rack on the floor.

Since she had no money to buy her coke I took pity on her and bought it for her. She took this as a hint to further break the communication barrier. I understood nothing she asked me.

'*Wo bu dong*' I told her '*I don't understand*'.

She just chortled. It seemed my response was the one she had expected from such an imbecile. Then I picked up a hand of bananas with one hand. So Ai Li picked up a hand of bananas with two hands.

'Go and play with your friends' I said

'Not have' she said. Then she giggled and ran away.

Later as I stretched in preparation for a run, Mrs. Ping the key-maker tipped forward and said finally

'I have seen you many times' she reckoned 'why are you running?'

'For my health' I said

'You can have medicine for health. Chinese or Western'

'True' I said 'but running is also good for health'

She did not look at all convinced, which was not surprising really considering conditions out here, and pulled back behind the safety of the key machine.

'Is business good?' I asked.

She shook her head and leant back on her chair to check on her son, who was poking a plastic bag with a stick. I noticed her stomach had inflated - something I had missed before.

'Another?' I asked, mustering a smile to offset my clumsy pointing. Her eyes bulged.

'Yes' she said, and she put her finger to her lip. Across the road Mr. Hong spluttered. He gagged like a cat ejecting a fur ball and then spit out a great gob of phlegm.

I ran onwards to find Kristel had beaten me to the supermarket by taking a quicker route through the middle of the warren. Lou Da was down there too: no girlfriend running him about in a shopping cart though today. He looked quite subdued without her.

'Have you come for the turtles?' he asked, feigning enthusiasm 'very good prices today'. I shook my head.

'How about some eel?' he asked. He leant over the trays of bullfrog and pulled out a live one, which he began to sniff distractedly.

'Where is Zhou Mei Xie?' I interrupted.

Da's face fell.

'She says she doesn't want to see me until I decide to protect her honour' he admitted.

'Are you going to protect her honour?'

'*Aiii*...' he said, and he shook his head sadly.

'*Aiii* what?'

Da rolled his head to iron out a crick and dropped the bullfrog back into the tank. There it began to slop about with the rest of them.

'Maybe I have some feeling for Zhou Mei Xie' he admitted 'She is not like the four beauties...' He smiled wistfully 'Xi Shi, so beautiful the fish stopped swimming; Wang Zhaojun, so beautiful birds fell from the sky...'

'So you feel strongly about Mei-xie?' I interrupted.

'I do not know' he said 'she is very argumentative. I do not like argumentative. Girls should not be so disobedient. Years ago she would do as I say and not make these difficult demands'

'I think you like argumentative girls Lou Da. You say you don't. But really you like the fight.'

'You do too'

'Maybe' I said

We continued taking Sunday afternoon strolls with Chang Wen by the lake. The drill was always the same. He would teeter up on the bicycle, climb off, lock it to some lamppost or another with four locks and turn his big head around searching for the shifty types hiding in the bushes, obviously waiting for the chance to steal a rust bucket should it come along. Then we ambled around its 8km circumference until called by one tea house or another. One day in the midst of the season I suddenly noticed Wen's oversized face had grown paler under the winter sun. It looked too as though he had lost weight.

'Are you tired?' I asked. He blinked.

'I'm working two jobs' he admitted 'I am saving for the house so I can get married. I've got to get married - and to think, her father is just a driver!' He shook his head in disbelief. On the White Causeway most of the visitors had vanished. Tour caps had disappeared from the Broken Bridge.

'I cannot buy a flat in the block Cheng Hualing's family want' he said 'they are already sold. All of them. I am in trouble' he continued 'house prices are already one and a half times what they were a few months ago'. The corner of his mouth twitched as though he were suppressing laughter. It was a universal truth: no man wanted to live with his in-laws.

We passed along the Su causeway and through the gardens and ponds of flowers harbour.

'Hualing is becoming very demanding' said Wen 'she says the house I wanted to buy is not big enough. So we lost time and now...' he threw his big hands in the air 'what can I do? It is costing my parents, my grandparents and me. It is already too much of our savings'. Marriage in one-child China was not an indulgence that could be left to the individual. It was an important matter of group strategy - in Wen's case, a dilemma for the entire family.

He called later in the week

'I may have found a place in the south' he said 'a new place' Indeed it was so new it would not be ready until 2012. We arranged to go see the building site with him next week instead of the usual lakeside walk. We stood on the hillside below the six harmonies pagoda and stared across the Qiantang river.

'They are moving the city core over there' he said 'my home is to be constructed behind it. Behind the new business district'. It was at present a muddy plain over which teams of workers hoisted beams many times the size of an individual.

In the afternoon Cheng Hualing came with her father to pick us up and take us back to the Cheng family flat. Mrs. Cheng cooked dinner in a kitchen hanging with a huge knitted knot. In the lounge CCTV 9 blared from a television (*'Chinese industrial output up 15% year on year...'*) while Kristel, Hualing, Wen, and I sat amongst the dishes Mrs. Cheng had worked so hard upon: soya pork, bamboo shoot, vinegar fish, flash-fried river shrimp. The Cheng parents eagerly watched us eat from the doorway, waiting to spring like mice upon the leftovers.

'When we get married...' began Hualing 'we must wear red underwear. Wen will buy it for us!' This was a lucky Chinese tradition. Hualing grinned playfully and stuck a finger in Wen's side. He did not look as though he recognised his luck though for instead he sat there glumly poking bamboo shoots with his chopsticks.

Next Sunday Wen locked his bicycle up beside the Autumn Moon on Calm Lake Pavillion.

'Cheng Hualing finished with me this week' he said.

'What will you do?'

'I must search for another woman' he said. We walked into the hills and sat in front of the stone pagoda. Wen mopped his brow.

'Maybe I can sell medical equipment' he mumbled vacantly 'you can sell medical equipment to me and I can sell it here for instance'

'I don't know anything about medical equipment' I said

He tried a new line.

'Maybe together we can sell boxes. I will post them to Britain. You can sell them'

'I don't think I can sell boxes either'

Down by the goldfish ponds we threw *baozi* to the mouths in the water.

'It finished when she said I am not earning enough money' Wen admitted 'I said maybe she should find herself a new boyfriend because I am not a businessman. I said in my heart I am a teacher. I make enough money. I said that the one I choose as my wife would accept this. So then we agreed we would not be getting married' he shook crumbs into the water 'we said to each other we will talk later. I think her parents are already encouraging her to meet new men, to find Hualing an acceptable husband. Hopefully a richer man'.

We did not meet next Sunday. Wen had called during the week.

'I'll be away over the next few weeks' he had said 'my Grandmother is dying of cancer. At this time she wants her family around. She wants to see that the family is strong together. I am sorry but I will not be able to watch over you at this time'

'How do you feel?'

He paused for some time.

'There is nothing that Chinese medicine can do. There is nothing that Western medicine can do' he said finally 'they are equally useless. We have already spent so much money. Now my Grandmother has asked for a spirit doctor'

'A spirit doctor?'

'Yes. To do prayers. But it is expensive. One month of salary for some prayers. My grandfather says he will not pay so much money. Aunt Mei says 'what good is prayers?' Aunt Zhu and Aunt Mei did not agree. I think Aunt Zhu is going to pay the money. Aunt Mei said that Grandfather needs the money more as he is still alive, that Aunt Zhu has been spoiled by the city'.

One cold evening Lei Shen and Tian Fei came round - and Chang Er too. They had all been busy. Tian Fei was organising a rowing trip. Lei Shen had organised a basketball competition. Chang Er had been busy too.

'Bo and me wanted to get married' she admitted 'But when Bo asked his parents if he can marry me, they refused!' Er blinked fast, trying to hold back tears. The girls moved to embrace her.

'So we agreed we can only be friends now. Not lovers'
Kristel fetched Er a mug of tea.

'Why did they refuse Chang Er?' I asked.

'My parents are blind' sniffed Er 'They met at a hospital for blind people. Bo's mother thinks that our children would have this problem too. They think my children will be born blind. But this is not scientific. When I try to say this cannot happen they do not believe me. They are superstitious and refuse the marriage'. She swallowed her upper lip inside her bottom one.

'There is still much superstition in our China' said Tian Fei. Then she half-smiled. 'Especially with boys. They do not have to be practical like women. A boy asked me to go out with him last week. He thinks it is easy to impress a girl. Just a matter of fate!'

Lei Shen sniggered.

'We must work harder now' he said 'no modern woman wants to go to a traditional restaurant. Now they want McDonalds or Kentucky Fried Chicken! But these things are not cheap. The other day I took a girl to the teahouse. She said we should go instead to Starbucks. It is better to be seen there'. We followed the old routine - gin, steak, *Tou Dofu* out of some masochistic nostalgia. We packed the girls off before curfew.

I caught Lou Da in his office the following day and asked him about the role of the blind in Chinese society. He seemed to have recovered from his nasty experience in the supermarket.

'Chinese people believe disabled people have heightened senses' he claimed 'if you are blind for example you will find a great job as maybe a piano tuner or a masseuse'. Every industry was a boom one in the new China, whether it be civil aviation, electronics, espionage, or blind massage.

Next day Tian Fei was back at the door. Lei Shen trailed at a respectful distance.

'Chang Xu has been telling the teachers that I do not believe in our leaders. I am extremely angry!' Suddenly this fiery Chinese girl seemed quite dangerous.

'Chang Xu is jealous' stated Shen, daring finally to catch up.

'Jealous?' asked Tian Fei, coyly drawing a piece of hair across her mouth.

'Yes. Maybe of your hair or something...'
She slapped him playfully.

'It's like the famous story of a golden cow' Lei Shen said 'Tian Fei is the golden cow'

'No. This is not like the golden cow' replied Tian Fei. Er put her hand over her mouth and I guessed she was smiling.

'What golden cow?'

'It's a story' began Shen 'about an official who left his three wives at home to take up a post far away. His first wife said she would bring him gold on his return. His second said silver. The third said she would bear him a son, which pleased him most of all. The other two were jealous and when she bore the son, the wives took it away and claimed it was in fact a lump of flesh. The 2nd wife wrapped the baby in straw and fed it to a buffalo. Then the official returned and his first wife gave him the gold and the second gave him the silver...' He stopped and flashed Tian Fei a grin.

'They told the official that the third had not given him a son' he continued 'instead she had provided a rotten lump of flesh which the buffalo had eaten. The official was very angry and sent his third wife to work in a mill to make rice flour as a punishment. But later the buffalo gave birth to a golden calf. The official was very wise and he guessed that maybe the buffalo had not eaten a horrid lump of flesh, but in fact, his own son...'

'So the official realised he made a mistake and brought his third wife back from the mill' interrupted Tian Fei.

'You are an impatient girl...'

'You make everyone impatient Lei Shen' Fei shouted impetuously. But it did nothing to hide her blushing.

Christmas

Soon the local brothels began to display pictures of Santa against the frosted glass, for Christmas was coming. The *'Merry Christmas!'* poster that had been up in the university canteen all year finally made some sense. So did the street washing trucks that had for much of the year spewed water to the tune of *'We wish you a merry Xmas'*. Now each morning I found the ground spattered in frost, and weather reports predicted that it might soon snow.

Teacher Nan taught a final Chinese lesson. During class she handed round chocolates, and afterwards Kristel and I followed her outside where she gave Kristel a bow from her hair.

'Come back soon Mi Jin' said Teacher Nan 'welcome you both again to Hangzhou another day!' Then she wobbled off over the frosty asphalt and into the congested traffic, off to collect her one daughter from nursery. She weaved in and out between the vehicles with her remaining plait dancing, merrily joining in with all the honking around her with a stream of ringing from her own little bicycle bell. The life of Teacher Nan seemed the epitome of a very modest kind of Chinese dream.

Then Betty called

'We have an idea to reward you for quality teaching' she said. She asked all foreigners to gather together at the foreign affairs office. Today seated beside her was a partridge lookalike, a plump man with a head as round and shiny as a bowling ball.

'This is Mr. Li' she said 'He runs the University restaurant'. But he wasn't just any old Mr. Li. Betty had been seeing this older man for some time. He had been showering her with gifts and she had been unable to resist, according to Lou Da's slightly dubious account.

'She is becoming like a modern concubine' Da had claimed contemptuously. It did not seem that he had a problem with Mr. Li's status as a married man and neither did he seem to care about the age difference.

Indeed Lou Da's main problem seemed rooted in simple irritation that Mr. Li had managed to conduct the whole thing on the cheap 'He doesn't even need to buy her a home!' he said 'it has been very easy for him'.

Back in her office, Betty began a pitch.

'We don't think the university will give you money for a Christmas party' she said. Neither Vice-President Yao nor Teacher Xu were committed multiculturalists she reckoned. Christmas was not only superstitious, it was foreign and superstitious.

'We'll have a party at the restaurant' she said kindly 'you foreigners will get the dinner for free. You can invite your students'. I had a feeling she had not put herself up to this hard sell.

'No thanks' we all said. We wanted a day of peace and quiet. Not commercial ventures. Baldy's mouth sagged. Betty shot him worried glances. These didn't seem to placate him.

'You need a dinner!' he thundered suddenly 'foreigners eat dinner at Christmas'. After all, if Christmas wasn't a time for making money, then what the hell was it for? But we still declined to support his idea.

Like clockwork the first flakes fell and the dirty streets became covered in thin snow. On Christmas day the heater failed but we lit candles and congregated in Richard's flat. Outside the kids built snowmen and started fights with blackened snowballs. We held our own party for the students, singing carols, drinking mulled wine, and eating cookies. We even dressed up the trees in the school park with tinsel and homemade angels while Dehuai watched quizzically from the gates.

But it was a subdued occasion. Most of our students were missing. The 25th was an important date in China, for it was the anniversary of Mao's birthday. It seemed though fitting that this Chinese messiah's birthday fell on that of the Christian one. Mao had occasionally celebrated by taking a swim in the freezing Yangtze. The University of Educated People was celebrating this special day by holding its final interviews to the communist party. Fei Lian had come to our party and sung enthusiastically along with these songs he did not know. I imagined he had been considered too much of a loose cannon for a communist party invite. But Chang Xu was gone, so were Lei Shen, Tian Fei, and Chang Er. Tian Fei though had dropped by earlier to help us set up.

'Westlife and China is not so different for politics' she had said 'America for instance has a two party system. Our China has a one party system. Just one party difference!'

'I see'

But when she paused she knew that I didn't, and took it upon herself to start elsewhere.

'Before we just had chaos' she said 'our country was abused and

233

we had nothing. It was like the story of Ah Q. Ah Q was like China itself. He showed us what it means to be trapped'. But there were more important conclusions to be drawn from Lu Xun's *'The true story of Ah Q'*. In his tale, the pitiful villager Ah Q tries his hardest to run with the flow, joining in enthusiastically with the forces around him - the other villagers, the Qing government, the rebels trying to bring them down. Ultimately Ah Q is caught out on the wrong side at the wrong time and executed for reasons he does not understand. Afterwards, Ah Q's death, like those of many others, is rationalised by others around him: *'All agreed that he had been a bad man, the proof being that he had been shot'* wrote Lu Xun *'For if he had not been bad, how could he have been shot?'*

'One party means stability' claimed Tian Fei 'one party can satisfy the Ah Qs of our China'. It was easy to see this as the self-fulfilling logic of the system. But on Christmas Day our differences seemed to unite the lot of us more clearly than ever: all were manipulated by social forces outside their control; and those that were not certain of the unique correctness of their own faith, often seemed beholden to those who were.

Wen's Ancestors

Early in the New Year we finally heard from Chang Wen.

'My grandmother died' he said 'We buried her in our home village'. He was going back to see those of his family who still lived out there. He asked us to accompany him and said

'You will see from where we come'

We travelled out there on an overcast weekend. We found grey cabbage plots, rows of vegetable wedged between the clogged canal and the dilapidated road - the farmland of Zhejiang. There were no hedges, no wooded areas, nothing natural save that sculpted by man. Chang Wen's home village lay beyond the city limits of Hangzhou, and beyond the Shaoshan exurbs. It lay out where overburdened tractors struggled on potholed roads, and families of four might ride into town on a single motorbike. There were no copses or hedgerows out here, just a few scrawny chickens pecking aimlessly amongst all this productive dullness.

'Nothing eats these chickens apart from humans' claimed Chang Wen with pride. Their natural predators had long been driven out by the human scourge. Even of flying birds there was little sign - just a single sparrow picking under a cabbage. Back in the Great Leap Forward the

Chinese had almost managed to extinguish even them in the 'four pests' campaign. Bashing gongs and saucepans the peasants had put the flocks to flight until they fell dead from the sky. But the sparrows it seemed, had not entirely given up on China, and had returned.

Aunt Mei lived in a typically weather-stained bunker. She had decorated it with red charms: fish for wealth, peanuts for fertility. It seemed neither had worked very well. Aunt Mei steamed us a turtle, which held medicinal value - one of the snouted creatures that was always trying to escape inside the supermarket. This one's snout had shrivelled in the steamer and its eyes looked faintly accusatory.

'Have some' ordered Mei. She looked at me.

'Not want thanks' I said 'I have allergies'.

Aunt Mei turned to Kristel and gestured encouragingly with the serving ladle. Kristel looked at the ceiling. It was no use. She was given a generous helping of turtle innards. At the sight of this, Uncle Wu, Mei's husband, sagged disappointedly in a chair, which shrieked under his weight. Aunt Mei rapped him over the knuckles with the all-purpose ladle. By the time Kristel was done, he finally remembered his manners.

'The heart' Wu exclaimed 'most delicious'. He stole Mei's instrument and ladled the leftovers onto Kristel's plate. I laughed. Kristel smiled sweetly and with her chopsticks, jabbed me in the leg.

That afternoon Wu drove us further into the country. Down the road, lived Great Uncle Bao. He came to us in a fraying green jacket and Wellingtons, another bear of a man whose resemblance with his great nephew was obvious. Great Uncle Bao had a face drawn in laughter lines. He cracked open bags of pistachio and monkey nut, and insisted on feeding us all eggs boiled in green tea.

'They are taking land' he said, waving at the monkey nuts 'for a new factory'. With the connivance of the authorities, developers were moving in on the land owned by the people, for the people - because all land in the Middle Kingdom was held in trust by the benevolent Chinese state.

'The villagers are not happy' explained Wen. Apparently some of the local hotheads had even threatened a protest.

Uncle Wu said his wife was buried across the fields close to where the constructions were going up.

'She always said she wanted to go the temple. But there wasn't

235

one before' he said. He pushed another egg into Kristel's hands. Five years ago a wealthy Taiwanese manufacturer of screws had come to the village in a parade of big black cars and tinted windows to declare the place his ancestral home.

'He donated money for a new temple' Wen boasted.

In the vegetable patch outside Bao's front door I pulled out my camera. Great Uncle wagged his finger sternly. I was disappointed by this until I discovered the ban was not permanent, for Bao had run back into the house. In a fit of mania he returned to exclaim

'I have not had a photograph for many years'

Bao pulled out a comb and ran it vigorously through his hair. Finally he grinned hard - a smile of three teeth - and gestured for the shot. I took it.

'How will I get it?' he asked. Chang Wen promised to send a copy in the post.

Great Uncle Bao had by now become infused with a childlike energy.

'I want to show you something' he said, and he beckoned us upstairs. There were no furnishings up here and the rooms reeked of damp. The windows had fallen to disrepair and Great Uncle had smothered the gaps between the panes with old newspaper. In one of these rooms he stooped under a mattress and, pausing for breath, hauled out a package. Behind protective cardboard were two oil paintings, one of a man, another of a woman, both painted in Qing dynasty finery - yellow robes and a Manchu hat for the man, and an elaborate headress for the woman.

'These are my parents' he reckoned.

'That was the formal style even in the twenties' said Chang Wen 'He hid these during the Cultural Revolution. Red guards came here looking but he kept them safe under the bed' The bridge of mother's nose had been scuffed in the hurry. But still Uncle Bao had managed to protect his parents from the revolutionaries and they remained immortalised here, regal courtiers hidden under a bed in a decaying room.

As we made to leave Great Uncle Bao thrust monkey nuts into our pockets.

'You will send the photo?' he asked uncertainly.

'Yes' we said.

'I once saw foreigners before' he claimed as he shook my hand 'But they had yellow skin'.

We walked away up the muddy lane while Great Uncle stood behind, watching us from the doorway.

'Foreigners...' Chang Wen repeated 'I think Uncle Bao is talking about officials. People from Hangzhou or even Beijing'.

Great Aunt Guolin was one of China's many graceful elders. She was Great Uncle Bao's even older sister, and she lived just up the road. She wore a rural uniform of old jacket and plimsolls, and lived with a daughter, granddaughters, great granddaughters. Together they occupied the largest house in the village, a three storey place that towered over all of the neighbouring properties. It had a tile floor and a built-in kitchen.

'This house gives my family a lot of face around here' reckoned Chang Wen.

At the age of eighty five, Great Aunt Guolin had last year been given a permanent break from the land. Her feet had been bound many years ago as a small girl and it was just getting impossible for her, hobbling out in the field. They really were tiny, and it struck me that her generation had been the last to suffer this experience. Soon the bound feet of China would be something read about only in books, along with eight legged tests on the Confucian classics, and palace eunuchs.

These days Aunt Guolin spent her days at the temple. She stayed there till the evening, making a few *mao* singing the sutras at formal events.

At this point Great Aunt Guolin's six year old Great Granddaughter wandered in to find two terrifying foreigners sat there in her house, drinking tea. She began to wail.

'I'll take you to the temple!' shouted Great Aunt Guolin with quick thought. So we left her home and trudged to it through patches of marrow and beans. The Taiwanese businessman's wooden temple had gone up beside the cemetery. It was guarded not only by the four heavenly guardians, but by a clutch of farmers sat on their haunches, and smoking. Great Aunt ran up the steps like a child, and spotting her friends, bowled over to join them.

With their gongs and woodblocks, the elders soon had an

ensemble on the go. Seated on yellow cushions they beat and clonked until a ragged little procession of monks filed out from an annexe. The chanting began and incense floated across the fields. It was burnt too next door in the graveyard where groups of farmers were making offerings to their forebears - a towel and a paper comb: objects that would make life easier for them in the afterlife, and perhaps help to gain spiritual assistance with those fields that were owed a ploughing, the children needing a schooling, the developers who required beating away. They linked themselves in this fashion with what had come before, integrating into a community that transcended any individual. But in the new China the most pious descendents were offering up paper cars and plasma screen televisions - for the ancestors seemed to have become as materialistic as everyone else.

Wen too was out there, setting fire to paper money. Only last weekend his Grandmother had been cremated close by and packed in here under a head of limestone. In plots not far away lay other family members: a Great Grandfather, a Great Great Grandfather, a Great Great Great Grandfather - the Chang line running back through the centuries.

11. *Guíhún*

Shaoxing opera was a positively new cultural phenomenon of eight hundred years old. It was told through the medium of song and this one was no different. I did not catch the title, which increasingly did not seem to matter - for the old folk beside us blabbered, people moved in and out of the auditorium at will, phones bleeped and were answered without shame at full volume. A child danced in the aisle. Then a horde of Ronald Mcdonald clowns mobbed the stage - actually part of the show it transpired. Meanwhile the leading couple took a romantic dinner underneath a pair of golden arches. In many ways this performance seemed a worthy distillation of Chinese urban life: frenetic ever-changing lives set against incoherent references and chaos.

The Next day CCTV 9 stated *'…a 20 year old bottle collector and recycler has been caught after robbing and killing ten of his competitors…'*

And Betty called once more

'Have you prepared for the end of year exams?' she asked

'I didn't know we had to deliver end of year exams'

'Ah yes' she said 'exams are part of the quality teaching. Please tell Kristel'

Outside frost had toughened the ground. But cloud had finally succumbed to sunlight. It streamed through my classroom window while outside hedge trimmers hummed and horns blared. The examinations were set and went off without a hitch. Afterwards, the desks were out of line and chalk splintered over the podium and the floor. It had fallen too upon the windowsill, in my hair and on my clothes. I stepped out of the classroom for the last time and realised both the place and the activity were about to become shuffled back to memory with all its selectivity and distortion. This is how it had always been. This here, was my Chinese life: mess, noise, and chalk.

Soon my students dispersed again to the far flung towns and villages of Zhejiang province. The temperature plummeted. Downtown the West Lake brooded once more under shrouds of 'mist' and the itinerants huddled for shelter in parks on its banks. Mrs. Ping bought herself a bomber jacket. Mr. Hong did not seem to notice. He had been donated a fraying Mao suit, and in it he kept his loyal vigil over the neighbourhood dump. We might have been able to work the heating these days, but the south of China was unprepared for winter. A national regulation stipulated that homes built north of the Yangtse river had to come with heating, those south of it, did not. It was as arbitrary a division as any given the great twists existing in the great river: Zhejiang province had been left on the losing side.

Yet in the far northern provinces of old Manchuria conditions had by now become more extreme. The temperature in Haerbin, capital of Heilongjiang, usually plummeted below minus 30 at this time of year. Yet it sounded as if the people were capable of bearing it. I heard that they had heating and military clothing; they were spirited and tough; they celebrated the cold with outdoor swimming and strong liquor. I imagined they did not whinge about the cold like pampered southerners or *laowai*.

Beyond the great wall where the horsemen had roamed there existed another Chinese front line - of humans against weather. As Hangzhou fell into the same bedraggled slumber we had found it in almost a year ago, the provinces of China's north were becoming places of magic, populated by heroes.

Russians

So we travelled north, beginning of course with a train. But not any old Chinese train: these express trains from Hangzhou to Beijing were modern - a generational shift. There were no nut shells, no itinerants, and less rowdiness. Instead there were plasma screens, illuminated posters for the *'Xitang wonderland'*, a wood-panelled restaurant car.

My brother Stuart joined us in Beijing, followed soon after by Josianne, a friend of Kristel's from Fontainebleau. With our party doubled we bought train tickets for the overnight to Haerbin. They were hosting an ice festival up there, a park of sculptures all cut from…ice. This festival was renowned across the land, and clearly an ingenious use of the city's most abundant resource. Nothing sounded more enticing.

Then I lost my ticket (berth 247) - probably in the melee passing the baggage screening x-ray machine. I retraced my footsteps and explained my predicament to the machine operators.

'Please stop the machine' I asked.

'Cannot' said the paunch nursing boss 'there are too many people coming in'. But a ticket was a ticket. So I dropped down beside it anyway and began flailing around for it. Kristel grabbed a broom from the wall and threw it to me. I got up and began to sweep. The masses streamed around. A fat man confused himself and fell over his own baggage.

'You cannot!' shouted paunchy again. But it turned out, I could. Kristel joined me to sweep with another brush that she had found. A group of security guards and police had gathered to watch, but it seemed they did not know what to do - after all, those *laowai* could be unpredictable. We swept. Dust rose. The machine, the group finally decided, should be shut down while the foreigners acted this way. The traffic meanwhile was diverted to the one other remaining machine, where it backed up considerably. Meanwhile I found plastic wrappers and a crushed chicken bone, but I did not find a ticket to Haerbin.

So I gave up and bought a new ticket for the same train. It turned out that this route had been demoted - the train was standard, a drab fifties affair clean, and without frills. But Kristel and I knew better how these worked. Someone else lay in birth 247. He was a businessman to judge by the shiny trousers and leather jacket.

'Where did you get your ticket?' I asked

'I bought it at the station'

'Where in the station?'

He narrowed his eyes and sized me up

'From a hawker' he admitted. I guessed somebody had quickly found my lost ticket. It seemed they had resold it to this gentleman. But I decided it would not be sensible to take things any further for I had no evidence, only a substandard grasp of the language, and therefore no leverage. Later I regretted this and cursed myself for behaving so rationally.

The onboard population was diverse. It was jammed with Russians heading back to Siberia. The men were afflicted by shaven heads and bomber jackets. The women wore bleached hair and a lot of cheap perfume. As well as these brawny Slavs, there were Asiatic Russians slouched in the corridors. Aside from their posture they were easy to differentiate from the Chinese due to their dress (puffer jackets and baseball caps), banter (aggressive, macho), and their modesty (gawping lustily at the Chinese girls).

Our girls fell asleep in bays opposite the cuckoo who had stolen my bunk. So my brother and I skirted the bays, dodging spit and seed husks. The train lumbered through the dark across frozen wasteland and the city of Shenyang passed, just a sea of muffled stars. We found the dining carriage where the weak bulbs hinted at some sort of cover up. A grey whiskered Russian leered into my face and said something. He was very drunk.

The carriage had been hijacked by four bear-sized men - naturally they were from Russia.

'Hey!' called one, 'please join us'. His name, ridiculously stereotypically, was Dimitry. He was from the border town of Blagovischensk, as were the others: Olexy, Vladimir, and Alexander.

'We live next door to China' Dimitry said, allotting himself the position of spokesman 'and we hate it' he added. It was 6pm. They were drunk already.

'Shitty people' he said 'Shitty vodka'. Olexy rolled forward and said

'There are too many Chinese'. Vladimir grunted, and Alexander shook his head

'They are too many' he agreed 'Too many now in Russia too'

'China wants land. And oil. And rock...how do you say?' his index finger waggled.

'Minerals?'

'Yes' he agreed 'China wants our minerals'

'Its good to see Europeans' purred Dimitry 'very good. We Europeans are the same'. I did not feel very much the same and I doubted if Stuart did either. But I did feel flattered by Dimitry's prejudice.

In any case Dimitry looked suddenly thoughtful - as though an idea was forming.

'Do you know how to say *I want to fuck you* in Russian?' he asked.

'No' I admitted.

'*Ya hachu tebya tray hate...*' he said.

'*Ya hachu tebya tray hate*' he repeated 'My girlfriend is a model. In Milan. I met her on the internet. I tell her this often...*Ya hachu tebya tray hate!*' The three stereotypes guffawed. Dimitry stared at me hard, soliciting the belief which I could not give him.

Olexy called for two more glasses which he filled with the last of the *baijiu*. He clapped them down in front of Stuart and I and we knocked them back. The Russians cheered and slapped their hands together sloppily. Olexy called for more. Outside rolled the plains where little villages of one storey brick homes hunkered down in a snowscape. The moon was busy separating all colour into black and white, the sky and the snow. Another bottle arrived. Alexander fished around in his pocket for change. He emptied the contents, carefully laying them out in the pedantic manner of the concentrating drunk. Out came the passport.

'Have a look' said Alexander. He flicked the passport across the table. We examined it like rampant stamp collectors: The gold wreaths of corn, the globe united under hammer and sickle, the star of world communism and the letters 'CCCP' all emblazoned on vermilion. This was a Soviet not a Russian one. Yet it had been issued in 2000 - nine years after the empire's dissolution.

'When we were powerful we were Soviet Union' said Olexy. He stabbed himself in the chest with his fist.

'Then Yeltsin came' said Dimitry.

'Yeltsin was a drunken fool' slurred Alexander, with masterful irony.

'Putin is a good man. A strong leader' continued Olexy 'Russia needs a strong leader'.

The next bottle of Chinese *baijiu* arrived. Dimitry shook his head in wonder.

'More shitty Chinese vodka!' he exclaimed. By now Vladimir's head was sagging but since he was tightly packed between his co-conspirators he would not slump. Olexy poured shots.

'You would love Russia' said Dimitry 'come with me to Kamshatka. We'll shoot geese'

'Yes!' shouted Stuart 'we'll do it. *Na sdarovie!*'

'*Na sdarovie!*' slurred the Russians. The shots were drained. The bottle was drained. The carriage was drained.

Alexander leant across to grapple Stuart in a bear hug and Vladimir slipped to the floor. Olexy screamed at the waiters for more.

'Not have' said the waiter 'not have alcohol'.

'Of course you have' insisted Dimitry. But he said this in English, and it seemed therefore, that the only part of it the waiter understood was the implication of menace.

'Over there' Olexy added in Chinese. He pointed at the display cabinet, which held two bottles of wine.

'Can't do' protested the waiter.

'Yes. Can do' insisted Olexy. The manager came out to see what was going on and the waiter filled him in. Recognising implacable drunkenness, the manager relented and sold out the display cabinet. The two bottles of Chinese wine were sweet and stale and they did not last long.

A group of young Asiatic Russians swaggered in and sat down at the opposite table. They too were steaming pissed and roaring with laughter.

Olexy frowned. 'From Yakutsk' he said, nodding at the Asiatics. Something shattered. One of the Asiatic boys had accidentally smashed a bottle. He sat there covered in shards, apparently as surprised as anyone. All conversation stopped. The background volume increased and I noticed the wheels squealing on the track below. Suddenly Alexander launched himself across the carriage, words spewing from his mouth. The Asiatics, still shaken, kept their eyes to the floor and their mouths open. Then the lot of them stood to gingerly and scarperred. Alexander pounded back, hauled Vladimir upright and sat himself back down.

'I told them to go and find us some more beer' he said.

'He told them we would beat them' chirped Olexy. Vladimir lifted his head especially for the occasion.

'No good' he chimed wagging a drunken finger.

'You don't like those boys' noted Stuart, in what I thought amounted to a dangerous level of facetiousness. Mercifully it went undetected.

'They are different' said Dimitry, and he grasped my shoulder 'they are not European'.

'They have Russian passports. But they are not Russian' added Olexy.

'If we go to their towns they beat us' said Alexander 'if they come to ours, they get the same'. The mood had darkened, and I wondered if our presence had simply encouraged bad behaviour. I nudged Stuart and we stood up to go.

'You'll come drink vodka with us again tomorrow' Dimitry predicted with confidence. Then he smiled.

'We will teach you how Russians say 'fuck your mother'!' he said, as we passed the Chinese waiter, who I noticed had barricaded himself into a corner. I wondered whether the aggression of the Russians stemmed from deep insecurity. The motherland was, after all, losing its place in the pecking order to the juggernaut rising in the south.

A pale sun was glowering over the snow plains when I awoke. It went on like this all morning, a sheen studded every so often with birch. Then about midday, industrial suburbs began to grope the earth. I got up to use the toilet and passed the Russian boys sound asleep in their bay. They were a tangle of smelly feet and damp luggage that spilled into the corridor. The train arrived in Haerbin. It was minus 25 on the streets, where exhaust fumes from taxis curled like dragon breath. I attempted to cash a travellers cheque. But the staff in China Industrial and Commercial Bank were having a late morning siesta, snoozing behind their desks. I rapped a counter window. A dozy cashier woke.

'Come back at 1pm' she burbled.

The typical life of a Chinese city had disappeared. The hawkers and the stall owners, the beggars and the pedestrians - they had all retreated to underground shopping centres which were protected from the weather by air locks of heavy fabric.

Haerbin had once been Russian run. Then the Japanese had humiliated them in the Russo-Japanese war and shown all of Asia that the European imperialists were not so invincible after all. But St. Sophia the Russian orthodox cathedral still remained. Her blue paint was flaking and the chandeliers had faded. The Chinese had been replaced in the cathedral and on the streets by people of fur, cheap perfume, and the odd bookish moustache. They peered through the windows of the solid townhouses and the sugar fairy terraces that their ancestors had left behind. They were not the quick-paced rabble of urban China.

But the big draw in Haerbin at this time of year was of course, the ice festival. We found its edges ringed in plastic drapes as if the site were awaiting redevelopment. The sculptures were lit only by the cold light of a northern evening. There was no-one else around. So we sat down disappointed on a small hill and watched as the sun faded. Then as the last silhouettes vanished, the lights switched on and the crowds began to roll in. Here was the wonderland – flush with colour: an ice frigate and an ice tank; an ice Aircraft Carrier several stories tall; but the true masterpiece was a replica Forbidden City decked in flying eaves and red lanterns. Unsurprisingly its steps were slippery. This whole place was as ethereal as the inspiration behind it - the ice lanterns the locals had been hanging on their eaves for centuries throughout the subjugations by foreigners. In a couple of months all of this would be gone.

Snow

Next morning we were back out there watching the birch breaking the plains. The bus was worn, and the passengers tiresome. They smoked and yakked and watched a karaoke movie about a Chinese policeman who had fallen in love with his Chinese homeland. At the town of Mudanjiang we changed for a train. Stuart and I tried the bank before it left. All staff present on the ground floor of the bank came to watch my transaction - four cashiers, a manager, cleaner, and a security guard, who was supposed to be watching the door.

'How much money are you changing?' asked the manager, his eyes lit greedily '...because foreigners often change a lot of money' I passed over the cheque to a raven haired cashier. She scrutinised it carefully before declaring

'Not so much'. This seemed to depress the audience and everybody was soon back to work, which meant only that they sat back down from whence they came. Two of the cashiers already had their heads buried in crossed arms, apparently trying to sleep. The manager began to tease another cashier over by the tea water boiler - she giggled behind a hand. As we made to leave the security guard called

'Have you been to Beijing?'

'Only for a moment' I admitted. This too seemed to disappoint him. We hadn't changed large sums of cash, nor had we visited Beijing - what kind of foreigners were we?

'I want to go to Beijing to live' he said. He was a young man with a strong posture and searching eyes.

'Why?'

'More money and better living. The girls are prettier' he said. The cashier giggled, and then remembered her manners by covering her mouth with a hand. I wished him luck. Out here the streets of China's cities seemed to be paved in gold.

Back at the station we met up once more with the girls. They had bought noodles for us all. It was a packed train, and our fellow passengers watched us slurp. As the train gathered speed I spilled noodle broth on the girl sitting opposite. She suffered it with such good grace I gained the distinct impression she had been expecting it.

This carriage was an unheated meat locker yet one hawker was doing a brisk trade in ice cream. As usual the floor was soon buried under seed husks. They were joined here in the north however by empty bottles of *baijiu*. Body heat seeped out to create an ice lining in the space between the carriages. We huddled for warmth like penguins, which made it quite difficult to write. My neighbours leaned over.

'He's writing Russian!' claimed an old drunk. One of those curious crowds began to form in the aisle, all straining to see what the devil I was up to.

'No, its German!' shouted someone else. It was French or even Italian, claimed others.

'Its English' I said. A murmur shot through the assembled. Suddenly the old drunk shouted

'He speaks Chinese!' and he pointed at me as if I might try to escape. After that they asked me the usual questions: where we lived, where we learned Chinese, and how much we earned. Kristel remained craftily mute while they asked me if I liked China, and whether I could use chopsticks. Then I asked them questions. I asked about the frightening cold, I asked about swimming in ice holes - which it turned out, no one had been foolish enough to try (in Haerbin it was apparently sport for the elderly). I asked them what it was like to live around these parts.

'Cold' said a skinny guy.

'Not so many jobs'

'There are Koreans' said a sharp cheeked young man wearing a Russian bear hat 'lots of Koreans'

'Tourists?'

'No' he said 'locals'.

'Some Korean tourists come in the summer' added some guy at the back.

'Yes' admitted bear skin 'they walk in the mountains and look over the border...'

'Koreans are very rich' butted in the drunkard 'but they can't

247

read Chinese characters!' He seemed to find this very funny and spent the next few minutes laughing at his own remarkable wit.

Meanwhile the snow plains passed. They were littered with steel mills and dead factories. Manchuria had once held an abundance of resources: iron, coking coal, soybeans, salt. It had been fought over by rapacious foreigners - Russians, then Japanese. Now the place had been worked dry. The booming industries had long been shipped to the interior, where Mao had considered them safer. The modern Manchuria was rust belt. It passed in the decrepit factories which stalked among shacks, trees and snow: it seemed unlikely to be so lusted after again by outsiders.

Yanji though did not seem to be standard rust belt. It was a Korean town, and less than twenty miles from the North Korean border. By the time the train wheezed in it was already dark. We said goodbye to a host of well wishers and found ourselves in a snowbound street in which the only street light framed a Western brunette on a street advertisement for skin cream. The flag of South Korea was strewn across shop fronts and the stripped down characters of Korea decorated the street signs. We found a guest house of pine and central heating that would not have gone amiss in Scandinavia. Apart from its serving of Dog stew perhaps, which was a house speciality. It was rich, and laden with *qi*: the perfect winter food.

We were to follow the summer footsteps of South Korean tourists to the Perpetually White Mountains, the *Changbai Shan*. Straddling the border, they were a sacred location. The Chinese had bestowed the fabulous title *'Emperor who cleared the Sky with Tremendous Sagehood'* upon them. As for the Koreans, they knew that their race had emerged from them at birth. This Korea, the North, battled hard to stop the outside world encroaching with its borders of radio jamming towers and barbed wire. And just as secrets are interesting no matter what, the possibility of ogling such a place from a point of beauty was a temptation too great to resist.

Next morning we jumped a bus. A man acting as baby comedy sketch was playing on the television: a fully grown man wearing nothing but a nappy cried for *mama*. Amidst this unnecessary bawling the vehicle stopped in every hamlet. It dropped off peasants bearing cabbage sacks, and picked up weathered men carrying *baijiu* flasks. Almost everybody decided to smoke their cheapest cigarettes and the fumes merged in a filthy cloud against the ceiling. From the back someone tried to catch our attention by calling to the *Lao Maozi* - the 'Old Hairy Ones'. It was slang for Russian foreigners in particular and therefore inaccurate. Since no response was received, a leathery gent toying a turnip took it upon himself to lean across the aisle and ask

'Are you from Vladivostok?'

'No'

'Would you like to buy *luobo* [turnip]?'

'No thanks' I said 'no need'

But he would not take no for an answer and was still wheedling when we arrived at the final stop, the town of Baihe, where we transferred to the single waiting taxi.

The driver of this taxi looked a little too young. Mr. Ju was his name. He was a rather flash looking tramp in a leather jacket and tracksuit bottoms which he tied up with a piece of rope. He drove like we had just raided a bank, hurtling across the snow without chains on the tires to a soundtrack of throbbing techno. Here there were dim-lit villages, thickets of white spruce, and thunderous logging trucks returning from the lonely mountains - they all rolled into one while Mr. Ju steered with one hand, and casually flicked ash from a chain of cigarettes between his legs.

The entrance to the Perpetually White Mountains National Park was locked. Fortunately the gatekeeper's house was not. He might have wished it had been for we discovered him asleep in his own bed in an otherwise empty room up on the first floor. He seemed surprised to find the lot of us in his room, staring at him while the northerly rays spilled through trees casting branches and gothic twig tangles against the walls.

'Not many people up here at this time of year' he said, pulling himself up 'going to Heaven Pool?' He warned us to be careful, and to take snow shoes too, which I first thought a wallet emptying wheeze. But then I tested my Chinese army issue boots in a snowdrift and my feet soaked through.

After sealing purchases, we climbed back in with Mr. Ju. He slammed the doors and raced us off through the great metal gates. Past the sign that said '*Protect ancient trees and benefit our offspring*' rose thick forests of spruce and Korean pine. But in turn these soon began to give way to small groves of birch where the trees had become stunted and the branches sprawled along the ground as though digging for the nourishment their roots could not find. Steam hissed from snow melt beside the road and the egg stink of hydrogen sulphide filled the air. Mr. Ju was still running the techno.

He stopped in a village at the foot of Mount Baekdu where the guesthouses ran mineral spas siphoning water from the mountain's hot springs. We chose to stay at the second guesthouse we checked out as with its mildewed walls and school gym showers, the first seemed to have modelled itself on some kind of Romanian orphanage. We agreed with Mr. Ju that he would pick us up around dusk the following evening. Then the girls holed up in bed. They were coming down with *ganmao* and worryingly, Josie complained of chest pain. I was disappointed to find that the spa was only lukewarm and its fibre glass floor irritated our backsides. The economy of the new China did not seem to extend up here in winter.

Still the next morning was a winter morning to solder itself in memory - bright sun, crisp air, a temperature so low it seemed to jolt the mind into a brilliant clarity. Kristel and I pulled on Peoples Liberation Army greatcoats which we had bought in Hangzhou where it was standard winter gear for itinerants and commuters alike. Then the four of us began the climb towards Heaven pool, the heart of the Perpetually White mountains. Crows had gathered around the pipes that carried hot water down the mountainside. Under the rich sunlight, the white Birch that had looked so bleak the day before now looked like ingenious artworks. We crossed back and forth across the frozen stream and passed through splintered copses.

Up ahead a rough door had been cut from the mountainside. But below it an old woman hawked boiled eggs she had cooked in a hot pool.

'Want or not want breakfast?' she shouted. But since most of them bobbed to the surface, we declined. Instead we trudged up steps and opened the door.

The path here twisted right through the side of the mountain. We began to ascend its coils and straights suddenly isolated from activity in the real world. Wind whistled outside, making this dank place of dim bulbs and melt water puddles seem cosy. From above came muffled thuds of the outside world, a brief whine, and a rush of wind as a door opened somewhere at a surface. It went on like this for some time - noise, and bulb after bulb passing like road markings. Eventually we turned into a long corridor. The exit was illuminated in snow. At this surface rested a spade wielder, his face stung red where scarves and goggles did not cover. He was part of a two man team trying to free the path of snow. But the wind was ferocious out there and so they were working in shifts, one shovelling while the other sheltered. This was the noise we had heard, the changing of shifts, a work routine eerily replaying into the bowel of the mountain.

The shoveller outside paused work as we opened the door, and stared.

'Hello' I said. He nodded.

'Come back within four hours' he said.

'Ok'

'Which way to Korea?' asked Kristel. He pointed into the snow. Gusts were raking it loose off the path and over the edge of the rock face. The shift changed again. It seemed the next shoveller would have a fight on his hands just to keep a scarf around his mouth. But it didn't seem to matter about the lack of traffic, they were doing this job in any case. In China, man could not submit to the weather: it was a matter of principle.

We continued into a valley. Flakes whirled like dust, glowing in orange eddies. Mottled pools of light flickered on streams of spring water and clouds of steam were cast into ice. Ahead lay a deep snow plain sculpted by the wind, frozen into a surface of choppy sea, the path staked in fluorescent path markers incongruously advertising some hotel *'Changbai Shan Dujuan Shanzhuang - doubles Y580'*. The plain funnelled down and across the lip of the caldera. Below us lay the frozen lake. It looked to be covered in cotton wool and on all sides it was encircled by stone.

North Korea sat just over the other side. It began half way across this frozen rink according to the map. Hidden hot springs bubbled under its surface and the ice was likely riddled with holes. Anyone going through it in this temperature would not last five minutes and it made sense not to stray from the edge. I had hoped quite unrealistically that we would be able to see it stretched before us, plains and villages beneath the clouds, a kind of corrupted, stricken, Shangri-La. I wished to see stretching from the peaks this older China, one from before reform and opening - one in which the leader was thought able to cure the sick and bring the dead back to life. And yet disappointingly North Korea from here was just a continuation of ice and stone. In the face of geography and weather, mere political demarcations had been rendered quite irrelevant.

Yet it was right here at the summit of *Baekdu* from which the Korean race had been born. This was corroborated by modern myth for the Dear Leader himself claimed to have been born just the other side of the mountain. It did not matter that both his parents were in exile in the Soviet Union at the time when Kim Jong Il must have entered the world, for facts have never intruded on a great personality cult: like many, I had for instance recently been impressed by the Dear Leader's fantastic reported golfing feats - apparently he had scored a hole in one on every hole of Pyongyang's brand new nine hole (and only) golf course.

The weather here was hardly conducive to a lengthy stay though, so we soon began our walk single file back across the deep snow of the plain. The wind blew into us now: it bit and clawed and burned. By the time we had traversed back across the blocked path and entered the safety of the tunnel, Kristel's ear had swollen. The diggers were nowhere to be seen.

But down below on the other side of the tunnel the wind was gone and the sky had fallen the colour of octopus blood. Beyond the shattered Birch stumps Mr. Ju waited with a near-empty bottle. His car waited further down the track.

'I've been waiting a long time! I finished the *baijiu*!' He shouted indignantly, as though it had been our negligence that had caused him to dispense with it. We gathered our backpacks from the guesthouse and jumped into his vehicle. Mr. Ju still played the same dance soundtrack and his driving had not improved over the last day. I hoped that he wouldn't hit the peasants out collecting firewood in the snow, or any one of the logging trucks that hurtled our way. Shamefully this was as much guilt as I could allow myself about travelling with a drunk at the wheel, for there was no other way out of the mountains.

Baijiu
Mr. Ju dropped us off in town. Really it was more of a pit stop

at the end of the line, a huddle of cabins and some trees. It turned out that there were no more trains out of Baihe today. We were just discovering this standing on the station platform through an excruciating study of the local railway timetable, when someone sidled up behind me and began poking me between the shoulder blades.

'Come to the guesthouse' this someone whined 'not far away. I'll cook anything you like'. This someone then stepped back and for a moment I thought I was safe. But it turned out that this was just a tactical feint, and so when he moved forward again to poke me some more, I became irritable.

'Go away' I said 'no need'

'Homemade *baijiu*' he tried. He was a thick set short fellow in a black bomber jacket that looked as though it had brought down from Russia. He tried a few other different ruses (fresh vegetables, warm rooms), but I still pretended he did not exist. He left to circle the others while they guarded the baggage, but then seemed to think better of disturbing them and left.

'The next train leaves tomorrow' warned Kristel.

'We'll need something' Josie added.

'There is not going to be a whole lot of choice' said Stuart. And in any case to see a hawker give up so quickly was almost heart-rending.

So I followed the man though the snow.

'Sorry' I said. He broke into smile. I said that we would in fact like to stay with him tonight and catch the morning train tomorrow. And because I had been so gruff, I redoubled my efforts at small talk.

'*Dongbeiren?*' (Northeasterner?) I asked

He nodded.

'The strongest' he said.

'The strongest?'

'In all of China' His name it turned out was Mr. Hu, and he owned a wicked grin. Baihe was a little bigger than it looked. Its wood cabins were hidden between clumps of rare Meiren Song, a species of pine that grew only around this town. Mr. Hu's dwelling however, was different. It was a whitewashed bungalow that would have blended with the ground had it been cleaner. It consisted of a couple of heated rooms and a kitchen. The centrepiece was the *kang*, a raised wooden floor heated underneath by a fire that smouldered continuously. Mr. Hu lived with a merry shawled wife and a young pony-tailed daughter. The daughter was highly excited by the arrival of foreigners, especially the female ones. There were also three large glass vats lining a wall.

'*Baijiu*' explained Mr. Hu. He grasped the first one, a milky brew 'This one is local'. He ran his hands over it lovingly, then moved on 'This one is also local. You cannot buy it'. He winked. Number two was the colour of formaldehyde. Finally Mr. Hu tapped the third vat. 'This one was made in Jilin' he said 'it is the strongest. It will put you foreigners on the floor in two minutes!'

From this third vat he poured three shots.

'Only for the men' he explained. For once Kristel did not argue.

Mr. Hu sat cross-legged on the *kang* and threw his drink back. Stuart and I copied him. We went through this procedure a couple of times while I remarked on the prettiness of the place, and told him how much I liked the colourful Daoist shrine hanging around in the corner. By the third round his tongue had loosened.

'*Dongbeiren* are simple' he said 'Not like southern Chinese. Not like Koreans either. These days we are not so important. It is poor here. We *Dongbeiren* have become poor. But we *Dongbeiren* used to govern China'

'You did?'

'Yes!' he said, waggling his fingers excitably 'We are Manchus' he said 'like the Qing'. Most of that race had since been swallowed into the great Han gene pool.

'...We are more tough than the Southern Chinese' he said. His daughter came back into the room with pen and paper and in an intense flurry of concentration began writing.

'Tough?' I prodded.

'Yes. Tough. They have it easy down in the South. No need for heating. No need for drinking. They read books and write poetry!' he said, as though these were the most unmanly habits one could exhibit. I translated for Stuart. He flung his head back and laughed raucously. Mr. Hu stared at him sullenly. Stuart caught a hold of himself: it seemed Mr. Hu was not joking.

'The Southerners cannot fight. They did not fight the Japanese' continued Mr. Hu. This was most inaccurate and I wondered what motivated him to say it, why he would wish to denigrate his compatriots in the eyes of foreigners. Perhaps I had found my first regionalist outside the minority areas: *Dongbei* first, China second.

Mr. Hu went out to the kitchen where his wife was busy chopping.

'Hungry?' he shouted, peering back round - he carried a withered old cabbage that he had surely found left on the bus. Yes, we all said.

A few minutes later he came back from the kitchen to pour another round. We discussed the cold and our trip to Heaven Pool, and Mr. Hu laughed when I complained about Mr. Ju's driving.

'Maybe he is a Korean' he shouted, as though that would explain it.

'There are many Koreans here?' I asked.

'In Yanji' he said. I told him we had come through Yanji and seen the signs.

'We have Chinese Koreans. But also new Koreans, ones that do not die as they come. We have *nan ming ying*' he said.

I got him to repeat this last word and then looked it up: *'Refugee camp'*.

His daughter pulled out a piece of paper which she handed to Kristel. *'Welcome you Foreign Friend'* it said. Kristel knelt down and hugged her.

'North Korea is a problem' I said.

'Yes' admitted Mr. Hu 'but the leader is a good man. He likes to drink. We say if a man likes to drink then he cannot be a problem'. But this argument seemed as logical to me as claiming a tiger that enjoyed a good feast could not be dangerous.

Mrs. Hu floated in carrying plates laden with vegetables and noodle which we munched on heartily. Then the girls retired, complaining that it was no use talking to anyone who slurred their words. We finished a last drink with Mr. Hu. Then we too made to retire.

'Don't go!' insisted Mr. Hu 'there is still so much for you to try'.

'We have to sleep' I protested weakly. But I lacked conviction and Mr. Hu knew it. He leapt up and refilled three glasses - this time with the formaldehyde.

'Ganbei!' he shouted. And down they went. Then before we could raise any other serious objections, Mr. Hu was already up to his feet

and refilling. We threw those back too. He repeated this routine until he could not get up to do any more refilling. Instead he closed his eyes and swayed where he sat. His wife and daughter were already curled up behind him on the *kang*.

'Two years ago I saw a Korean family come through Baihe' he slurred 'It was the middle of winter and the snow was very heavy'. He reached out for his empty glass but could not find it.

'They came across the border' he said 'like *guihun*' - ghosts.

The *Baijiu* leant us false strength. The four of us huddled together on the *kang* of a guestroom. But spending the night in a building heated by floorboards was trying - something like being trapped between a griddling iron and a deep freeze. Beside me Kristel talked feverishly while her frostbitten ear blistered. It burst in the night. By morning her ear was glued to the pillow. Josie too was sick. Mr. Hu though, seemed as bright as ever. He rose from the raised platform in the main room and offered us bowls of rice congee. But we declined for the train was soon to leave.

'I have a gift' said Hu as we were about to walk out. He passed Stuart a bottle: firewater from Jilin.

'Best stuff' he said with a wink 'you'll need it for the train'. We thanked Mrs. Hu for being such a sporting host. Mr. Hu walked us to the station and his daughter skipped beside him. We wandered down the track, past the shanty brick dwellings, through the trees where the scent of sap wafted. Mr. Hu's daughter tugged Kristel's arm - her plaits shook like a fat man's belly.

'Will you come again?' she asked.

'Maybe' said Kristel, bending the truth. It was unlikely. These people were stoics and toughies, but there seemed little reason for anyone else to join them in their winter.

Our ride was already waiting at Baihe station, and it departed a few minutes after we boarded. Mr. Hu waved us off while his daughter chased us along the platform. This was a mucky diesel and it soon picked up pace. It huffed across bridges until the rolling hills and soot blackened towns lay behind us. Manchuria was falling away, together with its ice, forests, and *baijiu*. Well, maybe not quite the *baijiu*, for half the carriage were still swigging the stuff. Its stench dominated the air. But there seemed to be only one garrulous drunk in this carriage. This one shouted and swore and when he saw the foreigners he came and shoved his red-eyed face into mine. He hadn't shaved in a while and sported one of those peculiarly Chinese fuzzes. His tipple of choice, it turned out, was wildly unconventional.

'Have a beer' he shouted 'made with Changbai Shan water!' I decided to take him up on the offer and drink beer brewed with Changbai shan water. It was after all, going to prove a distraction from *baijiu* from Jilin, which on the first sip had outed itself as a pretty unwelcome sort of kick in the head.

'Twenty years ago we didn't drink this foreign horse piss' exclaimed the drunk 'back then just *baijiu*. Plenty of it'. I could see why he might have been frustrated. The Germans had brought beer here, then the communists had standardised it. For in China, no matter what it was called, it all seemed to taste the same.

The drunkard offered me sunflower seeds. And he had some questions:

'Do you like the Northeast?'

'Is it the best part of China?'

'Are Northeastern men the strongest?'

Yes, yes, yes I said. Then abruptly he ceased being curious - the talent of the drunk. Instead he snatched a newspaper from a scrawny elder across the aisle. The old man smiled indulgently and everyone else smiled too, still bemused at the sight of the fool and the foreigner sharing a beer. But really it was liberating here sitting on the hard seats, drinking and crunching seeds as the forests dropped off. We were two outcasts together, both different: nails refusing to be hammered down. Our husks just happened to be going on the floor the same as everyone else's.

The train slowed and arrived in Tonghua. It was a town of relative prosperity for heavy industry had poisoned it with soot and grime. It looked like Manchester might have if the council's planning department had been hijacked by the cement industry. In this town we exchanged the draughty provincial diesel for a sleeping carriage bound for Beijing. Our fellow travellers wore furry hats, pulled long faces and swigged *Erguotai*, a more expensive brand of *baijiu*. Kristel began to feel nauseated. But when she tried to enter a toilet a sour looking attendant snapped

'Closed'. Later a floppy haired young man smoking alone said with reference to the attendants

'They close the toilets so they don't have to work. Half the toilets on this train are locked' he said. Then he pulled something from his pocket - a drop key.

'Look!' he demanded. He shoved the drop key into the toilet lock, fussed about a bit, then swung the door wide open. Kristel was very grateful. Josie, Stuart, and I took turns too. We soon became aware that people all over this train had brought their own drop keys and were unlocking and entering the toilets at will. The attendants roamed after these burglars, testing the doors and relocking those they found unlocked. It seemed they had initiated a draining game of cat and mouse – one far more exciting than cleaning toilets. Again, it was a Chinese game. There was no point tackling head on the ludicrous nature of bureaucrats and bureaucracy: rules were made to be bent.

Tonghua began to dribble away and the train rocketed head long into the dazzling white world of the plains once more. The speakers were on, piping out music for these happy people. Female voices began to screech all over it like cats caught on a wire fence. For some unfathomable reason Stuart had plenty of Mr. Hu's *baijiu* left. So we played cards and drank it. It tasted like run-off - a gift from the rust stacks still passing outside.

12. Hearts

Inside a box at the heart of Tiananmen Square lay a figure of plastic. It was stumpy, and quite bloated. Usually the same figure held everyone under quiet surveillance from *Renminbi* bank notes. Now I found it flat on its back with its eyes closed, a waxy kind of action toy. One that it was difficult to imagine had once respired and walked. This one in particular had definitely swum (in the great Yangtze), joked (coarsely), and issued decrees that would affect the lives of hundreds of millions. For lying here was Chairman Mao Zedong, embalmed, covered in a flawless scarlet sheet bearing the hammer and sickle of the international communist movement, revered forever. More than thirty years after his death, the Great Helmsman still appeared to have some sort of transcendental hold, for a minor miracle was unfolding here. There were no bleeping phones, raised voices, and barely the odd whisper. The only sound present was that of scuffling feet - hundreds of scuffling feet.

Unusually, our visit began with a queue. Our comrades, mostly domestic tourists - admirers, well-wishers, voyeurs, girls in fancy boots, leather-jacketed men - waited in the wind. They jabbered good-naturedly and danced to keep warm. Then came a bloodcurdling scream from the official kiosk. And another. Soon though I realised no crime was being committed, simply a bit of boisterous advertising.

'Flowers!' the shouter was shouting. It seemed to do the trick, for the impressive queue fell apart as quickly as a police clampdown on prostitution. And when it eventually reformed once more, it was in a completely different configuration. No matter. There was something resembling a queue again, and more importantly it was moving - or, more accurately, shuffling. Shuffling very slowly towards the gaudy block that was the mausoleum of the Great Helmsman.

This box had been constructed with granite from Sichuan, the porcelain of Guangdong, of pine harvested in Shaanxi and Jiangxi. It contained earth from the quake-stricken city of Tangshan, and milky quartz from the Kunlun Mountains. Just to reinforce Chinese territorial claims there were rock samples from Everest, and water and sand from the Taiwan Straits. 700,000 people from across the provinces and autonomous regions had built the place through symbolic voluntary labour. Certainly it had been symbolic, for these volunteers had come to the construction site, formed a human chain, and passed the bricks from one end to the other. The following day they had been replaced by a different group of volunteers ready to repeat a variation on the original task: passing the same bricks back to their original position.

Mao waited for us at the mausoleum entrance - here in marble, but inside, for real. The flowers, which had been purchased so hastily, were laid at the feet of this statue. And then, since they were not real flowers, but tough synthetic look-alikes, they were discreetly transferred back to the sales stall by an usher. It was a lucrative form of recycling. Flowers were bought and laid, returned, bought, laid - no-one wanted to look disrespectful when visiting a holy place. For in death the Great Helmsman had become venerated: a hallowed ancestor joining the pantheon he had for much of his life tried so hard to obliterate.

We were all ushered through at such speed there was only enough time for hat wearers to doff hats, or if they had forgotten, to find themselves reminded to. I tried to get up close to the glass, but another coach load of tourists squeezed into the way. Then the guards moved us all on. An ambush awaited at the exit - admirably set up, you had to hand it to them. The hawkers there had established overlapping fields of fire that covered every angle. Mao clocks, lucky Mao pendants, Mao kites, Mao cigarette lighters, watches featuring an imperious hand waving Mao who counted the minutes: first the Great Leader had suffered the indignity of deathbed display (he had wished to be cremated), then he had been trivialised in kitsch.

This whole circus plugged the route leading right into the old heavenly capital, blocked the artery and its carefully considered *feng shui*. The Forbidden City, home to the emperor and his court, had suffered sustained assaults on the flow of its *qi*. The communists had crushed the city walls and many of the guard towers. They had bulldozed and butchered the landscape and paved the gargantuan Tiananmen Square in front of it. Around this square they had positioned the odd soldier and huddles of alert-looking policemen. After all, one never knew when a *Free Tibet* activist or practitioner of Falun Gong might try to unfurl a banner. In a final insult the communists had stuck a painting of Mao's younger face above the Gate of Heavenly Peace and consigned the Forbidden City to history's abyss through its rebranding as the 'Palace Museum'. This was the new heart of China: the windswept square, the tomb, the body; coppers, hangers on and tourists, all collected here in the middle of the capital of the country that still seemed to consider itself the centre of the world.

Over a week we hunted duck restaurants in the back alleys where amongst the dollops of festive spit, hawkers were selling unidentifiable boiled animal parts, and birds hummed strangely over the telephone cables. We visited the temple of heaven where the emperor had divined the harvests, and the imperial observatory from which the ancients had divined the universe. We posed by the sign in the grounds of the Summer Palace with its solemn instruction to visitors, *'No Striding'*, and made a couple of excursions to the Great Wall: The Mutianyu section had been thoroughly restored. This meant the hawkers were numerous and go karts ran from its top. The Simatai had been paid less attention. It crumbled across steep mountainsides, occupied by only a single hawker who erroneously attempted to pass himself off as a Mongolian. For some reason I found this very funny, so I purchased a guidebook from him.

But around the centre of the world there were also whole cohorts of tramps - old ladies with gangrene and foraging men who hid piteously in the city's pedestrian tunnels. Within three hours of arrival in Beijing the taxi drivers had sharked us twice. Later I caught a scrawny pickpocket with his hand inside my camera case. I surprised myself by hauling him out of there by the scruff of his neck, and in a moment of rage, thought about hitting him. But he hung from my arms so meekly that I could not do it. The moment passed and someone (an accomplice?) disentangled us.

Later in the courtyard of the Dong Yue Daoist temple the early evening sun lit the head stone tablets - the *stellae* - like faces of the Madonna. At the enclosure labelled 'Department of Timely Retribution' Kristel threw in an offering.

'Who was that for?'

'the taxi drivers of Beijing' she said.

There were 300 wooden gods and demons depicted here, all acting scenes from the various departments of heaven - angels blessing the pious, demons carving out the innards of those less so; ecstasy, meditation, gore. It was the role of the spirits in the 'Department of Opposing Obscene Acts' enclosure to *'punish the culprits that overpower women'*. At the 'Department for demons and monsters' a sign explained *'this department controls and supervises them and forbids them to wander and bewilder people'*. Especially large piles of paper cash had been left outside the 'Department for Upholding Loyalty and Filial Piety' and the 'Department for Increasing Good Fortune and Longevity'.

But here away from the bustle of the street, with the deities and departments, the tranquillity of the light, was proof too that China was something greater than a political entity. China was a stable of ideas, an umbrella of practices, more than anything it was the continuation of a collective memory. For the roots of an original China which had existed continuously since the city states born on the banks of the Yellow River were apparently beyond destruction. These roots had survived political campaigning, scientific advance, economic progress. They were surviving also the communists - just as they had survived in earlier ages, nomadic conquerors from beyond the wall.

Hitting the Ground

One morning Kristel and Josie groaned and refused to get out of their hostel bunks. Illness had plagued both of them since the Great White Mountains. Only now did we take them to hospital where for an afternoon they were harassed with X-Rays, antibiotics dispensed from a drip, painkillers, blood tests. After many procedures the registrar had some news for us. I called Lou Da and asking him to translate, put him on the phone to the doctor.

'She wants Kristel to have to have a bone marrow test' he explained when the phone was handed back 'the situation is critical'. Since it was critical we put Josie on a plane for Singapore where her family would receive her, and Stuart sent himself back to the UK. Meanwhile we caught the next train back to the relative safety of Hangzhou where we checked Kristel straight into Number One hospital. I called Lou Da for another translation.

'These people say there is no problem with her white blood cell count' he said. Just to be sure we sought a second opinion, and a third translation.

'Bad case of flu' translated Da 'nothing more serious'.

A day later we met Chang Wen by the lake for the last time.

'Sounds like the northern doctors were trying to cheat you' he said 'happens often in our China. Doctors will always try to sell us medicines and treatments we don't need. Medicines the farmers cannot afford. They see foreigners like you and they see a walking bank. It is good practice especially for junior doctors: they can try new procedures and learn trickery at the same time'.

Back in the neighbourhood the word on the street was that a 19 year old girl from City College had just been raped and murdered. Her body had been dumped in a ditch just off Zhoushan road. A suspect - a taxi driver - had been arrested since and had apparently confessed.

'Would not have happened years ago' grumbled Mrs. Ho. Up in his office, Lou Da shrugged

'These things happen' he said 'maybe this student should have been more careful'

'Careful...?' began Kristel. Lou Da's eyes flickered anxiously. After a year he seemed to be getting the measure of her. Prudently he changed topic.

'I have been searching for your replacements' he reckoned, shuffling a stack of paper in his hands 'I've already found some'

'Who?'

'Canadians' he said 'they teach in Shaoxing at present. But they can't buy pet food there for their cat, or find a vet, they say'

'That's devoted' said Kristel

'They seem like Weirdoes' he said 'Most foreigners who live in China for a long time are. Then they cannot find jobs in their own country...'

'If you think they are strange why have you employed them?'

Da shrugged again.

'Couldn't find anyone else' he raised an eyebrow 'although there was an American man from Shanghai who was interested. When I contacted his school they said he is a good teacher. But he sniffed too much'

'Sniffed too much?'

'Sniffed. A healthy teacher does not sniff'.

At this stage of winter the cherry trees on the causeways were once more naked. Lovers paddled out on the water, the last heads of lotus had drowned, and the southern hills had vanished behind the screen. The lake had returned to the condition in which we had found it a year ago.

'Things will have changed by the time you return' claimed Wen. I expected so. There would be more cranes, more towers. There would be more itinerants, more tourists, more street hustlers. I had faith though that there were references that could be clung to: The West Lake most importantly, that constant amidst any change - just as it had been since the first glorious days of the Song, when Su Dongpo had dredged it and built the first causeway. Then poets had listened to birds in the hills, prayed in the temples and sat in pagoda shadows. They had fed the fish and regarded the blossom. Many generations down the line their descendents were conducting the same activities throughout the frazzled Hangzhou Summer - even if now they happened to come on a bus with a pack of noisy tour group friends.

On our penultimate evening in China another restaurant opened in mild firework frenzy. Stood in the street, Mr. Xo swapped a double happiness with Johann and shouted scornfully

'Good luck to them!' Then he ran inside and fetched Kristel a cartoon of tea. More sincerely, we wished him luck.

Later Ai Li saw me returning from my final run. She was seated on the curb munching a rather bedraggled looking tofu stick.

'Where are you going?' she called.

'Running' I said 'but tomorrow I'm going home. To *Yingguo* - to England.

'Yingguo?' she repeated.

'Yes' I said 'it's a different country'.

She snorted derisively. Then she threw the tofu stick into the gutter and ran off.

Before bedtime, Japanese Reiko invited us down to her flat. She poured us tea and when Kristel asked her how she had come to live in the Middle Kingdom, she folded her arms.

'One day I thought to myself, no longer am I a young woman' she began 'And what have I done? I have lived every day in this country with the same job. I decided I had to leave. The less I had and the more I left behind, the less I worried about the future. Before that I had no luck. Men did not like me and neither did women. I never found anyone to settle with and just accepted my life. When other Japanese hear I am from Nagasaki they become worried that I am dangerous to them, or have some defect. If you want to marry, your future husband may even hire a private detective, to make sure you are not from Nagasaki. I was glad to leave'. Reiko had run. Just like Darling, Johann, British Dave, us. Everybody in China ran: they ran to dream. They ran to get by. They ran hard from dawn through to twilight. They ran for wealth and status. Some sprinted to gain. Many struggled to run on the spot. In every direction they ran, the collective destination unknown. It was the greatest race on earth.

Attempting some sort of respect for our customs Mrs. Ho woke us up on our last morning with a rap at the door. I let her in. Singing to herself as she had always done, she began to sweep the kitchen with her broom. Stood by the heater Kristel and I finished a final mug of *Longjing* tea and left. On the way down we knocked on Professor Darling's door. The shoe pile had dwindled. No-one answered.

'Not there' said Lou Da from further down the stairs 'Darling said he needs time to himself. Two days ago he caught the bus to *Wutaishan*. He has gone to rest in the Buddhist mountains'.

Da pushed us outside. It was snowing. Betty waited for us out there. So did Lei Shen and Richard, Chang Er and Tian Fei. We said goodbye to them all. Betty said nothing about quality teaching. Instead she smiled sweetly and handed us each a glass sculpture of the thirteen storey library etched out in all its glory. It seemed as good a symbol as any of one year in China, a symbol of grand hopes, progress and mess. Mr. Ji had come along too. And for once he did not ask for anything. Instead he shook me by the hand. It was an exaggeratedly strong shake that was quite different from the standard Chinese dead fish. I imagined he had been waiting for an opportunity to try it out.

We climbed into the battered van that had once brought us to the University of Educated People. Chang Wen and Lou Da were already seated inside it. Flakes fell fast against the windscreen. The engine started, and we were on the move, past Dehuai standing there in a final stiff salute. We turned onto Zhoushan East Road where Mr. Hong still stared impassively over the refuse. Ai Li was sitting by the kerb and Mr. Xo was already out nattering with his customers.

At Shanghai Pudong Da and Wen waited while we sorted out the tickets. Finally they escorted us to the departure gate.

'Behave yourself' Kristel said to Da. He smiled mischievously.

'I leave that to fate' he said.

'I have been thinking of new ideas for trade between China and England' Chang Wen said in what appeared to be some sort of relapse. The modern elevation of business was proving a lure just too strong to resist.

He had printed up a pile of cards from which he now reeled one off clumsily.

'Wen Chang' it said in bold face. And underneath in italics, *'Managing Director'*.

'Together we can become rich' he reckoned, embracing us both in his bear arms. We walked through the gate and onto the plane, which passed from a future which had risen only recently from the marshes, taking wing above the smokestacks and skyscrapers, the masses still teeming below.

Acknowledgements

Great thanks to my Chinese Godfathers Chang Wen and Lou Da. Thanks also to my friends Lei Chen, Chang Er, and Tian Fei for helping me understand the many different ways that can be lived. To Kristel Pous, Chris Evans, Garfield Phillpotts, Clare McNaul, and my mother, Jane, please accept my most grateful thanks for all of your enthusiasm and encouragement.

Made in the USA
Charleston, SC
24 February 2012